Harmonica FOR DUMMIES®

by Winslow Yerxa

WILEY

Wiley Publishing, Inc.

Harmonica For Dummies®

Published by
Wiley Publishing, Inc.
111 River St.
Hoboken, NJ 07030-5774
www.wiley.com

About the Author

Winslow Yerxa is a harmonica player, performer, author, inventor, and teacher. His lifelong quest to understand the harmonica (and help others do the same) began early on, when he couldn't find a teacher and none of the available harmonica books taught anything about blues, country, Celtic, or jazz styles of harmonica he heard on records and wanted to emulate. His youthful experiences playing in waterfront bars in his native Vancouver, British Columbia, and with Cree guitarists and singers in the Canadian Rockies taught him how versatile the harmonica can be in playing blues, jazz, country music, popular music, and fiddle tunes. Composition, music theory, and jazz arranging studies at Vancouver Community College, at McGill University, and later, writing musical arrangements for Afro-Caribbean bands in San Francisco gave him the technical expertise to integrate harmonica into a wide variety of musical settings. Nowadays he spends a lot of time playing with the San Francisco Scottish Fiddlers.

From 1992 to 1997 Winslow wrote, edited, and published the magazine *HIP — the Harmonica Information Publication,* the most widely read harmonica periodical of its time. During that period, he transcribed John Popper's harmonica solos to musical notation and tab for the songbook to the Blues Traveler CD, *four.* He also authored the book and CD combination *Learn Blues Harp Effects in 60 minutes* and invented and marketed the Discrete Comb, a harmonica upgrade that unlocks all the note bending capabilities of a diatonic harmonica. Recently, in collaboration with Dix Bruce, he authored *Backup Trax: Basic Blues for Harmonica,* and he also recently worked with jazz harmonica virtuoso Howard Levy on his *Out of the Box* series of instructional DVDs.

In addition to teaching privately, Winslow teaches at harmonica seminars, such as Jon Gindick's Harmonica Jam Camp and David Barrett's Harmonica Masterclass. He also teaches at harmonica festivals, such as SPAH and the Buckeye festival. He is a regular contributor to the online harmonica magazine HarmonicaSessions.com, and he has contributed articles to *Harmonica World, Harmonica Happenings, American Harmonica Newsletter,* and *Echos France Harmonica.* He continues to contribute to the understanding and appreciation of the harmonica through such online forums as Harp-L.

Dedication

To my wife, Pat, who keeps my feet on the ground, and to our wee spirit guide, Alberto Duque.

I'd also like to dedicate this book to the memory of my dear friend, classical harmonicist Douglas Tate, and to the memory of that invaluable Québécois folklorist and peerless *joueur de la musique à bouche*, Gabriel Labbé.

Author's Acknowledgments

I'd like to thank Rob Paparozzi for recommending me for this project, along with acquisitions editor Michael Lewis and my agent, Carole Jelen McLendon of Waterside Productions. Thanks also goes to fellow *For Dummies* author Bill Evans for early orientation and advice.

The writing and editing processes ran smoothly thanks to the tact, organization, and sage advice of project editor Alissa Schwipps. The text was immeasurably improved by the advice of copy editor Jessica Smith and of technical editor and harmonica player extraordinaire Glenn Weiser.

A big thanks to photographer Anne Hamersky for capturing the tiny, hidden details of harmonica workings, and to Steve Malerbi, master harmonica technician, for the loan of the chord harmonica for the photo shoot. I'm grateful to my colleagues Damien Masterson and Chris Michalek for the loan of microphones and mixers for recording the CD, and Os Leguizamo of Suzuki for his responsiveness and dedication.

I'd also like to thank Jason Ricci and Ben Breyer for helpful suggestions, advice, and moral support.

Finally, I'd like to thank my students, from whom I am always learning.

Publisher's Acknowledgments

We're proud of this book; please send us your comments through our Dummies online registration form located at www.dummies.com/register/.

Some of the people who helped bring this book to market include the following:

Acquisitions, Editorial, and Media Development

Senior Project Editor: Alissa Schwipps

Acquisitions Editor: Michael Lewis

Copy Editors: Jessica Smith, Elizabeth Kuball

Editorial Program Coordinator: Erin Calligan Mooney

Technical Editor: Glenn Weiser

Senior Editorial Manager: Jennifer Ehrlich

Assistant Project Manager: Jenny Swisher

Assistant Producer: Angie Denny

Quality Assurance: Kit Malone

Editorial Assistants: Joe Niesen, Jennette ElNaggar, David Lutton

Cover Photo: ©Stockbyte/Alamy

Cartoons: Rich Tennant (www.the5thwave.com)

Composition Services

Project Coordinator: Patrick Redmond

Layout and Graphics: Carl Byers, Reuben W. Davis, Melissa K. Jester

Special Art: Kathryn Born

Proofreaders: Melissa Bronnenberg, Shannon Ramsey

Indexer: Slivoskey Indexing Services

Special Help: Todd Lothery, Christy Pingleton, Alicia B. South

---

Publishing and Editorial for Consumer Dummies

Diane Graves Steele, Vice President and Publisher, Consumer Dummies

Joyce Pepple, Acquisitions Director, Consumer Dummies

Kristin A. Cocks, Product Development Director, Consumer Dummies

Michael Spring, Vice President and Publisher, Travel

Kelly Regan, Editorial Director, Travel

Publishing for Technology Dummies

Andy Cummings, Vice President and Publisher, Dummies Technology/General User

Composition Services

Gerry Fahey, Vice President of Production Services

Debbie Stailey, Director of Composition Services

Contents at a Glance

Table of Contents

Introduction

· ·

Are you hankering to play the harmonica? Are you intrigued by that tiny, expressive instrument that you can take everywhere? Or are you maybe fascinated by that cool character in shades who gets up in front of a band and rips through an incandescent harmonica solo, or by the lass in bluejeans who plays a sweet, plaintive melody by the campfire? Have you finally decided that it's time to just go for it and become the person making that music?

If so, *Harmonica For Dummies* is the place to start. If you're a novice who doesn't own a harmonica yet, this book opens the door with solid advice and gives you a guiding hand into this fascinating new world. Even if you're already an accomplished player, this book shows you all sorts of techniques and approaches that can take your playing to the next level of excellence.

You can have a lot of fun making music with the harmonica, and it can enrich your social life. Over the last 40 years, playing the harmonica has introduced me to new friends worldwide. I've become friends with some of the world's greatest harmonica players, and I've noticed something remarkable about them: Even though they can comfortably rest on their laurels and bask in being called "world's greatest," they rarely do. They remain curious and open to new experiences. I imagine that you do, too. If so, I invite you to join me on the journey of discovery called playing the harmonica.

About This Book

Harmonica For Dummies gives you everything you need to get going with the harmonica. One great thing about this book is that it's a reference you can jump into and out of at will. Just head to the table of contents or the index to find the information you want. Here are a few more great things about this book:

- ✔ **Clear step-by-step instruction.** When I show you how to perform a certain task, such as playing your first note or bending a note, I provide you with easy-to-follow numbered steps. This way you don't have to wade through all the extras to get to the main points.

- ✔ **Helpful diagrams of tongue and mouth action.** When you play the harmonica, almost everything you do is invisible because it happens inside your body. So in this book, I illustrate the inner workings of your mouth and breathing apparatus when you play. Understanding what's going on inside can really help you as you gain mastery of the mysterious inner actions you use to play the harmonica.

✔ **Music notation and tablature for all the music in the book.** *Tablature,* also called *tab,* tells you what to do with your mouth to play the harmonica. It tells you what hole number to go to and whether you need to exhale (an arrow pointing up) or inhale (an arrow pointing down). Simple, eh? Everything you can play on the harmonica in this book is tabbed.

I include music notation for every piece as well. Being able to read notes on a staff isn't required to play harmonica, but it isn't difficult to learn either. Plus it's a useful skill — especially if you want to play a tune that isn't tabbed. So, throughout the book, I include the notation in case you want to check it out.

✔ **A CD full of examples you can play along with.** Every tabbed example is on this book's accompanying CD. Tab, tongue illustrations, and descriptions can carry you only so far. By listening, however, you can quickly comprehend what you're going for. In fact, by hearing the sound you're striving for, you'll achieve it more quickly.

Fool around with different sounds and techniques on your harmonica and note what happens. The greatest advances in harmonica virtuosity have come from players experimenting. Don't be afraid of doing something "wrong." Short of trying to swallow a harmonica or set it on fire, there's almost nothing you shouldn't try.

Conventions Used in This Book

The following conventions are used throughout the text to make things consistent and easy to understand:

✔ New terms appear in *italic* and are closely followed by an easy-to-understand definition.

✔ **Bold** is used to highlight keywords in bulleted lists and the action parts of numbered steps.

✔ All Web addresses appear in `monofont`.

It's also important to note that this book focuses on the ten-hole diatonic harmonica, which has — you guessed it — ten holes. Each hole on the harmonica should be numbered. When I refer to a note on the harmonica, I often state the hole number and the breath direction. For instance, "Hole 4 Blow" refers to the note you get when you go to Hole 4 and exhale into it. "Blow 4" means the same thing.

You'll notice that I use the terms "harmonica" and "harp" interchangeably throughout the book. The harmonica has many colorful names, and these two are the most popular (and the most likely to be accepted in polite company).

When I talk about high and low notes, I mean exactly those — the notes that people think of as high (a mouse squeaking, for instance) or low (a foghorn, or maybe Barry White). On a harmonica, the low notes are on the left and the high notes are on the right.

This book contains both figures and tabs, which are numbered sequentially within each chapter. Figures illustrate important points in the text. Tab, which is short for *tablature,* shows you the actions required to play each note (which hole to play, whether to blow or draw, and any other actions required). Each tab in the book shows you a tune, scale, chord, or sequence of notes that you can play on a harmonica. And if you aren't sure what the tab is supposed to sound like or whether you're getting it right, don't worry — each tab has a reference to the corresponding track on the CD so you can listen to the tab being played.

What You're Not to Read

You don't need to read the music notation in this book — unless you want to. The tab tells you exactly what hole on the harmonica to play, whether to inhale or exhale, and when to bend a note.

You can also skip the paragraphs that have a Technical Stuff icon attached to them (and most of Chapter 3) if you just want to get right down to playing. Pay no attention to the man behind the curtain — unless you get curious about how he's creating all those special effects.

Sidebars, those gray boxes you see scattered in the chapters, can be fun to read if you're interested in harmonica lore, but you don't need the information in them to play.

Here's the bottom-line tip: Skip anything that doesn't look important to you at the moment. If you focus on what matters to you now, you'll start getting familiar with the subject. Later on, things that didn't initially seem important may take on new significance — and you can always go back to them when you're ready.

Foolish Assumptions

I'm going to stick my neck out and assume that you like the harmonica and that you wouldn't mind being able to rip out some cool licks. But I won't assume that you know anything at all about where to start or what sort of a harp to get (oops, I mean what sort of *harmonica* to get — maybe you don't know any of the inside lingo yet, either). Maybe you don't know anything about music except that you like it. Don't worry — that's not a problem.

At the same time, I won't assume that only a greenhorn will ever read this book. You may be an intermediate player who has the basics down but who's looking for a few tips to feed your ever growing harmonica fascination. I also won't assume that you're interested in blues, campfire tunes, or any other style of music. The core techniques you need for every kind of music are covered; though I do include chapters specifically on blues, rock, country, and folk styles.

I do assume that you're interested in the most widely played type of harmonica: the ten-hole diatonic harmonica (which includes such popular brands and models as Hohner Marine Band, Blues Harp, Special 20, Golden Melody, Lee Oskar, Suzuki, Huang, Seydel, and Bushman). While I do touch briefly on other types, such as chromatic and tremolo harmonicas, this book focuses on the ten-hole diatonic.

How This Book Is Organized

Harmonica For Dummies is organized so that you can easily get the information you want. The chapters are grouped into seven parts that focus on different aspects of the harmonica — acquiring, mastering the basics, going beyond the basics, performing with and for others, fixing and upgrading, and hearing some really great harmonica music in different styles. The following are the different parts you can skip in and out of.

Part 1: Getting Started

This part orients you in the world of the harmonica. You get a dab of history and some basic advice about choosing a first harmonica from the multitude of types and models. You also try making your first sounds on the harmonica. Just to set the stage for what's coming, you have the option of getting acquainted with harmonica tab and with some basic music terminology. Do you need to know a lot of music terms and symbols to start playing? Not really. But as you gain playing ability, musical knowledge can help you advance.

Part 11: Starting to Make Some Music

Part II starts with rhythm and melody (and a rite of passage for all harmonica players: getting one single note to sound all by itself). You then can build on these foundations by shaping your sound with the harmonica player's secret weapon — the amazing organic amplifier called the human body. Next I show you the variety of sonic textures you can create with your tongue. Finally, I round off the part by getting to the heart of what every harmonica player wants to master and every listener wants to hear — the thrilling wail of bending a note so that it slurs and cries as it slides down in pitch.

Part III: Growing Beyond the Basics

In this part, you get to apply your skills to making music. I show you how to play one harp in multiple keys and how to hone your ability to blaze away on melodies while navigating the structure of a song. I also show you how to master complex melodies and how to jam and make stuff up as you go along. Finally, you get to experiment with another important technique — *overblows,* or bending notes up.

Part IV: Developing Your Style

After you master essential harmonica techniques, develop a few cool moves, and understand how songs work, you're ready to play the most popular harmonica styles — blues and rock, country, folk, and traditional music. What you discover in this part can be applied to many other styles of music as well. For instance, you could experiment with jazz, classical, or even klezmer, which is a lively, gypsy-influenced style of Yiddish music (*Fiddler on the Roof,* anyone?).

Part V: Taking Your Music to the World

How do I develop a repertoire of tunes to play? How do I go about making music with my friends and playing for audiences? How do I deal with sound equipment so I can be heard or even go electric and make my harp sound even cooler? How do I get my harps fixed if they break? Can I hot-rod my harps for higher performance? What other harps should I own, and what gear and accessories are helpful? This is the part to get answers to all these questions.

Part VI: The Part of Tens

No *For Dummies* book would be complete without the trademark section: the Part of Tens. This part includes chapters with top-ten lists of important, but fun, information. For example, do you want to network with other players? You're in luck! In this part, I show you ten ways to connect with the larger world of the harmonica — locally and worldwide and online and off. And suppose you want to feed your head and get some inspiration. You've come to the right place. In this part, I take you on a tour of ten different musical styles and their greatest harmonica players, and I also recommend some of the best CDs to check out in each style.

Part VII: Appendixes

You only need one harp in the key of C to learn and play along with the music in this book. But if the harmonica bug bites you (and I think it will), you'll want (and eventually need) harps in all 12 keys. In this part, you can see how the notes are laid out and where the bent notes are in all keys of harmonica. I also give you the rundown of the tracks on the CD to help you get the most out of the audio examples.

Icons Used in This Book

In the margins of this book, you find icons to help you spot important information — or even information that you may want to skip. Like those neon signs that depict a shoe or a martini glass in a shopping district, these icons point out things you may want to get into or skim over as you read. Here are the icons I use and what they mean:

This icon highlights important points that are key to the understanding and skills you want to acquire.

Every now and then I offer a tip that can get you where you're going more quickly or can put things in the right perspective. This icon helps you spot these golden tidbits.

This icon highlights long-winded technical explanations. If you want to skip the tech talk and just try out a new technique, that's perfectly fine. Later you may get curious about how things work. When that happens, you know where to look.

When you see this icon, exercise caution to avoid damaging your harmonica or, more important, your eyes, ears, or other sensitive body parts (including your ego).

This icon helps you relate what you hear on the CD to the examples and techniques in the book. The book describes and the CD demonstrates — what a combination!

Where to Go from Here

If you're a beginner and don't know much about harmonica, go to Chapter 1 or Chapter 2. They provide you with the basics to get you up and running. If you already play but can't quite figure out how to play what you're hearing on CDs or at live shows, check out Part III, where you discover how players use positions to play in many keys.

If you're fascinated by the secrets of bending notes, check out Chapter 8. (*Tip:* Working first with Chapter 6 will give you a big advantage.) And if you want to learn some tasty tongue textures, flip to Chapter 7.

If you already play fairly well but haven't yet developed a repertoire of tunes, hooked up with a band, or played in a jam or onstage, check out Part V. And last but not least, if you're an experienced player who wants to pick up on more advanced techniques, head to Parts III and IV.

Still not sure where to head? Simply check the index or table of contents for the topic you're most interested in.

Part I
Getting Started

The 5th Wave   By Rich Tennant

"I don't know who they are or where they come from, but they start showing up every time David plays his harmonica."

In this part . . .

Sometimes the best thing you can do is start at the beginning, especially if you're new to playing the harmonica. In this part, you get a little background on what's cool about the harmonica and where it came from, and then you find out which end is up and what sort of a harp to buy. After you've purchased your new harp, you can get a guided tryout. I round out this part with an introduction to harmonica tab and some basic musical theory and terminology.

Chapter 1

What Is This Thing Called Harp?

In This Chapter

▶ Discovering what makes the harmonica such a cool little instrument

▶ Considering what it takes to play

▶ Understanding how to take your playing beyond the basics

▶ Sharing your music with others and visiting the virtual harmonica village

Maybe you're attracted to the sweet yet wailing sound of a harmonica. Or maybe you dig the image of a harmonica player onstage who somehow manages to strike a hip-looking pose while apparently eating a sandwich that's hidden in his or her hands. Either way, you know you love harmonica, and you're dying to find out more. For a little background on the harmonica (or as players call it, the harp) and why it's such a great instrument to play, read on.

Considering the Harmonica's Coolness

What makes the harmonica one of the world's best-selling musical instruments? Let me count the ways! Here are just a few reasons that the harp is so cool:

✔ **Its sound has immediate appeal.** Its haunting, plaintive wail, which alternates with sweet, soothing tones, makes the harmonica attractive and easy to identify. Even a beginner on harmonica can rock a roomful of listeners for a few minutes. Expert musicians can play on the immediate emotional connection of the harmonica to create extended intimacy and depth of expression. That emotional appeal is one reason the harmonica is so often featured in film scores and on popular records.

✔ **It automatically sounds good.** The harmonica was designed to sound, well, harmonious. It's designed to play several notes at once in combinations that are pleasing and make intuitive sense because they automatically support the melody notes. Playing a harmonica is like riding a bicycle that you can't fall off of.

✔ **You can take it anywhere — even outer space.** The harmonica is one of the most portable instruments around. In fact, here's a tidbit most folks won't know: The harmonica was the first musical instrument in outer space. On a Gemini space flight in December 1965, astronaut Wally Schirra reported an unidentified flying object in a polar orbit (Santa's sleigh, perhaps?) and then played "Jingle Bells" on a harmonica that he had smuggled aboard.

✔ **It's cheaper than dinner out.** Seriously! You can buy a decent harmonica for less than the cost of a restaurant meal. You can't say that about a guitar or synthesizer.

✔ **It's close and intimate with the player.** You can enclose a harmonica completely within your hands, and its sound comes out closer to your ears than that of any other musical instrument. Playing the harmonica can be an intimate act, almost like writing in a secret diary.

✔ **It has the allure of the outsider.** The harmonica seems to bring out the rebel and the lone wolf in some players. In fact, harmonica technique is built on doing things the designers never imagined and may not even approve of! The harmonica embodies the triumph of creativity over orderly procedures.

✔ **It has the appeal of tradition.** Despite the lone wolf aspect, the harmonica expresses musical traditions beautifully, and it's also well accepted within the comfortable confines of community values.

Harmonica ancestors in the Stone Age

Possibly as early as the Stone Age (and probably in Southeast Asia), someone discovered that if you plucked a bow string and held it up to your open lips, your mouth would amplify the vibrations. Eventually, a clever musician developed a more compact sound source. This person made a simple jaw harp by taking a flat piece of bamboo and cutting a narrow flap (or reed) into its surface. When plucked or blown, the reed would swing freely and its vibration would sound a note. Eventually, people made these *free reeds* out of metal and installed them in bamboo tubes to create mouth-blown instruments, such as the *khaen* (several tubes bound together in rows like a pan pipe) and the *sheng* (a cluster of tubes inserted into a gourd, which looks like a forest of bamboo growing out of a teapot). To this day, the khaen is used in Thai and Laotian social music and courtship rituals, while the sheng remains an esteemed instrument in Chinese opera. The metal free reeds used in khaens and shengs are thought to be the ancestors of the reeds used in harmonicas today.

Becoming the Next Harmonica Idol: What It Takes to Play

Playing a musical instrument doesn't take supernatural abilities. It simply takes desire and application (and, okay, maybe a little talent). So, if you want to play the harmonica, trust your desire — you can totally do this. Once you're willing to try, you just need a few things:

- **A harmonica.** If you go shopping for a harmonica, you may encounter a bewildering array of types and models at prices that range from the equivalent of a hamburger to a small car! So when you're ready to buy your own harp, check out Chapter 2 for a buying guide to help you select a decent-quality harmonica of the right type at a sensible price.

- **A little music know-how.** Chapter 3 shows you how to read basic harp tab, which is the main thing you need to understand in order to read the examples and tunes in this book. If you read through all of Chapter 3, you also can pick up some basic music theory (which never hurt anyone).

- **Your body.** It may surprise you to know that most of the sound you hear when you play a harmonica comes from your lungs, throat, mouth, and hands — not the harmonica. After you get the hang of breathing through the instrument, you can start developing a little rhythm (Chapter 4), and then you can zero in on single notes to play melody (Chapter 5). From there you can start using your body to shape and amplify your sound. At that point, you're ready to tackle just about anything on the harmonica.

- **Regular practice — and unstructured fun!** The most important thing you can do to become better at playing the harmonica is to play regularly. Keep a harmonica in your pocket, car, purse, briefcase, carry-on bag, or fanny pack — it can pretty much go wherever you do. Find spare moments to play a little. Instead of watching reruns on TV or drumming your fingers on the dashboard at red lights, play your harp. Then, when you have time, try to spend half an hour just playing. As long as you do it frequently and regularly, you'll start to develop some playing ability.

Make sure to have fun and experiment. A regular practice session with goals is great, and I encourage it. But set some time aside for unstructured play. When you explore the instrument, you can have fun discovering new sounds, and you'll learn things about the harmonica that you won't get by sticking to the guided tour.

Harmonica in the Western World

No one really knows when the free reed made it from Asia to Europe (see the sidebar "Harmonica ancestors in the Stone Age" for more on the free reed's start in Asia). However, it had certainly arrived by 1636, when a khaen-like instrument was clearly described by French philosopher Marin Mersenne.

Then, in the mid-1700s, a Russian organ builder named Franz Kirschnik fashioned a new kind of free reed. Instead of being cut from the surface that surrounded it, the reed was made separately and attached above the surface. This new type of reed could respond to air flow without being mounted in a tube, which created all sorts of new possibilities. Kirschnik's reed was incorporated into organs, pitch pipes, and (starting in the 1820s) harmonicas and accordions.

Credit for inventing the harmonica usually goes to a German teenager named Friedrich Buschmann, who in 1821 strung together a series of pitch pipes to play a scale. By the 1870s, when mass production began and the Hohner company started aggressive overseas marketing, the harmonica had taken on today's familiar form. By the 1920s, Hohner was making 20 million harmonicas a year, and people worldwide were using them to play folk, popular, and even classical music. Since then, the harmonica has been a fixture on the world music scene.

Taking Your Talent to the Next Level

After you can play some chords and melody, you're ready to take your harmonica skills on the road. You may not be ready for the 30-cities-in-15-days kind of road, but you're definitely prepared to travel the road to greater mastery and satisfaction.

When you're ready to take your talent to the next level, consider mastering tonguing techniques, which allow you to take full advantage of rhythmic chording to accompany, vary, and accentuate melodies. (Check out Chapters 4 and 7 for more information on these techniques.) Your lungs, throat, tongue, and hands all play a part in making the harmonica one of the most expressive, voice-like musical instruments you can play. So be sure to explore ways to use your body to shape your sound as you advance. (Chapter 6 can help.)

Other important techniques include bending notes up and down in pitch, both to make an expressive wailing sound and to create notes that weren't designed into the harmonica. Experienced players also regularly play the harmonica in keys that it was never designed for, which works surprisingly well. (Chapter 9 has more information on the art of playing in *positions,* or multiple keys.)

As you master harmonica techniques, you'll likely want to start using them to play tunes. To work up your melody chops (your playing ability) in the high, low, and middle registers of the harmonica, spend some time with Chapter 10.

To see how song structures work, go to Chapter 11. Then you're all set for choosing songs and tunes to include in your repertoire (Chapter 16).

Hanging Out in the Harmonica Village

Wouldn't it be nice to step out of your practice room and amble down to the main street of the nearest harmonica village? There, you could chill at a harmonica coffeehouse where you make music with your friends, visit a harmonica accessories boutique with all the latest harmonica belts and cases, hit the music store to find great harmonica CDs or get new harps, and maybe hang out at the local harmonica garage to check out the vintage models that have come in for a wash and wax or the hot rods that are being souped up for horsepower and speed. Some parts of this ideal village probably exist in your town, while some parts may require a trip to far-off cities. Still others exist only online. So the village is a virtual place, and one you have to assemble for yourself. The following list sheds light on some tips for finding (or creating) parts of the village, and it shows you how to deal with what you find when you get there.

✔ **Sharing your music with others locally:** Getting together with other folks to play music can be enormously satisfying. When you're ready to take the plunge, you need to assemble a repertoire of tunes and understand the musical etiquette of playing with your friends. Also, when you get up in front of an audience, you need to be prepared, read the mood of the crowd, make a good impression, and know how to keep your cool when you make mistakes. If you suffer from stage fright, you need to overcome it as well. Chapter 16 explains all this and more.

An important part of playing for audiences is using sound systems and amplifiers (although playing amplified is also just plain fun). Chapter 17 guides you through the workings of microphones, speakers, amplifiers, and sound systems so you can deal with sound technicians, hear and be heard, and sound great while you strut your stuff.

✔ **Making the worldwide connection:** Harmonica players are like other groups of folks who share a common interest — they simply want to connect with others to talk shop, share tall tales, jam, teach and learn from one another, and just hang out. The Internet isn't the only way to do this. In fact, face-to-face encounters can be much more rewarding than cyberspace encounters. How do you connect with other harmonica players locally and nationally? Find out in Chapter 20.

✔ **Visiting the repair shop and the accessory store:** Harmonicas can be leaky, and they occasionally go out of tune or even break a reed. However, even if your harps are working okay, you can still spruce them up for better performance, including faster response, brighter and louder tone, easier note-bending, and sweeter sounding chords.

Harp techs usually live in out-of-the-way places where they can concentrate on their work. Instead of shipping your harps away and waiting for several weeks, why not fix them yourself? You can save time and money (and feel empowered by your self-reliance). Check out Chapter 18 for some hints on fixing and upgrading your harmonicas. When you're ready to purchase some accessories to make playing even more fun, check out your local music store. However, you may find a greater selection from online specialty retailers and manufacturers. (Check out Chapter 19 for some information on available harmonica gear.)

✔ **Feeding your head (and ears) at the music store:** Over the years, harmonica players have recorded some really great music in an amazing array of styles, from classical harmonica quintets to heavy metal and jug bands. To discover some of harmonica's greatest players and how to hear the inspiring music they've made, check out the recommended listening in Chapter 21.

Why is it called a harp when it doesn't have strings?

Both "harmonica" and "harp" are borrowed names, and neither one is the only correct name. The harmonica was invented during the Romantic era of Beethoven and Schubert. This was an era when home and garden décor included the *Aeolian harp,* which is a stringed harp that you set outdoors where the wind makes the strings vibrate. Even though the harmonica has reeds sounded by a player's breath instead of strings sounded by the wind, some early harmonica makers referred to their instruments as Aeolian harps by way of poetic association. Other early makers used the term "mouth harp." Still others borrowed the name of the *glass harmonica,* which is played with a moistened fingertip rubbed on the rim of a glass. Since those early days, Germans have referred to the harmonica both as a *mundharmonika* (mouth harmonica) and as a *mundharfe* (mouth harp). Meanwhile, American books were comparing the harmonica to a harp as early as 1830, and the introduction of a model called the "French Harp" in the 1880s may have helped to popularize calling it a "harp" in the American South.

Chapter 2

Your First Harmonica

. . . .

In This Chapter

▶ Buying a diatonic harmonica

▶ Trying out your new harp

▶ Exploring the nuts and bolts of a harmonica

▶ Keeping your instrument in good shape

. . . .

*I*f you want to try playing the harmonica, you probably should buy one. I mean, you could hum falsetto sounds into your hands like I did when I first started, but after a while people will start giving you funny looks. Trust me, I speak from experience.

Once you decide to take the plunge, your first challenge is figuring out what kind of harmonica to get. You can buy hundreds of different models and dozens of different types, in all sizes and shapes and keys. A harmonica can cost less than a hamburger or more than a small car. In this chapter, I tell you what to look for and what to avoid.

After you get a harmonica, or *harp,* as it's often referred to, this chapter can also help you get your first sound out of it. And if you're curious about how a harp actually makes that sound, I show you how a harmonica is put together. Your harmonica doesn't need vaccinations or a license, but you do need to know how to care for it, so I give you some easy guidelines for keeping it in good playing condition.

Shopping for Your First Harmonica

A good harp to begin with (and the only one this book includes instructions for) is a ten-hole diatonic harmonica in the key of C. And that's the one you should buy. Get one that has a plastic comb. Expect to pay an amount roughly equal to the price of this book.

Understanding the construction of the ten-hole diatonic

I wrote this book for the most popular kind of harmonica: the *ten-hole diatonic harmonica*. This harp is about 4 inches long, which makes it easy to cup in your hands. A diatonic harmonica is designed to play in just one key (but in Chapter 9, I show you how to play one of these harps in at least three keys). A diatonic harp looks like the one shown in Figure 2-1.

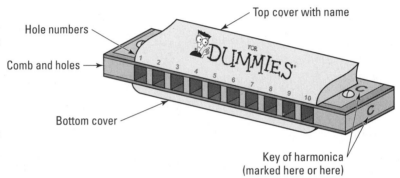

Hole numbers

Top cover with name

Figure 2-1:
A typical
ten-hole
diatonic
harmonica.

Comb and holes →

Bottom cover

Key of harmonica
(marked here or here)

Diatonic harmonicas come in many configurations. Yours should have:

✔ **Ten holes in a single row:** If your harp has more than one row of holes, it won't work with the instructions in this book. If it has more or fewer than ten holes, such as 4, 6, 12, or 14 holes, it may or may not work with this book. So just be safe and get one with ten holes.

✔ **A comb that's made of plastic, not wood or metal:** The *comb* is the middle layer of the harmonica. (Refer to Figure 2-1 to see what I mean.) I recommend a plastic comb because it won't swell, and plastic is the material that's most often used for mid-priced harmonicas of good quality.

Wood combs are beautiful, but when they get wet they can swell up and cut your lips. In fact, new players often produce a lot of saliva, so wood isn't a good choice until you get over the waterfall stage. Metal-combed harps are expensive. If you want to fork out the extra cash, however, I won't stop you. It's your money, and it will probably be a good harp. (See the later section, "Getting to Know You: Discovering How a Harmonica Works," for more information on combs.)

Choosing a harp in the key of C

Harmonicas come in all 12 keys, but all you need to get started is a diatonic harmonica in the key of C. You'll see this type referred to as a *C-harp*. The key is labeled on the top right or right side of the harp, as shown in Figure 2-1. The key will either be a single letter, like C or A, or a letter followed by a sharp (♯) or a flat (♭), as in B♭ or F♯. (Are you curious what a key is? If so, check out Chapter 3 for more details.)

All the examples on this book's CD are played on a C-harp. You can use a harp that's in another key, but then what you play won't sound like what's on the CD, because the notes will be different. Nearly all harmonica music books are written for a C-harp, and C is in the middle range of harmonica keys, so it's less likely to give you trouble than a low-pitched or high-pitched harp when you first start playing.

After you start getting the hang of playing on a C-harp, you can try other harps in different keys. Luckily, everything you learn on the C-harp will apply directly to other diatonic harps. However, do remember that anything you play on another key of harp automatically comes out in a different key.

Pricing a harmonica

Your first harmonica doesn't need to be gold-plated or encrusted with rubies, but it does need to be airtight, responsive to your breath, and in tune. The cheaper the price of the harp, the more likely it will be leaky, unresponsive, and out of tune. But that doesn't mean you have to take out a loan to buy a harp that plays well.

Prices for decent harmonicas range from the price of this book (you can find the price on the back cover of the book, near the bottom) to about twice that amount. Use that price as your guide for what to pay. You can pay a little more or a little less, but be aware of the following guidelines:

- ✔ If you buy a harmonica that costs less than half the price of this book, you may get lucky and find a decent harp. But the odds aren't good, and they get much worse as the price goes lower.

- ✔ If you pay more than twice the cost of this book, you'll get a good harp but it may be more than you need right now. New players often damage harps from breathing too hard, so you may as well start with something economical (as long as it's airtight, responsive, and in tune).

Among the better known manufacturers that consistently produce good quality instruments are Hering, Hohner, Lee Oskar, Seydel, Suzuki, and Tombo.

Determining where to buy a harp

If you're unsure of where to buy your first harmonica, remember that your local music store likely has some good harmonicas for sale. Its prices may be higher than you'd find online, but you'll come to realize the following three advantages to buying locally:

- ✔ **You won't have to wait.** You can walk in and walk out with a new harmonica in a matter of minutes. And the more you and your fellow harp players buy locally, the more likely it is that your local store will stock harmonicas and have them available when you need one. And think of it: If your harp breaks just before a gig (you're quitting your job and going pro tomorrow, right?) or you quickly need a harp in a key you don't have, that local shop can be a lifesaver.

- ✔ **You won't pay shipping costs.** Online retailers may charge for shipping, which can eat up any cost savings on the price of the harp.

- ✔ **You won't have to guess at quality.** By buying at a local store, you get to see a harmonica before you buy it, and you can examine it for obvious damage or flaws. You can sound the notes using the store's harmonica tester, which is a bellows that lets you sound out individual holes or several holes at once without actually playing the harp. (You may be relieved to know that your lips will be the first to actually touch your newly-purchased harp.) You push the bellows for the blow notes and let it spring back for the draw notes. This test allows you to determine whether all the notes work. And if you sound several holes at once, you can tell if the harp is in tune. If it sounds bad, it's probably out of tune.

Even though you benefit from shopping at your local music store, remember that it may not stock all the models and keys you want. You may find a wider selection and lower prices from mail-order sellers online, especially the ones that specialize in harmonicas and related accessories and equipment. However, don't forget that you may have to pay for shipping, wait for it to arrive, and then hope that it isn't defective.

Always check out the reputation of an online or mail-order seller. You want to ensure that the seller has quick delivery, is accurate in sending what was ordered, provides good communication with customers, and has a willingness to solve problems when they occur. To check a seller's reputation, go to some of the online harmonica discussion groups and ask around, or read the group's recent archive of postings. (For more about online resources, check out Chapter 20.)

Making Your First Sound

Got a shiny new harp all snug in its box? I'll bet you're eager to crack the lid, pull out that harp, and start playing. I get you officially started playing in Chapter 4, but in case you just can't wait to try that new harp, the following sections provide some basic pointers.

You don't need to break in your harmonica. Just warm it up first by cupping it in your hands or putting it under your arm for a few minutes. If you've had something to eat or drink recently — especially a sugary or thick beverage or anything oily or with a lot of fragments (such as nuts) — you should rinse your mouth out or even brush your teeth before you try your new harmonica. Food residue can clog up your harp — not to mention make it smell and taste unpleasant. Are you and your new harp all warm, clean, and fresh? Then read on!

Holding the harp

Before you do anything, look at the harp and the printing on the covers. It has a top and a bottom. On the top cover, the name of the harmonica is engraved. For instance, you may see the name Special 20, Lee Oskar, or Golden Melody. Just above the holes in the front of the harp are the numbers 1 through 10, from left to right. (Figure 2-1 earlier in this chapter shows an example of a harp.) Locating these items helps you learn how to hold a harmonica.

To hold your harmonica, be sure to follow these steps:

1. **When you pick up the harp, make sure the name and hole numbers are on top.**

2. **Hold the harp in your left hand with your index finger along the top and your thumb along the bottom, as shown in Figure 2-2.**

    Keep your finger and thumb back far enough on the covers that you have room for your lips. (I show you more about holding the harp in Chapter 4. For now, I just want to make it easy for you to get the harp in your mouth.)

Putting the harp in your mouth

As you're holding the harp between your thumb and forefinger, raise it to your lips. To get a good sound without letting air escape, your lips should form an airtight seal around the harp. The following steps can help you form a good seal:

1. **Open your mouth wide like you're going to yawn.**

2. **With your mouth wide open, put the harp between your lips until you feel the harp touching the corners of your lips, where the top and bottom lips meet.**

3. **Let your lips close gently over the covers.**

Your fingers should do all the work of holding the harp, so keep your lips relaxed, resting gently on the harp covers without any lip pressure. If your lips and fingers are fighting for space, back your fingers away to give your lips more space. Just make sure to keep enough of a finger grip so that the harp doesn't fall out of your mouth.

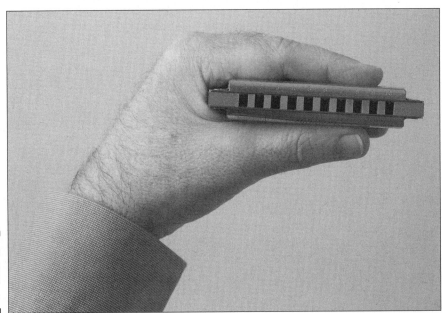

Figure 2-2:
The classic way to hold a harp.

Breathing through the harp

After you have the harp in your mouth, you can get it to make a sound simply by breathing in and out. No special techniques are required. Just follow these steps:

1. **Try inhaling gently like you're taking a normal breath.**

   As you breathe, you should hear a *chord,* which is several notes sounding at once.

2. **After you've inhaled for a few seconds, gently exhale like you're breathing normally.**

   You should hear a different chord.

You've just discovered one of the coolest things about the harmonica: You get notes and chords by both breathing in and breathing out. (Chapter 4 discusses in more detail how to breathe while you're playing.)

Leave the harp in your mouth for a while and gently alternate between inhaling and exhaling. Feel the sensation of the harp in your mouth, focus on your breath moving in and out, and listen to the sound of the harp. You do this to get comfortable with the feeling of breathing through the harp and to become familiar with the sounds you're making.

In Chapter 5, I show you a better way to hold the harp and how to play some chords in rhythm. In Chapter 6, I show you how to isolate just one hole for a single note. And in Chapter 7, I delve into breathing and show you how to get a big sound. I also show you how to start shaping the sound with your lungs, throat, tongue, and hands.

Getting to Know You: Discovering How a Harmonica Works

A harmonica can seem like a small, mysterious box — you breathe through it and music comes out. Knowing what goes on inside that little box can help you understand how to play it. So in the following sections, I take you on a tour of the hidden workings of the harmonica.

Making a five-layer tin sandwich

A harmonica has five layers, as shown in Figure 2-3.

The center layer of the harmonica sandwich is a slab of wood, metal, or plastic called the *comb*. Ten channels are cut into the slab. These channels form the holes that direct air from your mouth to the notes in the harmonica. The comb gets its name because the dividers between the channels look like the teeth of a comb.

The layers above and below the comb are the two *reedplates,* which are stiff plates of brass that enclose the top and bottom of each channel in the comb. Ten *reeds* are mounted on each reedplate, and the reeds vibrate to sound the notes. (You can read more about reeds and reedplates in the next section.)

The *covers* (or coverplates) form the top and bottom layers of the harmonica sandwich. The covers help to project the sound of the harmonica to the listener. The covers also protect the reeds and allow you to hold the harp without interfering with the reeds. The covers are made of thin, shiny metal that reminds people of tin cans (hence the nickname "tin sandwich"). Actually, though, the covers are either stainless steel or brass plated in chrome or nickel.

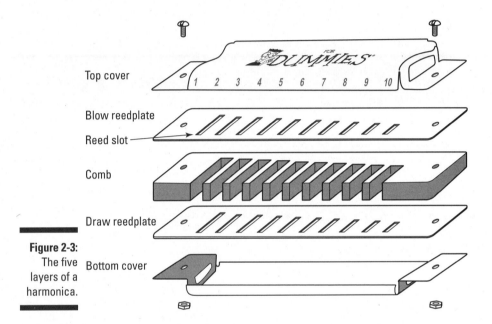

Top cover

Blow reedplate

Reed slot

Comb

Draw reedplate

Figure 2-3:
The five
layers of a
harmonica.

Bottom cover

Taking a closer look at the reeds that make the sound

Each note in a harmonica is sounded by a *reed,* a thin strip of brass that vibrates when you breathe into the harp. One end of the reed is fastened to the reedplate with a rivet. The rest of the reed is free to vibrate. A *slot* is cut into the reedplate directly under the reed. This slot allows air to get through to the reed and gives the reed a space to swing up and down as it vibrates. Figure 2-4 shows an example of a reedplate and reeds.

Each reed sticks up slightly from the reedplate. Your breath drives the reed into its slot, and then the reed springs back. This cycle is considered one complete vibration. Each note you hear is a reed vibrating hundreds or even thousands of times per second in response to your breath.

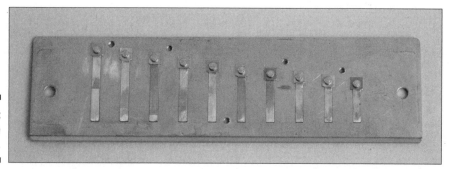

Figure 2-4:
A reedplate
and reeds.

Each hole has a *blow reed* and a *draw reed* mounted in its air channel. The blow reeds are mounted inside the air channels in the harmonica, on the upper reedplate. Exhaled breath pushes blow reeds into their slots and sets them vibrating. The draw reeds, on the other hand, are mounted on the outside of the air channels, on the lower reedplate. When you inhale, your breath pulls draw reeds into their slots to make them vibrate.

The *pitch* of the reed (how low or high the note is) is determined by how fast the reed vibrates. For instance, a long reed vibrates slowly and plays a low note. And if you add extra weight to the tip of the reed, it vibrates even more slowly and plays a lower note. A short reed vibrates quickly and plays a high note. If you look at the reeds on a reedplate, as shown in Figure 2-4, you can see that they progress from long (low notes) to short (high notes) as you go from left to right.

Tuning in to the key of the harp

Each diatonic harmonica is designed to play the notes that belong to one key, such as C, D, or A. If you learn to play a tune in C on a C-harp, you can easily play it in A. To do so, you just get an A-harp, play it exactly the same way that you did on the C-harp, and it will automatically come out in the key of A. (Not sure what a key is? Find out in Chapter 3.)

Having harps in different keys makes playing in different keys on the diatonic harmonica easy, but you do need a harmonica for each key. That's why you may see harmonica players onstage constantly picking up and putting down different harmonicas between songs, switching harps in the middle of tunes, or wearing vests or bandoliers festooned with pouches containing a dozen or so harmonicas.

Locating different notes

Ten-hole diatonic harmonicas are like hotel chains (or *For Dummies* books). No matter which one you go to (or pick up), they're all organized the same way so you know what to expect and where to find everything. For example, on a C-harp, C is the home note, and it's always the blow note in Hole 4. The next note up in the scale is the draw note in the same hole (which happens to be D). Similarly, on an F-harp, F is the home note, and you'll find it in — you guessed it — Blow 4. Draw 4 is the next note in the scale (which, in the key of F, happens to be G). This consistency of organization is what makes switching harps easy.

Figure 2-5 shows the note layout for a C-harp. It shows all ten holes, with each hole number above the corresponding hole. Each hole has one note name above another note name. The upper note name is the draw note, and the lower note name is the blow note. I go into more details about how notes relate to one another in Chapter 3. I show where all the notes are on all keys of a harmonica in Appendix A.

Figure 2-5:
The note layout for a diatonic harmonica in C.

	1	2	3	4	5	6	7	8	9	10
Draw	D	G	B	D	F	A	B	D	F	A
Blow	C	E	G	C	E	G	C	E	G	C

Safe and Sound: Caring for Your Harp

The better you care for your harps, the longer they'll last and the better they'll work. Here are a few tips to keep your harps in good shape:

✔ **Warm your harp before you play.** You can warm harps in your hands, in a pocket close to your body, under your arm, or even in a warming pad. Why should you warm your harp? A warm harmonica resists moisture buildup and clogging, and it may respond more readily than a cold harp.

Don't get your harps too hot. You don't want to melt any parts or set your harps on fire (at least not literally — we all want that creative fire). And you don't want a harp so hot that it burns your lips and tongue. Never place a harp on a heater or a radiator.

✔ **Keep your harp clean.** The first line of defense in keeping your harp clean is not blowing food chunks or syrupy liquids into it. If you've just had a snack, be sure to rinse your mouth out or brush your teeth before you play. The second line of defense is playing with clean hands. Most viruses are picked up by your hands and then rubbed on your eyes or lips. Germs can also be transferred from your hands to your harp to your lips. So washing your hands before you play helps you avoid illness. And not getting sick means you have more play time.

I don't recommend washing harmonicas, because some of the inner parts can rust. Some players periodically take their harps apart and clean all the parts with alcohol, but this isn't really necessary. (I go into harmonica maintenance in Chapter 18.)

✔ **Remove excess moisture during and after playing.** The longer you play, the more breath moisture you build up in the harp. This moisture can clog the reeds, corrode some of the metal parts inside, and make wood parts swell and warp. So between tunes and after playing a harp, tap the loose moisture out of it. To do so, simply hold the harp with the holes facing out (see Figure 2-6a) and tap the holes gently against your palm (see Figure 2-6b). Then allow the harp to dry in the open air before putting it away.

✔ **Store your harp properly.** It's best to carry a harp in a pouch or box — like the one the harp came in. Properly storing an instrument helps protect it from getting clogged with hair, lint, and other foreign particles. It also protects the harp from damage. As your harmonica collection grows, you can get cases, wallets, and even belts to carry your harps. See Chapter 19 for more on harp-carrying systems.

Figure 2-6:
Tapping moisture out of a harp.

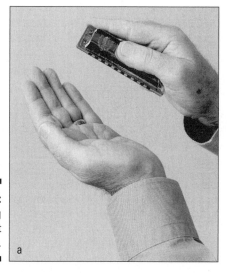
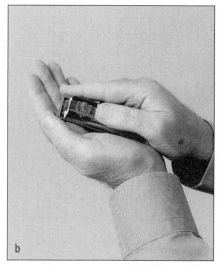

Chapter 3

The Language of Music: Surveying a Bit of Theory

*P*eople say that music is an international language because it has a strong, immediate effect on its listeners. In this chapter, I take you on a tour of the language *behind* the music. I show you:

- ✔ **How to read harmonica tab.** *Tab,* which is short for *tablature,* shows you the physical action you take to play each note. I use tab throughout this book.

- ✔ **How to find the key of a song.** Most music is organized around a key note, and knowing the key of any tune you want to play is essential.

- ✔ **How to read rhythms.** Throughout this book, I use written rhythms to help you know when to play a note and for how long to play it.

- ✔ **How sound is organized into notes.** The vast spectrum of audible vibrations is organized into note names using a few simple principles.

- ✔ **How to read basic music notation.** *Notation* is the lines, spaces, dots, and squiggles of written music. You don't need notation to master the tunes in this book, but it's included in case you find it helpful. I encourage you to acquire the knack of reading notation because thousands of tunes are available in music notation, whereas only hundreds of tunes are available in harmonica tab.

Reading Harmonica Tab

Harmonica tablature, or tab for short, tells you how to play each note in a melody by showing you which hole number to play and whether to blow or draw in that hole. (Tab can tell you more about how to play a note, but the hole number and breath direction are the most important things to know.) Basic tab is shown in Figure 3-1.

When looking at basic tab, such as in the figure, an arrow pointing up tells you to exhale breath into the harmonica. A note that you play by exhaling is called a *blow note.* An arrow pointing down tells you to inhale air through the harmonica. A note that you play by inhaling is called a *draw note.* The number under the arrow tells you which hole to play; each number corresponds to the number directly above each hole on the harmonica.

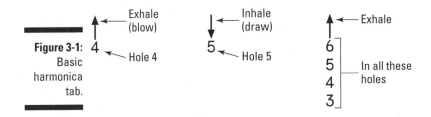

Figure 3-1: Basic harmonica tab.

Basic tab works for notes that are built into the harmonica. However, as you may know, harp players *bend* notes up and down to create additional notes. Tab for bent notes is shown in Figure 3-2.

In tab meant for bent notes, one slash through the arrow indicates that you should bend the note down one semitone. (I explain semitones in more detail in the later section, "Measuring the distance with semitones and whole tones.") Two or three slashes tell you to bend the note down two or, you guessed it, three semitones. A circle through the arrow shaft indicates a note that's bent up (which can be an *overblow* or an *overdraw* note depending on the direction of the arrow). Have I made you curious about bending? Check out Chapter 8 for more on bending notes down and Chapter 12 for bending notes up.

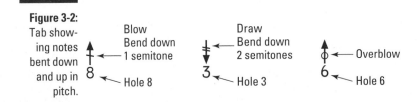

Figure 3-2: Tab showing notes bent down and up in pitch.

I use other tab symbols in this book, but I introduce them along with the techniques they depict.

Tab tells you how to play notes on the harmonica, but it doesn't tell you how long to play them. So nearly all the tab in this book also includes written rhythms that tell you how long to play each note. To take advantage of this rhythm information, check out the section "Exploring Rhythm Basics" later in this chapter.

Finding the Key of a Song

People casually say things like "Let's play in the key of E major" or "Was that really played in the key of B♭ minor?" Hearing these types of comments probably makes you realize that a key must be associated with a note, such as E or B♭. But what does that mean? Don't worry — I can explain.

In a piece of music, the key is the *tonal center,* the one note among all the others that feels like home. This home note — the *tonic* — feels like a place of rest. But the tonic is also a place of power. When you're on the tonic note, you can feel all the other notes orbiting in the gravitational pull of the tonic. This feeling is more important than the specific identity of the key because the distances, or *intervals,* between the other notes and the tonic are more important than the notes themselves. Each interval creates a unique impression when it interacts with the tonic.

When you're listening to music, try to feel where the tonic note is. It's usually the note you hear most frequently in the bass, and it's often the note that starts and ends the tune. Listen for that note, and when you find it, hum it and feel how it defines everything else going on in the music. After you define the tonic note, try humming or playing other notes, and then notice how they interact with the tonic. If you want to identify the key by name, find an instrument (such as a keyboard) that allows you to match the note and easily identify which note you're hearing.

For information on how to choose a key of harmonica to match the key of a song, check out Chapters 9 and 11.

Exploring Rhythm Basics

Rhythm is just the relative durations of notes. Whenever you play a note, then follow it with another note, you create rhythm. In this section, I take you through the most important rhythm concepts, and I show you the ways you'll see them written throughout this book.

Counting time with quarter, half, and whole notes

Music uses *beats* to count time. These beats come at a steady rate — just like with walking, a heart beating, or a clock ticking. When you measure how fast the beat goes by, it's called *tempo*. The smooth swimming exercise in Chapter 4 has a fairly slow tempo of 60 beats per minute. A tempo of 120 beats per minute is a common dance tempo (disco, anyone?), and something like 220 beats per minute is a very fast tempo (think white-hot jazz or a bluegrass barnburner).

The most common way to represent a beat is the *quarter note*. A quarter note has a note head and a thin stem that can stick up or down from the note head. When you see a series of quarter notes, it looks a bit like an army of legs and feet walking along, as shown in Tab 3-1.

In Tab 3-1, I include tab under the quarter notes that tells you when to inhale and exhale through the harp. Try tapping a steady beat with your foot that isn't too fast. Then raise the harp to your mouth and try breathing in and out through the harp according to Tab 3-1. Don't worry about trying to isolate a single hole. Let your mouth cover several holes. You'll hear a combination of several notes sounding at once, which is a chord.

You can hear Tab 3-1 being played on Track 1 of the CD.

When you have two chords in a row that are on the same breath (both blow or both draw), don't stop breathing between them. Play one continuous breath, and use your tongue to say "T" at the beginning of the second chord.

Tab 3-1:
Inhaling and exhaling on the quarter note beat (Track 1).

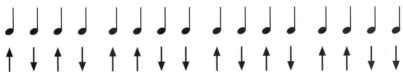

When a note lasts the same amount of time as two quarter notes, it's a *half note*. A half note has a head that's hollow instead of solid. The half note head looks heavy, like it can only walk half as fast as the quarter note.

Tab 3-2 shows an exercise for playing quarter notes and half notes. While looking at the tab, play two quarter notes. Then hold one half note for the same amount of time as two quarter notes without interrupting your air-stream. The counting numbers above the notes in the tab may help.

You can hear the exercise in Tab 3-2 on Track 1 (0:13) of the CD.

Tab 3-2:
Playing
quarter
notes and
half notes
(Track 1,
0:13).

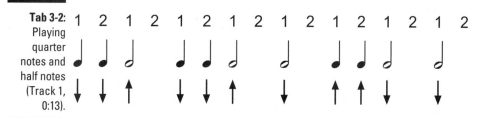

When you have a long note that lasts four quarter notes (or two half notes), you have a *whole note.* This type of note has a hollow head and no stem. It looks sort of like a big egg that just lies there and can't go anywhere.

Try playing Tab 3-3 to get a feel for playing quarter notes with whole notes. You can hear this tab on Track 1 (0:26) of the CD.

Tab 3-3:
Playing
quarter
notes and
whole notes
(Track 1,
0:26).

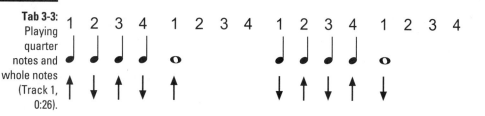

Counting silence with rests

Sometimes you don't play; you just *lay out,* as musicians say. In some types of music, you may play for three beats, and then lay out for a beat. In any case, silent time is shown with *rests,* and each note value has a corresponding rest symbol. Figure 3-3 shows quarter- and half-note rests, with just one note played in each measure. The last measure is silent — it's a whole note rest.

Figure 3-3:
Quarter-,
half-, and
whole-note
rests.

Quarter rest   Half rest   Whole rest

Extending notes with ties and dots

All the notes in a measure have to fit inside the measure. After all, you can't put five beats in a four-beat measure. But what if you have a note that starts in one measure and ends in the next? You write the beginning of the note in one measure and use a *tie* to connect it to another note in the next measure, as shown in Figure 3-4.

When two notes are tied together you play them as one long note. Several notes in succession can be tied together as well, and the notes can be of different individual durations. Ties allow you a lot of flexibility in specifying how long a note should be, when it starts, and when it ends.

Figure 3-4:
Using ties
to extend
notes.

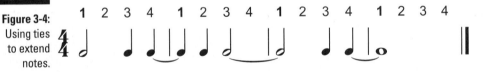

Another way to extend a note is to add a *dot* after the note. When you do this, you increase the value of the note by 50 percent, as shown in Figure 3-5. If a half note has the value of two quarter notes, a dotted half note has the value of three quarter notes. Any note value can be dotted. (See the later section, "Grouping beats with measures, bar lines, and time signatures," for more on using dots with notes.)

Figure 3-5:
Dotted
notes.

Dividing quarter notes

In this section, I show you how divisions of the quarter note are organized. The beat of a tune is often a quarter note, and dividing the beat into smaller units is something that makes music exciting. Imagine you're walking along to a beat, and you start drumming your fingers on your chest or leg faster than the walking beat. You can come up with all sorts of fun rhythms.

Getting eighth and sixteenth notes

When you divide a quarter note in half, you get two eighth notes. An *eighth note* looks like a quarter note, but it has a flag flying from its stem. It's almost as if an eighth note moves fast enough to leave a motion blur streaking in its wake. Two eighth notes in the same beat are joined by a beam instead of having individual flags. An *eighth note rest* is sort of like a little stick with one twig to match the flag or beam on an eighth note. Figure 3-6 shows an eighth note, a set of eighth notes joined by a beam, and an eighth note rest.

Flag   Beam   8th Rest

Figure 3-6:
Eighth notes
and rests.

Eighth notes divide into . . . (wait for it) . . . sixteenth notes! A *sixteenth note* has two flags or beams instead of one, and a *sixteenth note rest* has two twigs instead of one, as shown in Figure 3-7. By adding more flags, beams, or twigs, you can also create 32nd, 64th, and even 128th notes and rests.

Flags   Beams   16th Rest

Figure 3-7:
Sixteenth
notes and
rests.

Using triplets

Sometimes, instead of dividing a quarter note in half, you need to divide it into three equal parts. Dividing a quarter note by three gives you a twelfth note. But wait a minute. There's no such thing as a twelfth note!

Luckily, musicians have a practical solution to this problem. They simply put three eighth notes in the beat and call it a *triplet* (three notes in the space where two notes would normally fit). Any note value can be divided into triplets in the same manner, but eighth note triplets are the ones you're most likely to encounter. A triplet has a 3 written above or below it, as shown in Tab 3-4.

Tab 3-4 shows a melody that starts out dividing the beat in half and then employs triplets. You can hear this melody on Track 2 of the CD. If you can play single notes, try counting time and playing along.

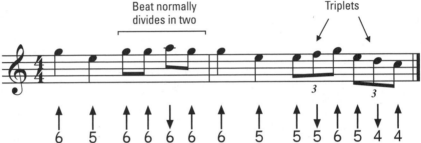

Tab 3-4: Playing a melody with triplets (Track 2).

Grouping beats with measures, bar lines, and time signatures

A steady procession of beats is kind of dull. Beats are more interesting when they're grouped in twos, threes, or fours (though in some cultures, groups of 7 and even 11 are highly favored). To make the beginning of each group obvious when you're playing, you give the first beat of the group (the *downbeat*) more emphasis than the rest. Usually you give that emphasis by playing the note slightly louder.

Each group of beats is called a *measure* (or *bar*). Written music uses a vertical line, called a *bar line,* to mark the end of each measure. This line allows you to easily see where one measure ends and the next one begins (see Figure 3-8). The last measure of a piece of music always ends with a heavy double bar line, also shown in Figure 3-8.

How do you know how many beats are in a measure and what kind of note represents the beat? You get this information from the *time signature,* which is written at the beginning of the first measure of a piece of music. The time signature looks like a fraction, with one number above another. The top number tells you how many beats are in each measure, and the bottom number tells you which note value represents the beat. Figure 3-8 shows an example of 4/4, with time signature, bar lines, quarter-note beats, and some division of the beat into eighth notes.

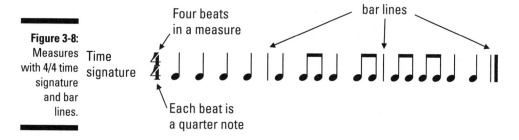

Figure 3-8:
Measures with 4/4 time signature and bar lines.

Sometimes 4/4 is indicated by a symbol that looks like a capital "C," which stands for *common time*. Whenever you see the C instead of a time signature or encounter the term "common time," you know it refers to 4/4.

Some other common time signatures that use the quarter note as a beat are 2/4, which is used for marches, and 3/4, which is often called *waltz time* because waltzes are played in 3/4. You can see 2/4 and 3/4 time signatures in Figure 3-9.

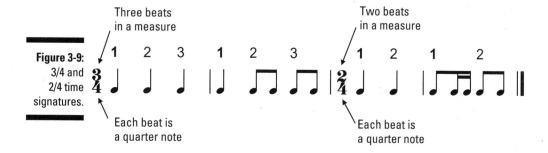

Figure 3-9:
3/4 and 2/4 time signatures.

Cut time is the common name for the time signature 2/2. A measure of 2/2 has two half-note beats. When you write cut time, you use a special symbol for the time signature. It looks like a capital "C" with a vertical slash through it. Figure 3-10 shows a few measures of cut time.

Figure 3-10:
An example of cut time.

Time signatures that divide the beat into three equal parts use a dotted note as the beat. (For instance, when you hear a jig, such as the "Irish Washerwoman," you're hearing a tune where the beat divides into three.) When you put a dot after a note, its length is increased by half, so a dotted quarter is three eighth notes long instead of two. Time signatures that use a dotted note for the beat are called *compound time signatures.*

When you write down a compound time signature, you can't represent the beat as a 4 with a dot after it. (Why? Who knows — it just isn't done.) Instead, you write down the total number of divisions of the beat. For instance, a jig has two beats, and each beat is a dotted quarter, for a total of six eighth notes, so the time signature is 6/8. Figure 3-11 shows a few measures of 6/8.

Figure 3-11:
An example of 6/8 time.

Dividing the beat unequally to get swing

Sometimes when the beat normally divides in two, divisions of the beat are played so that the first "half" lasts a little longer, while the second "half" comes a little later and is a little shorter. This unequal division of the beat is called *swing.* The difference between swing and an equal division of the beat can be almost imperceptible. Swing is the rule in blues and jazz, but it can be heard in many other kinds of music as well.

Because swing is a matter of feel, it's difficult to write down accurately. You may see a piece with "Swing" or "swing 8ths" written at the beginning. Or a piece of written music may have no indication that it's to be played with swing. However, when you hear knowledgeable musicians playing it, you'll hear them swing the notes.

Tab 3-5 shows a tune played with a type of swing called *shuffle rhythm* (because the rhythm sounds like you're saying "Shuffle, shuffle"). Shuffle rhythm is especially common in blues. Many of the examples in this book are played with a swing or a shuffle rhythm. If you can already play single notes, pick up a harp and try playing the rhythm. If you need an idea of what the rhythm sounds like, you can hear it on Track 3 of the CD.

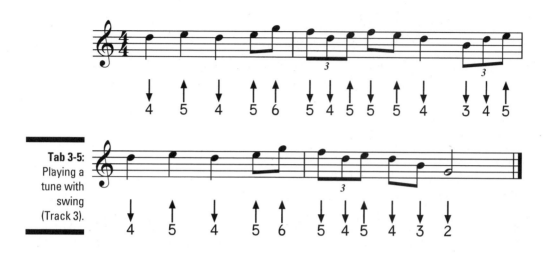

Tab 3-5:
Playing a
tune with
swing
(Track 3).

Counting off a tune

Whenever you start a tune, you need to count aloud at least one measure of time before you begin playing. How you count tells you and anyone else playing along what the tempo and meter are for the song. For instance:

- To count off a tune in two (or in 6/8), you may count like this: One, two, one, two.

- To count off a tune in three, you may count like this: One-two-three, one-two-three.

- To count off a tune in four, you may count like this: A-one, a-two, a-one, two, three, four.

Some tunes have a *pickup* — a few notes of melody that start while you're still counting off the tune. Tab 3-6 shows a pickup while a tune is being counted off. Try counting it off and playing it, and then listen to it on Track 4 of the CD.

Tab 3-6:
Counting off
a tune with
a pickup
(Track 4).

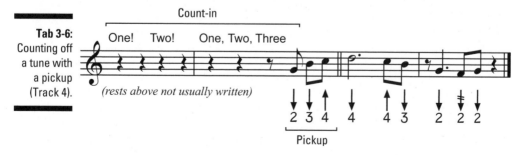

Mapping the Universe of Notes

You're likely aware that music is played with notes, and that the notes are named for letters of the alphabet. Only the first seven letters are used — A, B, C, D, E, F, and G — and yet, those seven letters are used to name over 100 different notes. How can you tell one note from another? And how are the note names organized? The next few sections help to answer those questions.

Naming the notes

When you play a note on a harmonica, you're making a sound that vibrates at a steady speed, anywhere from about 100 to about 4,000 times each second. The speed of vibration is called its *frequency*. Instead of referring to so many "vibrations per second," people refer to a specific number of *Hertz*, abbreviated Hz.

A low note, or low frequency, is one that vibrates slowly, and a high note, or high frequency, vibrates quickly. We humans can hear sounds vibrating at frequencies anywhere from about 20 to about 20,000 Hz. We can sing notes over a range from about 80 to about 1,000 Hz, and we use frequencies ranging from about 30 to about 4,200 Hz for instrumental music.

When you play two notes and one vibrates twice as fast as the other, you hear these as being the same note only in lower and higher versions. In other words, the note vibrating twice as fast sounds like the same note, but it's played an octave higher.

For instance, the note called "A" can be one that vibrates at 110 Hz. A note vibrating twice as fast, at 220 Hz, is also called "A" but is an octave higher. You can keep doubling the frequency of A to 440 Hz, 880 Hz, 1760 Hz, and so on through the range of human hearing. Each of these notes is a *pitch*. A pitch has both a name and a specific frequency.

In between two pitches called "A" that are located an octave apart, ancient musicians filled in other pitches and called them "B, C, D, E, F, and G." The sequence A B C D E F G A totals eight notes, or an *octave* (from the Latin for "eight"). The notes contained in an octave are called a *scale*. You can start a scale or an octave on any note; you don't have to start on A.

Music spans more than eight octaves, or roughly 100 notes. Instead of trying to find (and remember) 100 or so unique note names, we just reuse the same seven names over and over, taking advantage of the fact that each note in each octave vibrates half or twice as fast as the same note in the octave below or above.

Altering notes with sharps and flats

Even though music uses 7 note *names,* the octave really divides into a total of 12 named *notes.* At this point you may be wondering, "In what universe does 7 equal 12?" All I can say is that human ideas don't always evolve in a straight line. I'll attempt to explain here.

If you look at one octave of a piano keyboard, you see eight white keys, one for each note in the scale, as shown in Figure 3-12. These are the *natural* notes that musicians identified sometime during the Dark Ages. Why are these notes white? Maybe the light in those dark times was too dim to see anything else. Anyway, medieval musicians based all their scales on the white notes and called those scales *modes.* Modes are important on the diatonic harmonica (check out Chapter 9 for more on modes).

Figure 3-12:
The notes on a piano keyboard.

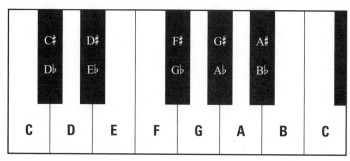

But what about those black keys that have two different names? Where did they come from? Well, over the centuries, people began to notice that lurking between some of the natural notes were additional notes that hadn't been identified. (What took people so long to notice these notes? Who knows. Maybe their hearing improved as the light got better.)

By the time these new notes were discovered, the natural note names were already standardized, and it would have been confusing to redistribute them to accommodate the new notes (sort of like having to change your address because someone built a new house next door). But adding new names, such as J or K, in between A and B would have been confusing as well. So these new black-key notes were named for *both* of their closest neighbors.

For instance, the black key between C and D can be called C♯ (C-sharp), meaning C raised in pitch but not all the way to D. However, that same note can also be called D♭ (D-flat), meaning D lowered in pitch but not all the way to C.

C♯ and D♭ are two different ways to *spell* the same note. Any two notes that are different spellings of the same note are said to be *enharmonic.* (Just think of all the fancy new vocabulary you can start tossing around!)

Measuring the distance between notes with semitones and whole tones

The distance between notes is measured in semitones and whole tones. A *semitone* is the smallest distance between two notes. For instance, if you look at the piano keyboard in Figure 3-12, each key is one semitone away from its closest neighbor. C is a semitone away from C♯, and E♭ is a semitone away from E. Notes E and F are also a semitone apart. A *whole tone* is two semitones. For instance, C and D are a whole tone apart. E and F♯ are also a whole tone apart, and so are B♭ and C.

Semitones are sometimes called *half-steps* or *half-tones,* while whole tones are sometimes called *whole steps,* or simply *tones.*

Writing Notes Down

Music notation tells you which notes to play and when to play them. However, notation doesn't tell you how to get the notes on the harmonica or on any other instrument; those specifics are left up to you. Because notation doesn't have to be written for any specific instrument, you can learn music written for flute, piano, or voice on the harmonica. In this section, I show you the basics of reading written notes and relating them to a *C-harmonica* (a harmonica built to play in the key of C). I also show you where to find the notes in notation. You can find out about rhythm and time in the earlier section, "Exploring Rhythm Basics."

Placing notes on a staff

Notes are written on a stack of five horizontal lines called the *staff.* The notes are represented by oval shapes that are placed either on the lines or in the spaces between the lines; low notes are placed low on the staff and high notes are placed high on the staff (the staff is a little like a ladder).

A staff can represent any range of notes, so a *clef* is placed at the beginning of the staff to indicate the location of one specific note, such as G, C, or F. From that note you can count up and down to figure out which notes lie above and below. For instance, the *treble clef* is a stylized letter G, and it wraps around the line where G above Middle C is written. From that G you can count up and down to figure out where the rest of the notes are. A staff with a treble clef is often called the *treble staff.* You can see a staff with a treble clef and notes in Figure 3-13.

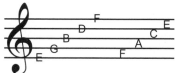

Figure 3-13:
A treble
staff with
note names.

Here are some simple ways to remember which notes in the treble staff are on which lines and spaces:

- The lines are used to write these notes: E G B D F. And here's the common mnemonic device folks use to remember the ascending order of the notes that go on the lines: Every Good Boy Deserves Fudge.

- The spaces are used to write the notes F A C E, which together (obviously) spell "face."

Some high notes go above the staff, while some low notes go below the staff. You write these notes by adding more lines above or below the staff and then writing the notes on or between the added lines. These added lines are called *ledger lines.* You use them whenever you have notes that extend above or below the staff. Figure 3-14 shows you ledger lines both above and below the staff.

Notes on ledger lines
above the staff

Figure 3-14:
A treble
staff with
ledger lines.

Notes on ledger lines
below the staff

Reading notes that go into multiple ledger lines is like scaling the dizzying height of some tall peak. To make things easier to read, you can write the notes above the staff one octave lower. To show that these notes should be played an octave higher than written, the phrase "8va" is placed above them along with a dotted line to show which notes should be played an octave higher. In Figure 3-15, you can see one staff showing notes written at actual pitch and another whose notes have been transposed an octave.

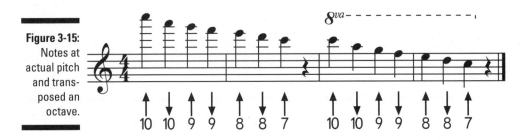

Figure 3-15:
Notes at
actual pitch
and trans-
posed an
octave.

Writing sharps and flats on the staff

On the staff, sharps (♯), flats (♭), and naturals (♮) are symbols placed in front of a note to raise or lower its pitch by a semitone. (See the earlier section, "Altering notes with sharps and flats," for more details.) Here are some guidelines to follow when reading these symbols:

✔ Assume that a note is a natural note unless you find out otherwise.

✔ A flat is used to lower the pitch of a natural note by one semitone.

✔ A sharp is used to raise the pitch of a natural note by one semitone.

✔ If a note has been flatted or sharped and is now going back to being a natural note (as you were, soldier!), the natural symbol is used.

Figure 3-16 shows G♭, G♯, and G♮ on the treble staff.

Sharp
raises pitch
one semitone

Flat
lowers pitch
one semitone

Natural
cancels a sharp or flat

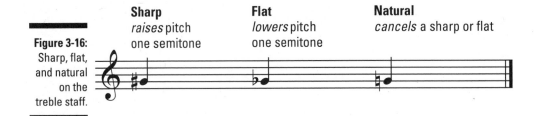

Figure 3-16:
Sharp, flat,
and natural
on the
treble staff.

When sharps, flats, or naturals are written in front of a note, they're called *accidentals*. An accidental applies only during the measure in which it occurs. If you were a note walking down the street, you might accidentally bump into an accidental, say "Hey, how's it going, dude?" and then forget about it and go on with your day.

Unlocking key signatures

A *key signature* is the group of sharps or flats needed to create a major scale in a particular key. On the staff, a key signature appears at the beginning of the line as one or more sharps or flats. It tells you which notes are automatically changed to sharps or flats to fit the key. (See Figure 3-17 for an example.) Chapter 11 goes into more detail about key signatures.

When you contradict the key signature to temporarily raise (sharpen) or lower (flatten) a note in the scale, you use an accidental. (Refer to the earlier section, "Writing sharps and flats on the staff," for more on accidentals.) If a note is flatted or sharped in the key signature and you're changing it back to a natural, you use the natural sign, ♮, as shown in Figure 3-17. You see accidentals a lot in harmonica music because a lot of it — blues especially — uses a scale that's a little different from the major scale. Plus, when you bend notes (see Chapters 8 and 12), the bent notes are often outside the scale.

Figure 3-17:
A key signature and an accidental.

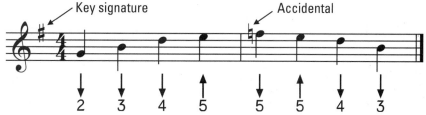

Finding harmonica notes on the staff

Figure 3-18 shows all the notes in a C-harmonica on the treble staff. The draw notes are shown on a staff above the harmonica and the blow notes are shown on another staff below. The arrows point from each note to the hole in the harmonica where the note is found. If you want to read music notation on the harmonica, this figure can help you relate the written notes to the notes on a C-harmonica.

The harmonica is designed to play *chords* — harmonious groups of notes — whenever you play three or more holes at a time. The most basic type of chord is called a *triad*. The chords on a harmonica are useful in music. However, when you play chords, you should be aware of which chords they are. This way you can be sure they don't clash with the chords being played by guitar or piano when you play music with others.

The draw notes contain the following triads:

- ✔ Holes 2, 3, and 4 form a G major triad (G-B-D), written on staff lines.
- ✔ Holes 3, 4, and 5 form a B diminished triad (B-D-F), written on lines.
- ✔ Holes 4, 5, and 6 (and also 8, 9, and 10) form a D minor triad (D-F-A).

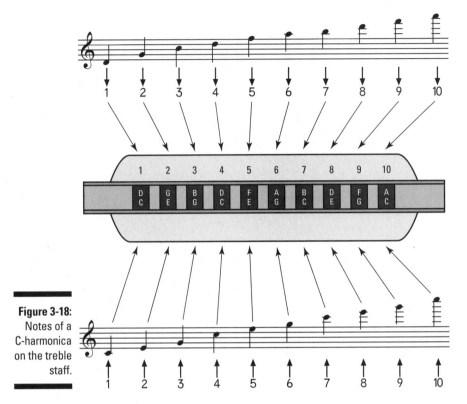

Figure 3-18:
Notes of a
C-harmonica
on the treble
staff.

✔ Holes 7, 8, and 9 form another B diminished triad (B-D-F), written on spaces between ledger lines above the staff.

✔ Holes 8, 9, and 10 form another D minor triad (D-F-A), written on spaces between ledger lines above the staff.

The blow notes form the following series of C triads:

✔ C, E, and G in Holes 1, 2, and 3 are written on lines, starting with Middle C on a ledger line below the staff.

✔ C, E, and G in Holes 4, 5, and 6 are written on spaces.

✔ C, E, and G in Holes 7, 8, and 9 are written on ledger lines. Hole 10 is C, which is written on a space above a ledger line.

Part II
Starting to Make Some Music

The 5th Wave   By Rich Tennant

"Okay, did you feel that rhythm on the way down?
That's the syncopation I'm looking for."

In this part . . .

This part is where you and the harmonica start getting to know each other by playing together. You get your basic breathing and rhythm together, and then you discover how to play simple melodies. After that you begin to focus and shape your sound and use your tongue to create textures. Finally, you delve into the not-so-mysterious art of bending notes, which is one of the signature sounds of harmonica expression.

Chapter 4

Relaxation, Breathing, and Rhythm

. . . .

. . . .

In Chapter 2, I give you a brief lesson in getting your first sound out of a harmonica. In this chapter, I get you to pick the harp back up and guide you through everything you need to develop good posture, to hold the harp in a hand cup that lets you shape the sound, and to breathe deeply while concentrating your breath for maximum efficiency to get a powerful sound out of the harp — all with minimum effort. You get to try out your new skills by having some fun with rhythm patterns, including one the harmonica is famous for, the chugging sound of a train. I top it off by showing you how to use your hands to add intensity to your rhythms.

Preparing to Play: Relax, Breathe Easy, and Hold the Harmonica

Can you get more if you give less? In a word, yes. If you find the minimum effort needed to accomplish an action, you'll have energy left over. In fact, if you can gently persuade the harmonica to do your bidding, you'll get a bigger and better sound than if you bludgeon it into submission. As you're preparing to play, relax and you'll have more concentration and more energy. When you relax, you'll notice more about what you're doing, and you'll have more fun.

When you're trying something unfamiliar, such as playing harmonica, you may be apprehensive. You may be afraid of failing, or you may simply feel uncomfortable making your body do something it has never tried before. There's nothing wrong or unusual about any of those feelings. But if you pay attention to what your body is experiencing and to what you're thinking, you can work to relax and clear your mind. Then you'll be more receptive to learning.

Relaxation starts with posture and breathing. So, in the following sections, I prepare you step by step for playing some basic harp sounds.

Perfecting your playing posture

When getting ready to play a harmonica, be sure to stand or sit so that you feel no physical tension or discomfort and so that your entire upper body can breathe deeply and fully. This means standing (or sitting) erect with no part of your body slumped.

Try this simple exercise to relax and prepare your body before you pick up a harmonica to play:

1. **Stand with your arms at your sides, and lift your heels so that you're standing on the balls of your feet.**

2. **Take a deep breath as you raise your arms over your head until your hands gently touch.**

3. **Slowly lower your arms and your heels as you let out your breath.**

4. **Let your arms dangle at your sides, and let your shoulders relax.**

5. **Keep your head erect so you feel no tension in your neck, and gaze confidently at something that is at eye level. Imagine that it's far away but crystal clear.**

Maintain this posture when you play standing up. When you play sitting down, keep your upper body erect, your upper legs level, and your feet on the floor.

Breathing deeply and gently

In the previous section, I show you how to attain a relaxed, erect posture. Now I want to turn your attention to your breathing. The following exercise gets you breathing deeply, fully, and gently.

1. **Yawn and notice how your throat opens wide to increase airflow. Keep your throat open while you breathe.**

2. **Breathe in slowly and gently, and feel your rib cage and your abdomen expand (your abdomen is the area between your rib cage and your waist).**

   As you inhale, notice your shoulders — they may rise slightly as your rib cage expands.

3. **Exhale gently and allow your abdomen to deflate inward, but keep your rib cage and shoulders expanded.**

   Don't allow your shoulders to become rigid. Let them be relaxed and expanded at the same time.

Keep breathing deeply and evenly from your abdomen with your shoulders relaxed and your chest expanded. Now pay close attention to your breathing by doing the following:

1. **Breathe from your abdomen.**

   Let your abdomen expand as you breathe in and contract as you breathe out. This gentle, deep breathing gives you a lot of oxygen, and gives the sound from the harmonica a big space to vibrate.

2. **Breathe evenly.**

   Each breath should have the same intensity from beginning to end. Avoid sudden bursts as you begin new breaths, and make sure that your breath doesn't fade at the end.

3. **Take long breaths so you can feel the air in motion. While you breathe, observe your sensations.**

   Try to take at least three seconds as you inhale and three more seconds as you exhale. You can try breathing longer, but only if you're able to keep the entire breath relaxed and at an even intensity. If you're gasping or having difficulty making your breath last the full count, try beginning the breath with a lower volume of air, and make the breath a little shorter.

To find the right intensity of breathing for harmonica playing, try the warm hand exercise. Hold the palm of your hand about two inches in front of your open mouth. Exhale gently. You should feel warmth on your hand from your breath, but you shouldn't feel any air.

Deep gentle breathing supports your sound as you play the harmonica. You can achieve proper breathing sitting down, as long as you sit up straight and don't hunch your ribs down over your abdomen or your chin down on your chest. (And keep your elbows off the table, or you won't get any dessert! Well, maybe you will, but your harmonica won't sound as good.)

Concentrating air flow in your mouth

When you play the harmonica, you direct all the air into the harmonica through your mouth — not through your nose. Any air that isn't going through the harmonica weakens the sound and reduces your control over the instrument. But you probably breathe through your nose most of the time, so you may wonder how you can turn off the air to your nasal passages. The body parts that do this are invisible, and you may never think about them, but you can learn to control them with the following simple exercises.

Blow up a balloon. You can't do this without shutting off your nasal passages. If you have a balloon handy, give it a try. You nasal passages will automatically close so that you can direct all your breath through your mouth. When you play the harmonica, you concentrate all air flow through your mouth in the same way, though you shouldn't blow as hard as you do when blowing up a balloon.

If you don't have a balloon, or if you're reading this book in public and don't want to attract attention to yourself, try the "P" explosion exercise. Whisper the sound "Puh." Your closed lips stop the air from escaping from your mouth, and when they let go, the resulting burst of air makes the "P" sound. You can do this without closing your nose, but you'll get a sound more like "Buh" or "Muh." If you do close your nose, the "P" is more concentrated. Now, keeping your lips closed, try to exhale air. If your nose is closed, the air can't get out and pressure builds up until you open your lips.

Cupping the harp in your hands

In Chapter 2, I show you briefly how to hold the harmonica in one hand and play chords. Here, however, I show you the standard harmonica *hand cup*. This cup helps you to hold the harp securely, and it improves the sound of the harmonica. In Chapter 6, I show you how to use your hand cup to shape and amplify your sound. Similarly, in Chapter 17, I show you how to cup the harp and a microphone together.

When attempting to make a basic harmonica hand cup, follow these steps:

1. **Stand with your arms relaxed at your sides.**

2. **Bring your hands together at chest level and cup them together, as shown in Figure 4-1a.**

   You should be able to hold water in the cup your hands have formed.

3. **Bring your thumbs together, as shown in Figure 4-1b.**

   You should be able to see where the harmonica goes — between your thumb and forefinger. Don't pick up the harp yet, though; you have one more thing to do.

4. **Make a slight opening in the back of your hands, just below your little fingers, as shown in Figure 4-1c.**

   You can see the opening through the space between the thumb and forefinger of your left hand. This opening is the *edge opening,* which lets you focus the sound coming out.

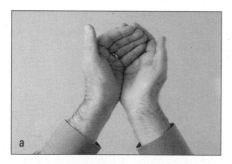
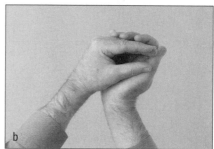

Figure 4-1:
Forming
a basic
hand cup.

Congratulations! You've formed a hand cup. This cup gives you a lot of power over the tone of the harmonica. But don't get too excited yet! You still need to add the harmonica. Here's how:

1. **Pick up a harmonica and hold it between the thumb and forefinger of your left hand. (Remember, the name and hole numbers should be on top.)**

   Don't jam the left edge of the harp into the webbing between your thumb and forefinger. Let it poke out a little, as shown in Figure 4-2. Doing this helps prevent joint pain and deformity from pressure, and it also helps you cup the harp if you have small hands (or when you play a big harp).

2. **Place your fingers as close to the back edge of the covers as possible.**

   Don't grab the harp with all your might. Relax your hand and hold the harp gently but firmly, just enough so that it doesn't fly out of your hand while you play.

3. **Wrap your right and left hands together so that your hand encloses the harp, and then make an edge opening below the little fingers.**

   When you level the harmonica into playing position, your hands will look like Figure 4-2.

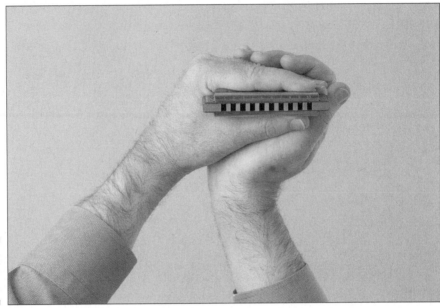

Figure 4-2:
Cupping the
harmonica.

Playing Some Big, Fat Chords

A *chord* is composed of several notes all sounding at once. Both the blow chord and the draw chord in Holes 1, 2, 3, and 4 sound big and powerful. In this section, I show you how to play those chords and get a big, relaxed sound with them.

Preparing your breathing

Before you begin, flip to Chapter 2 for pointers on putting the harp in your mouth and forming an airtight seal. When you're ready, open your mouth wide like you did in Chapter 2, and then follow these steps:

1. **Raise your hands to your mouth, and put the harp between your lips until the front edge of the harp makes full contact with the corners of your lips.**

2. **Let your lips drop onto the harp so that the moist inner part of your lips is touching the harp to form a seal around the covers and front of the harp.**

   Are your lips touching the edges of your fingers? They probably are. This is fine as long as your fingers aren't fighting with your lips for space — and as long as your lips don't drag against your fingers as you slide the harp from side to side in your mouth.

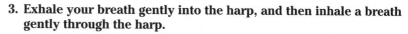

3. **Exhale your breath gently into the harp, and then inhale a breath gently through the harp.**

As you breathe, the only body part that should move is your abdomen, which will be moving the breath in and out. As you change breath direction, from blow to draw, or from draw to blow, remember that you don't need to move your hands, your lips, your jaw, your tongue, or your throat. Everything stays relaxed and motionless while you simply breathe in and out with the harp in your mouth.

Making a big sound with the smooth swimming exercise

You can use some of the easy, relaxed breathing from the previous section to play some big, lazy chords in a long, simple rhythm. The exercise I introduce here, called the smooth swimming exercise, gets you breathing evenly and lets you feel your breathing and hear the harp. It also helps you develop a big, rich sound simply by listening for it. Here's what you do.

Look at the harp and find Holes 1, 2, 3, and 4 at the left side of the harp. These are the holes you want to put in your mouth. As you raise the harp to your mouth, Holes 2 and 3 should pass under your nose.

If you aren't sure whether you have the right holes in your mouth, don't worry. Just try to get lots of holes in your mouth and you'll be fine.

Now you're going to breathe while you count time. Follow these steps:

1. **Prepare to start playing by counting off.**

   You always count off to set the *tempo* (the speed of the beat) and to get ready to play. Count (either out loud or mentally) "One, two, three, four" at a relaxed pace. For this exercise, you start where the next "one" would come. If you aren't ready yet, keep counting to four until you're ready to start playing.

   Avoid tapping your foot when you do this exercise. You want to breathe at a regular, steady rate, but breathing should be your only physical activity.

2. **When you're ready, start breathing on one. Inhale gently and steadily through the harp through a count of four.**

3. **When you reach the next one, switch breath direction and exhale for a full count of four.**

   Don't pause between ending one breath and starting the next. Your breath is always in motion and the harmonica is always making a sound.

Keep alternating between inhaled and exhaled breaths, always breathing for the full count of four and switching breaths on the one without a pause. After you have your breathing going steadily, pay attention to the airflow. No air should be escaping through your nose or at the corners of your lips. ***Tip:*** If you hear a telltale hiss or breathy sound, keep playing but try to determine where the sound is coming from, and then either close your nose or get your lips and the harp into a snug (but gentle) seal.

As you keep alternating between inhaled and exhaled breaths, concentrate on steady, even breathing. In other words, don't start with a big blast of air and don't let your breath fade away at the end. Each breath should start and end at the same level of intensity — just like you're swimming smoothly across the surface of a pool of water. You never dive down and you never jump up; you just glide smoothly and evenly from one end of the pool to the other, breathing in and out evenly.

As you breathe, listen to the sound that the harp makes, and relax your hands, arms, shoulders, neck, lips, jaw, tongue, and throat. Do this for at least five minutes. And always count to four for each breath. As you listen to the sound of the harp responding to your breath, allow the sound to enlarge. Don't increase your volume of breath, however. Just listen, open your mouth and throat, breathe deeply, relax, and let the sound reach deep and expand. You're not *making* the sound enlarge; you're *allowing* it to happen.

Listen to the sound of the smooth swimming exercise on Track 5 of the CD.

Discovering Rhythm

One note (or chord) follows another. Each one has its own duration. For instance, one note could be long, while the next one is the same length or longer or shorter. As you sound a series of notes, their durations form a pattern called *rhythm*. I guide you through an exploration of some simple rhythms in the following sections.

Breathing in rhythmic patterns

In this section, I show you three simple rhythmic patterns. Then you combine the patterns to create a sort of rhythm tune. All three patterns use the same rhythm — you just play one chord on each beat. But for each pattern, you use a different sequence of blow and draw chords. At the end of each pattern, you hold a chord for four beats.

In all three patterns you play two consecutive chords on the same breath, either two blow chords in a row or two draw chords in a row. How do you make two chords on the same breath sound distinct from each other? Don't stop breathing between the first chord and the second chord. The smooth, easy way to play these two chords is to play them on a single breath and say the syllables under the tab, like "Ha-ta" on two blow chords, or "Ah-ta" on two draw chords.

The tab for these patterns only shows the arrows for breath direction (up for blow and down for draw). After all, you already know you're playing Holes 1, 2, 3, and 4. Each of the notes above the arrows is one beat, which is represented by a quarter note. The big hollow note at the end of the tab is a whole note, which lasts for four beats. (For more on reading rhythms, have a look at Chapter 3.)

When you first try playing these patterns, start out with a slow tempo of 60 beats per minute. Always learn music at a slow tempo that allows you to make all the moves in synchronization with the beat. When you get the hang of a piece of music at a slow tempo and you're ready to speed it up, increase the tempo only by the amount that you can handle. If you lose your place or coordination with the tempo you've chosen and can't recover, or if you're scrambling at the new tempo, try slower tempos until you find one that gives you a better chance to play through the piece with confidence and few or no mistakes or stumbles.

Note: For now, just ignore the Xs and Os above some of the notes in the tab. They're for closing and opening your hands around the harp while you play. I explain this notation later in the section "Using a hand cup to intensify a rhythm." After you read that section, you can come back and try these patterns using your hands.

Rhythm pattern #1

The first chord pattern is shown in Tab 4-1. It alternates two draws and two blows. Here's the sequence:

- ✔ Play the sequence of the first four notes three times. Count these mentally as they go by.
- ✔ Hold the long ending chord for four full beats. This gives you a resting point.
- ✔ When you finish the complete pattern, start right in again and keep repeating it without a pause. This helps you develop a feel for the rhythmic pattern.

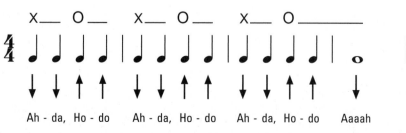

Tab 4-1: Rhythm pattern #1 (Track 6).

Track 6 on the CD plays it first at a metronome marking of 60 (60 beats per second), then at 120, and finally at 224. When you first try speeding this rhythm up, you may want to try something between 60 and 120.

Rhythm pattern #2

The second breathing rhythm, shown in Tab 4-2, reverses the breathing pattern so you start and end on blow chords. As with the first pattern, you play the initial four-note sequence three times, and then you end on a blow chord that lasts four full beats.

You can hear this pattern on Track 6 (0:41) of the CD. It's played at 60, 120, and 224 beats per minute.

Tab 4-2:
Rhythm
pattern #2
(Track 6,
0:41).

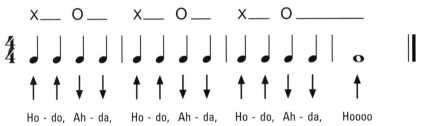

Rhythm pattern #3

So far, the breathing rhythms have all occurred in the same place on the harmonica: Holes 1 through 4. In this pattern, I ask you to play the first breathing rhythm again but to do it one hole to the right. You do this by moving the harp slightly to the left and playing the rhythm shown in Tab 4-3.

When you move to a different hole on the harp, you move the harp, not your head. In other words, to move to the right on the harp, you keep your head in the same place and move the harp to the left. (I explain more on moving the harp in Chapter 5.)

You can hear this rhythm pattern on Track 6 (1:23) of the CD, played at 60, 120, and 224 beats per minute.

(shifted up one hole)

Tab 4-3:
Rhythm
pattern #3
(Track 6,
1:23).

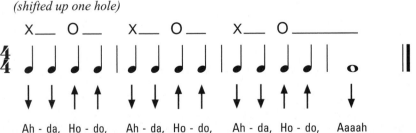

Connecting the three rhythms into a rhythm tune

In this section, I ask you to connect rhythm patterns 1, 2, and 3 into a sort of rhythm tune. Each rhythm forms a phrase in the tune, and by connecting phrases you create a complete sentence, or *verse*.

The verse has the following three parts:

- **First part:** In this part, you play the first breathing rhythm twice.
- **Second part:** Here you play the second breathing rhythm once, and then you play the first breathing rhythm once.
- **Third part:** In this last part, you shift over one hole and play the third rhythm once. Then you shift back and play the first rhythm once.

You can hear how this verse sounds on Track 6 (2:04).

Sounding like a train

Tab 4-4 shows two chord rhythms that are often used to imitate the sound of a train. The rhythm on the first line starts and ends with draw breaths. The rhythm on the second line starts and ends with blow breaths.

You can hear these two rhythms on Track 7 of the CD.

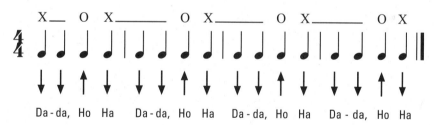

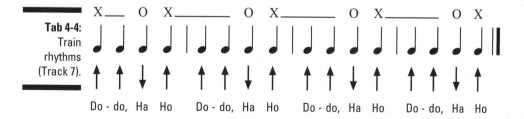

Tab 4-4: Train rhythms (Track 7).

Try playing either the blow or the draw version of this rhythm for a while to get the feeling of the train moving. If you start to feel like you have too much breath building up in your lungs, move the harp away from your lips a little and make a hissing sound as you exhale. By doing so, you create the sound of the steam engine blowing off excess steam.

After getting used to the train moving, you may want to make the sound of the train whistle. To do this, follow these steps:

1. **Move one or two holes to the right and play the draw chord you find there.**

2. **Narrow the opening in your mouth to just one or two holes.**

   Do this by pushing your lips outward — sort of like you're pouting. Pushing your lips outward will push the harp out a little as well.

3. **Relax your lips again to get a wider chord.**

Remember that going from wide chord to narrow chord and back to wide chord again happens very quickly, and it sounds like "Aah-Ooh-Aah."

To hear the steam blowoff and the train whistle played with the train rhythms, listen to Track 7 (0:18) on the CD.

Using a hand cup to intensify a rhythm

Earlier in this chapter, I emphasize the power of a hand cup (see the section "Cupping the harp in your hands"). After you've mastered some of the rhythms earlier in this chapter, you can try using your hand cup on them.

Your cup can be *closed* (with your hands closed around the harp), or it can be *open.* A closed cup sounds dark and muffled, and an open cup sounds bright. You can see what a closed cup looks like in Figure 4-3a. When you open the cup, you keep your thumbs together — they're the hinge — and you pivot your right wrist slightly to move the edge of your right hand away from the left, creating an opening, as shown in Figure 4-3b.

Remember those mysterious Xs and Os that you saw above some of the notes in the rhythms you played earlier in the chapter? I told you I'd get to them sooner or later! Here's what they mean:

X = close your hand cup and keep it that way for now

O = open your hand cup and keep it that way for now

Try going back and playing each of the rhythms in the earlier section, "Breathing in rhythmic patterns," using your hands as shown in the tab.

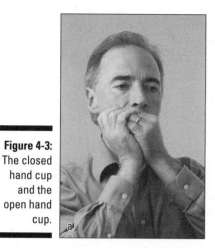 

Figure 4-3:
The closed
hand cup
and the
open hand
cup.

On Track 8, you can hear rhythm patterns 1, 2, and 3 as well as the train
rhythms with hand cups (0:41).

Chapter 5

I Hear a Melody: Playing Single Notes

*W*hen you first start getting sound from a harmonica, you get several notes at once. But if you want to play melody, or a sequence of single notes, then you focus on isolating one of those tiny holes and start figuring out where all the notes are. One cool thing about the harmonica is that you can do both at the same time.

Whoever designed the note layout of the harmonica was very smart. He (or she, or they, we don't really know who was involved, though there are plenty of legends) knew that it wasn't easy to get single notes right away, so he arranged the notes in neighboring holes so that almost any two, or even three, holes produce harmony notes when you play them together. On piano or guitar it takes special study to play harmony notes along with melody. However, you have the opposite problem with harmonica: You get to make pleasing harmonies right away, and your job is to pare down those harmonies so you can play one pure melody note at a time. Then you can add harmony whenever you want it.

When you first try to play melodies on the harmonica, you may feel like you're fumbling around in the dark — there's nothing to see and not much to feel. So it's a big help to know what you're trying to find. In this chapter, I explain how to play single notes, and then I give you some simple, well-known tunes to play. You probably already know what these tunes sound like, so all you have to do is try to find the notes in the harmonica.

Shaping Your Mouth to Single Out a Note

Musicians have a word for what you do with your mouth when playing a musical instrument — *embouchure,* pronounced *awm*-boo-shure. (It's a French word, so you can feel sophisticated when you casually mention to your friends that you've been devoting hours of study to your single note embouchure.) Embouchure is one thing guitarists can't brag about — making painful grimaces to impress the audience doesn't count; your embouchure actually has to help make a sound come out of the instrument.

Don't worry if you can't isolate a single note right away. The skill will come over time — perhaps in a few days. If you can hear the tune in what you're playing, you're doing okay. Start in on the tunes in this chapter whether you can get a single note or not — don't wait! You can develop your embouchure as you go.

The two most widely used embouchures are the *pucker* and the *tongue block;* they're both valuable for different reasons. With a pucker, as the name suggests, you pucker your lips like you're going to kiss your mother on the cheek. When you tongue block, you put your tongue on the harp to block out some of the holes. Tongue blocking offers all sorts of cool effects, as detailed in Chapter 7. I show you the basics later in this chapter.

Forming the pucker embouchure

I recommend that you learn the pucker embouchure to get started, because it's easy and straightforward. Here's how you do it:

1. **Open your mouth wide, leaving your lips relaxed.**

2. **Place the harmonica between your lips so that the front of the harmonica touches the right and left corners of your lips, where your upper and lower lips meet.**

3. **Let your lips drop onto the harp so they form a cushion that lets the harp slide when you move it to the left or right.**

   The cushion should be relaxed, but it should also form an airtight seal with the harp.

4. **With your lips on the harp, inhale or exhale gently.**

   You should hear a chord (several notes sounding at the same time).

5. **As you play, let the harp slide forward as if it's slowly slipping out of your mouth (but keep an airtight seal between your lips and the harp).**

Your lips will make a smaller opening as they get closer together — it may feel like you're pouting. As you do this, make sure that the corners of your lips still touch the harp. As you continue to breathe through the harp, you should hear fewer notes; it will sound like less overall sound is coming out of the harmonica.

6. **To isolate a single note, you may have to push your lips forward a little more — be especially pouty (like your kid sister used to).**

   Keep your lips as relaxed as possible while maintaining an airtight seal.

As you work on the pucker, listen for air escaping around your mouth. It will make a sort of hissing sound. Try to keep your lips, especially the corners, gently sealed on the harp so that all the air from your mouth goes through the harp.

You may need to move the harp a small amount to the left or right to line up a hole on the harp with the hole in your mouth. If you aren't quite getting a single note, experiment by sliding the harp just a little as you push your lips forward.

The farther you can get the harp inside your mouth and still get a single note, the better the harp will sound. After you get a single note, try pushing the harmonica a little farther back inside your lips. The harmonica should always be inside your lips and in contact with the moist inner parts of the lips. It should never feel like the harmonica is pressed against your lips from the outside.

A relaxed, airtight seal with full sounding tone takes time to achieve, but don't hesitate to make it a goal. Look at my lips in Figure 5-1. I played a single note and then took the harp away from my mouth. The opening in my lips is much bigger than the holes in the harp, and yet that's what I use to get a single note with a pucker.

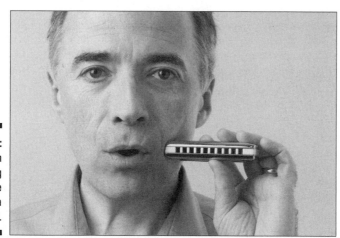

Figure 5-1:
The mouth opening for a single note with a pucker.

Producing a tongue block embouchure

Even if you're just playing single notes with no special effects, tongue blocking has one advantage: It configures your mouth to promote a full, rich tone. Sure, you can get a good tone with puckering, but tongue blocking makes it almost automatic.

To get a single note by tongue blocking, follow these steps:

1. **Open your mouth wide, leaving your lips relaxed.**

2. **Place the harmonica between your lips so that the front of the harmonica touches the right and left corners of your lips, where your upper and lower lips meet.**

3. **Let your lips drop onto the harp so they form a cushion that lets the harp slide when you move it to the left or right.**

   The cushion should be relaxed, but it should also form an airtight seal with the harp.

4. **With your lips on the harp, inhale or exhale gently.**

   You should hear a chord (several notes sounding at the same time).

5. **Touch the tip of your tongue to your bottom lip and press your tongue forward gently.**

6. **Gently press the top of your tongue against the harp.**

   When you do this, the top of your tongue will make a broad surface that glides against the harmonica without poking into the holes.

7. **Touch the left edge of your tongue against the left corner of your lips, leaving an opening between the right edge of your tongue and the right corner of your lips.**

   This is where air will pass through to the harmonica.

Listen for air escaping, and move the harp a little to the left or right to help align a single hole with your mouth opening. Try to make the opening between your tongue and the right corner of your lips small enough to isolate a single note but large enough so that air can flow freely and produce a clear, strong note. Figure 5-2 shows my tongue block embouchure with the harp removed from my mouth.

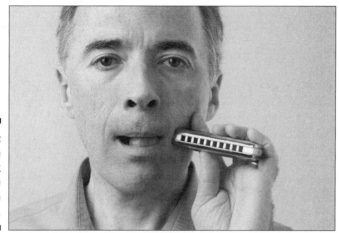

Figure 5-2:
Tongue
block
embouchure
for a single
note.

The Elements of Motion: Moving from One Note to the Next

Getting a single note is great, but there aren't many one-note melodies out there. To make the most of your new skill, you want to start moving from one note to another to play melodies. On the harmonica, the following are the three most important ways to move from one note to another:

- ✔ **Change your breath direction from blow to draw or from draw to blow.** When you change breath direction, you don't move your hands, lips, tongue, or anything else. You just stop breathing in one direction and start breathing in the other. (You can read more about this in Chapters 2 and 4.)

- ✔ **Change holes by sliding the harp left or right in your mouth.** I show you how to do this in Chapter 4, but without measuring how far you move. Now you have to start aiming for specific holes and notes.

  Again, when you move to another hole, the only things that move are your hands sliding the harmonica a tiny amount to the left or right. Your lips stay put and form a gliding surface.

- ✔ **Change holes and breath direction.** You have to coordinate changing your breath with moving the harmonica. You'll probably pick up on the combined action pretty quickly.

Exploring the Three Registers of the Harmonica

The diatonic harmonica has three overlapping *registers,* or segments of its range. Each register covers eight notes of the scale, which is an *octave* (see Chapter 3 for more about octaves). Here are the different registers:

- ✔ **The middle register:** The diatonic is designed to play melodies mostly in the middle register, which covers Holes 4 through 7.

- ✔ **The high register:** This register, covering Holes 7 through 10, allows you to play melodies that extend beyond the middle register. Some melodies can be played entirely in the high register.

- ✔ **The bottom register:** Holes 1 through 4 make up this register, which is designed to add accompaniment chords to the melodies you play in the middle register (you do this with tongue blocking).

In the remaining half of this chapter, I start with simple melodies in the middle octave, and then I move up to melodies in the high octave. But I stop there, because playing melodies in the bottom register is tricky. Why? Well, because the bottom register omits two notes from the scale to make its chord sound better.

I show you how to use the bottom register for chording in Chapter 7. And because you can do more with melody in the bottom register after you can bend notes down (Chapter 8), I delve into melody playing in the bottom register in Chapter 9.

Playing Familiar Tunes in the Middle Register

You probably already know how to whistle or hum dozens of tunes. So the best way to get started playing melody on the harmonica is to try to find some of those melodies in the harmonica. In this section, I take you through several familiar tunes that are played in the middle register.

The harmonica tablature (or tab) under the written music tells you the holes and breaths to play (see Chapter 3 for more on tab). If you want, you can try reading the musical notation as well. If any of the tunes are unfamiliar, the notation tells you how long to hold each note (basic notation is covered in Chapter 3 as well). And the words to the first few songs are included to help get you started.

"Hot Cross Buns"

When playing the tune "Hot Cross Buns," which is shown in Tab 5-1, your first move is to go from Hole 5 to Hole 4 as you change from blow to draw. Later, when you repeat the same note several times, play the notes all on one long breath and touch your tongue to the roof of your mouth for each new repetition. You can hear this tune on Track 9 of the CD.

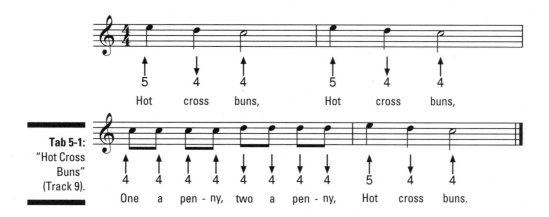

Tab 5-1:
"Hot Cross
Buns"
(Track 9).

"Good Night, Ladies"

The first several notes in "Good Night, Ladies" allow you to practice sliding to a neighboring hole. (See Tab 5-2.) **Remember:** When you move to a new hole, use your hands to move the harp. Don't move your lips or your head. This tune introduces Draw 5, the highest note you've played so far. Listen to this tune on Track 10 of the CD.

Tab 5-2:
"Good
Night,
Ladies"
(Track 10).

"Mary Had a Little Lamb"

"Mary Had a Little Lamb," shown in Tab 5-3, takes you farther into the middle register, all the way to Blow 6. You can hear this tune on Track 11.

Try stringing "Good Night, Ladies" and "Mary Had a Little Lamb" into one long tune. They fit together, so you'll have your first medley!

Tab 5-3: "Mary Had a Little Lamb" (Track 11).

"Frère Jacques"

"Frère Jacques," shown in Tab 5-4, is an old French tune that's also known as "Are You Sleeping, Brother John." Notice the clues that the notation gives you. You can see the shape of the melody, almost as if it were on graph paper. If you'd like to hear this tune played, check out Track 12.

Tab 5-4: "Frère Jacques" (Track 12).

Each phrase in this tune repeats once, so you only have to learn half the tune. The second phrase uses a set of moves similar to the first phrase, just moved one hole to the right, and it sounds similar as well. The notes in the third phrase move much faster than the first two phrases. You may want to study this phrase all by itself until you can navigate it confidently. After you have the moves down, try playing the third phrase at the proper speed relative to the other parts.

"When the Saints Go Marching In"

The tune "When the Saints Go Marching In," which is shown in Tab 5-5, is a spirited New Orleans tune that's fairly easy to play. Why not give it a try? The first phrase comes three times in the tune, with the first three notes leading up to that big arrival note in Blow 6. This tune doesn't introduce anything new; it's just a great tune to use the skills you've already learned. Take a listen to this tune on Track 13 of the CD.

Tab 5-5: "When the Saints Go Marching In" (Track 13).

Making Your First Multi-Hole Leaps

Before now, you've probably never moved more than one hole — at least not on purpose. So you're probably peering into the darkness and asking something like, "When I need to jump to a distant hole, how do I tell how far to slide the harp? There's nothing to look at or even feel!" Don't worry. If you know where you're starting and where you're going, you can slide toward your goal, and you'll hear your target note when you get there. The tunes in the following section let you practice leaping to nearby holes.

After you slide from one hole to another a few times, you'll get a feel for the size of the leap. Once you can make the leap accurately, you may start noticing something else. When you slide from one hole to another, you end up playing the notes in the intervening holes as you travel across them. How do you keep those notes from sounding? You could stop your breath completely, but then the tune may sound choppy. Instead, keep breathing as you traverse the intervening holes, but lower the intensity of your breath so that the note doesn't sound. You may not grasp this skill right away, but it will come with practice.

"Twinkle, Twinkle, Little Star"

As long as you're learning something new, you may as well start with something easy, eh? The leap you make in "Twinkle, Twinkle, Little Star," shown in Tab 5-6, is from Blow 4 to Blow 6. To make the move, just start on Blow 4, continue to exhale, and then slide up until you hear your target note in Blow 6. Listen to this tune on Track 14.

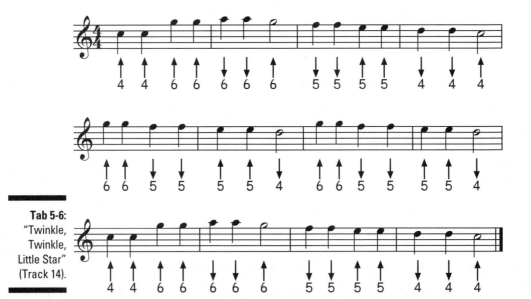

Tab 5-6: "Twinkle, Twinkle, Little Star" (Track 14).

"Taps"

"Taps" is all blow notes, and that means playing it can help you develop breath control. Notice the little apostrophe-like symbols after some of the notes in Tab 5-7. Those are good places to take a breath. Plus, with this tune, you have a new leap to work on: Blow 5 down to Blow 3. Another important thing about playing all blow notes is that you can work on just moving smoothly through a series of neighboring holes without having to think about your breath direction. See if you can think of ways to add some expression to those long notes. Chapter 7 goes into detail about some expressive possibilities, but see if your imagination can suggest some things to you as you hold those long notes. You can hear "Taps" on Track 15 of the CD.

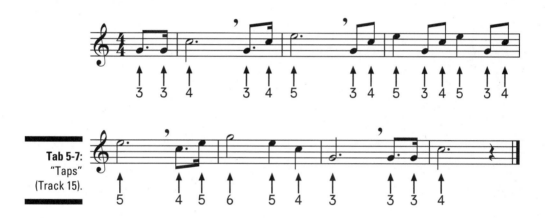

Tab 5-7: "Taps" (Track 15).

"On Top of Old Smokey"

The leaps in the middle of "On Top of Old Smokey" (see Tab 5-8) aren't as obvious as in the two previous tunes. One is a leap down from Blow 6 to Blow 4; another is a leap down from Blow 6 to Draw 4. This tune, which you can hear on Track 16, reaches a new high note that you haven't played before: Blow 7.

Try counting beats during the long notes in this tune. This way you're sure to hold them for the full length.

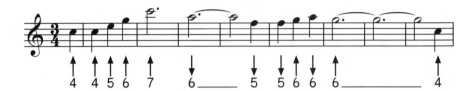

Tab 5-8: "On Top of Old Smokey" (Track 16).

Shifting Up From the Middle

So far in this chapter, I've managed to shield you from *the shift* — the place in Holes 6 and 7 where the breathing sequence changes as you go from the middle register to the high register.

Here's an important fact to remember about the shift: When you go up the scale from Draw 6, the next note is Draw 7 (instead of Blow 7). It's easy to forget this shift, because this is the first sequence in the scale that goes from one draw note to another. In Holes 1 through 6, you always go from a draw note to a blow note as you go up the scale. Suddenly you have to go to a draw note instead. And when you play Draw 6 and Draw 7 together, they create the only discordant combination of neighboring holes on the harmonica — yikes!

The next two tunes are played mostly in the middle register (though "Shenandoah" creeps into the high register), but they both use the shift. Before trying these tunes, take some time to get comfortable with the shift by playing Tab 5-9 a few times. It simply walks you through the four notes in the scale that approach, travel through, and leave the shift. You can hear the note shift exercise on Track 17.

Tab 5-9: A note shift exercise (Track 17).

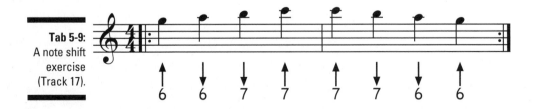

The tunes in the following sections help you navigate the shift with confidence (perhaps even with aplomb). ***Note:*** You can also play the first eight tunes in this chapter in the high register. I encourage you to try them out.

"Joy to the World"

To get better acquainted with the breath shift in Holes 6 and 7, try playing "Joy to the World" (see Tab 5-10). This traditional Christmas tune is attributed to Handel. This tune starts in Blow 7 and plays all the way down the scale to Blow 4 — the complete middle register, including the shift. Then it comes all the way back up before moving around to different parts of the scale. Who knew that playing a scale could sound so glorious? Listen to this tune on Track 18.

Tab 5-10: "Joy to the World" (Track 18).

"Shenandoah"

"Shenandoah," which is shown in Tab 5-11 and played on Track 19 of the CD, is a classic ballad that is usually played very slowly. It plays downward through the shift early in the tune. The last six notes break into the high register above Blow 7.

Tab 5-11: "Shenan-doah" (Track 19).

Floating in the High Register

The high notes in Holes 7 through 10 can make some beautiful music, but they also pose some challenges. People sometimes associate these high notes with high tension and tiny size — as if the holes were smaller and closer together and they took more force to play. But look at the holes on a harmonica. They're all the same size. Getting the high notes to respond doesn't take force, either. Instead, it takes relaxed, gentle breathing that lets the notes float out. There's no need to drag them out under protest.

Tab 5-12 is a little study to help you get used to where the notes are in the high register. Each group of four notes is all blow or all draw and moves to neighboring holes. Play each note as long as you like, but leave enough breath for the other three notes that share a breath with it. If the highest notes don't sound, try yawning to open your throat. Keep your mouth relaxed and breathe gently. Let the notes float out on your breath. You can hear the tab played on Track 20 of the CD.

Tab 5-12:
High reg-
ister float
(Track 20).

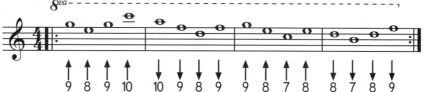

The next two tunes help you explore the high register. Both tunes spend time in both the middle and high registers but go farther into the high register than previous tunes.

In the high register, you can find the draw notes one hole to the right of where you expect them to be. When you go from a draw note to a blow note, the blow note will be one hole to the left of where you'd expect.

"She'll Be Comin' 'Round the Mountain"

"She'll Be Comin' 'Round the Mountain," shown in Tab 5-13, is a tune that centers on Hole 7. Even though it travels equally into both high and middle octaves, this tune mostly avoids the shift and doesn't contain any hole leaps. The melody goes all the way up to Blow 9, one hole from the top. Note the "8va" and dotted lines above the tune. They tell music readers that the notes written should be played an octave higher (to write them where they really sound would be way above the staff and hard to read). The tab isn't affected though. You play the tab exactly as it's written. You can hear this tune on Track 21.

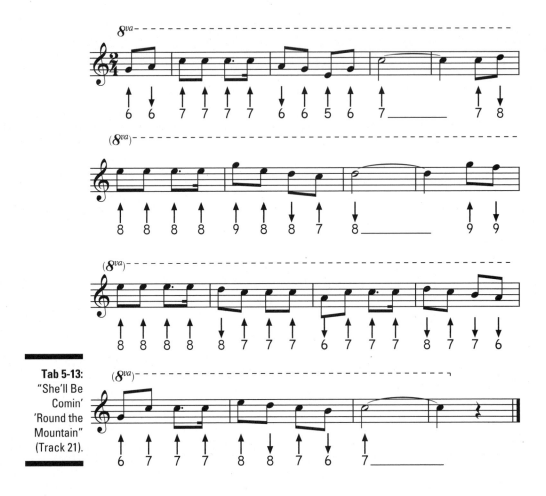

"Silent Night"

The classic Christmas tune "Silent Night" (see Tab 5-14) plays with Holes 6 and 7. It also contains two leaps: one from Blow 6 to Draw 8 and another from Blow 5 to Draw 8. Listen to the tune on Track 22 of the CD.

Start inhaling as you slide up to Draw 8 from Blow 6 or Blow 5. As long as you're looking for a draw note, you may as well be inhaling so you can hear it when you arrive. After you get comfortable with the leaps, try to minimize the sound of the notes in between. (See the earlier section, "Making Your First Multi-Hole Leaps," for more info on how to minimize the sound of the in-between notes.)

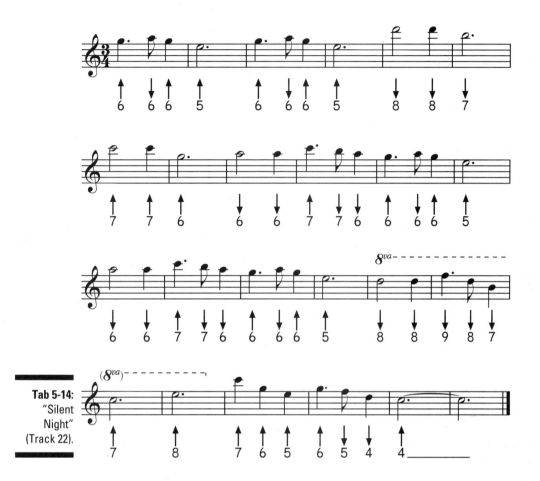

Tab 5-14: "Silent Night" (Track 22).

Chapter 6

Shaping Your Sound

- -

In This Chapter

▶ Getting a big sound with resonance

▶ Using your diaphragm, throat, tongue, and hands to shape sound

▶ Pulsating notes with vibrato

- -

*U*nlike most musical instruments, the harmonica doesn't use its body to project its own sound. Consider, for example, the guitar. It has a big sound box to amplify the sound that the strings make. And a saxophone reed sends its sound down a long vibrating column of air that ends in a big bell to amplify and direct the sound.

A harmonica, on the other hand, hardly has a body at all. It's just a little box of tiny reeds that barely can make audible sounds by themselves. But the harmonica has you, the player, to amplify its sound. Your lungs, throat, mouth, tongue, and hands form and control a powerful acoustic amplifier called the *air column,* the moving mass of air that carries and amplifies the faint vibration of harmonica reeds. In a very real way, the sound of your harmonica is your sound. In this chapter, I help you explore your air column. I show you how to use it to shape and amplify your sound.

Try the exercises in this chapter first without a harmonica to focus on your body sensations and breathing. After you have a feel for the action, add the harmonica to hear and refine the musical result.

Developing Deep Resonance with Your Air Column

As you may know, the reeds in a diatonic harmonica move a tiny amount when they vibrate. Even the longest reed playing its loudest note moves only two or three millimeters. However, every time a reed vibrates, it briefly stops the air flowing past it. That interruption in the air flow has a ripple effect that passes back through the air flowing through your body. The deeper it can go into your body, the more air will vibrate, making the sound much louder and fuller.

Musicians often use the word *resonance* to describe the reinforcement that sound receives from a hollow body, such as the body of a guitar or your air column when it's coupled with the reeds of a harmonica.

The air column in your body is like a hollow tunnel that extends from the bottom of your lungs to the harmonica, and the bigger and more open you can make the air column, the more resonance you create. If you simply breathe from your mouth or chest, you don't get the full air column moving, and you don't get a full sound from the harmonica. To get the entire air column moving and vibrating, you need to breathe from the bottom of your lungs.

In Chapter 4, I show you good playing posture. I also show you how to breathe deeply and evenly by keeping your rib cage expanded and by breathing from your abdomen. Posture and breathing are the beginning of air column exploration, so if you haven't explored these basics, now would be a good time to do that.

Your air column extends from your abdomen all the way up to the harmonica. From the bottom of the air column upward, there are several control points where you can shape the sound that's vibrating in the column. These control points can be used individually or in various combinations for a variety of effects. Here are the main control points:

- ✔ **Your diaphragm is the sheath of muscles beneath your lungs that moves air in and out.** Breathing deeply from your diaphragm gives power and volume to your sound. The diaphragm can also be used to start and stop notes and make them pulsate.

- ✔ **Your throat, which is halfway up the air column, can start, stop, and pulsate notes.** It gives definition to the power of the abdomen in starting and stopping notes. Your throat also can make pulsating notes throb.

- ✔ **Your tongue and mouth cavity can start and stop notes, adding clarity and crispness to the power of your diaphragm and throat.** The tongue and mouth can change the tonal qualities of the sound and can form speech-like vowel sounds. They also can lower or raise the pitch of a note, as I show in Chapters 7 and 12. Your tongue can select individual notes on the harp and create all sorts of percussive and chord textures.

- ✔ **Your hands aren't part of your air column, but they can still help your playing.** They amplify your sound, shape your tone, produce vowel sounds, and create pulsations as well.

Using Your Diaphragm

Like your heart, your diaphragm is always working. It gently propels your lungs to inhale and exhale each breath. When you use your diaphragm to start, stop, and pulsate notes, you're moving the entire air column (see the preceding section for more details on the air column), so you have a huge amount of power supporting every diaphragm movement.

Starting and stopping notes

To develop an awareness of your diaphragm, try panting rapidly like a dog, and as you do, notice where the motion is coming from. It comes from the area that's below your rib cage but above your navel. Each time you exhale or inhale when panting, your diaphragm starts the breath with a little thrust of your abdomen. Of course, you don't usually pant when you play the harmonica.

To help you harness the power of the abdominal thrust, in this section I take you through some explorations that give you a powerful way to start and end notes. Later, I also show you how to use your diaphragm to *pulsate,* or put a wave into, the notes.

As you learn the abdominal thrust, be sure to breathe deeply and bring the vibration of the reeds down into the depths of your lungs to give the vibration maximum amplification.

To do an abdominal thrust, you don't have to breathe hard, and you don't need to move your head, shoulders, or chest. The only body part that should move is the area between your ribs and your waist. And even then, it should move very gently.

To get the hang of starting an exhaled breath with an abdominal thrust, try this exercise without a harp:

1. **Whisper "Hah!"**

   Notice the little push inward that comes from the area below your rib cage. Keep your throat open like you're yawning. Note that the sound of the "Hah!" will be faint, because it's produced entirely by air moving.

2. **Try sustaining your exhaled breath for a few seconds after you give it that little push start.**

   It should sound something like "Haaaaaaaaaaaaaa."

Now try doing the same thing while inhaling. Start off by panting again. As you do, notice the sensation of starting the inhaled breath with a slight outward thrust of your abdomen. Now try doing a single inhaled breath with an abdominal thrust — the inhaled "Hah!" with a whisper. It may feel like the sudden intake of breath that you might make involuntarily when something surprises you. The place just under the apex of your rib cage will suddenly bounce outward and air will rush down your throat. Finally, try starting a long inhaled breath with your diaphragm: "Haaaaaaaaaa." Again, your throat should be open and the only sound will be air moving.

After you try this while breathing, pick up a harmonica and try it while playing. At first you may want to try it while playing a chord of two or three notes, then while playing a single note.

Now try using your diaphragm to start and stop a series of short bursts of breath, first just by breathing, then with a harmonica. Do this while both inhaling and exhaling. Follow these steps:

1. **Start a breath with an abdominal thrust, and end it abruptly.**

   The breath should sound like "Hah!"

2. **Perform a series of these short thrusts, both inhaling and exhaling.**

   Stop the flow of breath at the end of each "Hah!" Then resume with the next "Hah!" Your thrusts should sound like "Hah!" "Hah!" "Hah!" "Hah!" "Hah!" The series of starts and stops should be like parts in a longer breath. Each time you start again, you continue that longer breath.

3. **Now try it with a harmonica.**

   Try playing a single note while doing a series of "Hah!-Hah!" abdominal thrusts, both while inhaling and while exhaling like you just did without the harp. You could do this in any hole, but I suggest you try Hole 4.

 After you've tried playing breath bursts just breathing into the harp, try playing the scale in Tab 6-1. Play each note with a single "Hah!" You can hear what it sounds like on Track 23.

Tab 6-1:
Pulsing long notes and playing a scale with articulation (Tracks 23, 25, 27, and 28).

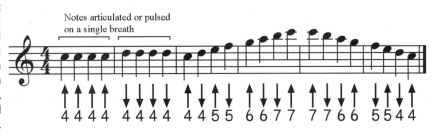

Notes articulated or pulsed on a single breath

4 4 4 4   4 4 4 4   4 4 5 5   6 6 7 7   7 7 6 6   5 5 4 4

 In Chapter 4, I take you through a series of rhythmic breathing exercises. In these exercises, each repeated chord is *articulated* (separated from the ones before and after) with your tongue. Try those same exercises using abdominal thrusts instead of your tongue. The sound will have a lot more power.

 To hear the sounds from Tab 4-1, listen to Track 6, which is played with diaphragm articulation, and then compare it with the same pattern played with tongue articulation on Track 24.

Pulsing a note

When you pulse a note, you don't start or stop it. Instead, you use a series of gentle pulses to create a subtle ripple or undulation in a long note. You do this using the same motions as when you start and stop notes, but you do it more gently.

Try using your diaphragm to pulse a note, following these steps:

1. **Take a deep breath.**

2. **As you start to exhale, begin with an abdominal thrust.**

3. **Continue to exhale, but do a series of gentle thrusts without stopping the flow of breath.**

   This breath should sound like one long note with evenly timed pulses rippling through it. It should sound like "HaHaHaHaHa."

   Try going through the steps while inhaling. However, note that you don't need to start with a deep breath, because you'll be breathing in while you play the note.

4. **Try it with a harmonica, playing long blow and draw notes in Hole 4.**

   Hold each note long enough to let the rippling effect occur. Listen to it and see if you can make the ripple occur at faster and slower rates.

Putting Your Throat to Work

The abdomen delivers power, but the throat delivers throb. Your throat is positioned in the gateway between your lungs in the lower part of the air column and your mouth in the upper part. Your throat can couple with both parts to influence the sound of the harmonica.

The throat does its work with the *glottis,* which is the opening between your *vocal cords.* (Note that vocal cords aren't actually cords but folds of tissue.) For instance, if you try to cough politely without disturbing the person next to you on the bus or in a movie theater, you're closing and opening your glottis while exhaling.

To experience what using your glottis feels like, try saying, "Uh!-Uh" (as in "no way"). Now whisper "Uh!-Uh" without using your voice. To heighten the sensation, keep your throat open as if you're yawning. Notice that your glottis closes twice, at the beginning and the end of the first "Uh." When you stop the airflow with your glottis, you've produced a sound called a *glottal stop.* *Note:* In this section, I use an exclamation mark (!) to indicate a glottal stop.

Starting and stopping notes

On the harmonica, try starting a long note with a glottal stop. For example, try "!Aaaaaaaaaahh" while both inhaling and exhaling. At first it may seem like the note starts very loudly with the glottal stop. Try breathing fully to make the note strong but relaxed, and make the glottal stop as mild as possible so it doesn't overpower the rest of the note.

You can also practice starting and stopping by doing a series of glottal stops as you play a long note, both inhaling and exhaling. For instance, you may try "!Aa!aa!aa!aa." This should sound like a series of repeated, connected notes. To hear this series on both inhaled and exhaled notes, listen to Track 25. Also try playing the scale in Tab 6-1; start each note with a glottal stop. This scale is also on Track 25.

Now try starting and stopping a note with a glottal stop. Without the harp, the note will sound like !Uh! !Uh! !Uh! The beginning and the end of the note are much crisper than with abdominal action. You could actually call these ways of starting and stopping notes *attacks* and *cutoffs*.

Play a long inhaled or exhaled breath, and try breaking it up into a series of shorter notes. Start each note with a glottal stop, and then cut it off and interrupt the breath flow. Then start again and continue the longer breath. To hear what this sounds like, listen to Track 25 (0:15). Try playing Tab 6-1 again, attacking and cutting off each note with a glottal stop. When you play a note for the briefest possible moment with a sharp attack and cutoff, it's called a *staccato* note. This staccato scale is also on Track 25 (0:15).

Pulsing a note

When you pulse a note with your glottis, you don't stop the air flow; instead, you just narrow the air passage. Pulsing a note with your throat sounds different from pulsing with your abdomen. When you pulse with your throat, the sound throbs.

To see what I mean, try whispering "AhAhAhAhAh" on a single breath. Notice that your glottis narrows the air column for each "Ah." The breath never stops; it just pulses. While you practice this, make sure your abdomen moves smoothly without pulsing — all the action is in your throat. Your glottis does the politest almost-cough imaginable.

To hear throat pulsation on the notes of Tab 6-1 in the middle range of the harmonica, listen to Track 25 (0:31).

Using Abdominal and Throat Action Together

When you combine the power of the abdominal thrust with the throb of the glottal stop (I explain both earlier in this chapter), you get a sound that's stronger than both. When you use your throat to pulse a note, you may notice your abdomen reacting. It's a bit like the echo is making your stomach and rib cage bounce. This sympathetic vibration is a sort of passive reinforcement, and it's definitely worth cultivating. You can control it by either trying to isolate the action in your throat or by letting your chest and abdomen help out a little.

After you develop your abilities to do both abdominal and throat pulsation, you can coordinate the two. For instance, you can play a steady rhythm with your throat while you give certain notes emphasis with your abdomen.

Grab your harp and try the rhythmic combination in Tab 6-2. Your throat provides the steady rhythm while the abdominal pulses that give emphasis are indicated with angle brackets (>) over the notes. You can hear the rhythm on Track 26.

Tab 6-2:
Combining a throat rhythm with an abdominal rhythm (Track 26).

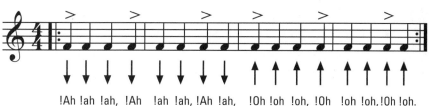

!Ah !ah !ah, !Ah !ah !ah, !Ah !ah, !Oh !oh !oh, !Oh !oh !oh, !Oh !oh.

Coloring Your Sound with Your Tongue

When you talk, your tongue forms consonants, like "T" and "K," and vowels, like "Aaah," "Oh," and "Eee." When you play harmonica, you can use consonants to *articulate* notes (start and stop them), while vowel sounds change the *tone color* of notes, making them sound darker or brighter. If your tongue isn't on the harp, you have more freedom to form these sounds. However, even with your tongue on the harp you can still do a lot to articulate and color your notes. (When your tongue is on the harp, you can also use it to select and combine notes, as I describe in Chapter 7.)

Starting and stopping notes

When you play harmonica using a *pucker embouchure* (using your lips to isolate a single note; see Chapter 5), your tongue is free to make all the sounds of speech. The most useful sounds are T, K, and Dl (as in "diddle"). When you repeat T or K, you're single tonguing. But when you combine them, you get double tonguing (ooh, la, la — who said musicians were nerds?).

Single tonguing

When you use one type of tongue action to start or stop a note, it's called *single tonguing.* The sounds of "T" and "K" both work well for single-tonguing articulation. For example, try playing a long note while you whisper "Tatatatata." Do this while both inhaling and exhaling. This is the *T articulation.* Now try playing a long note while whispering "Kakakakaka." That's the *K articulation.* The two articulations are similar, but the "T" has a bit more snap.

To hear the scale in Tab 6-1 played first with a "T" attack and then with a "K" attack, listen to Track 27 on the CD.

Try starting and stopping a repeated note — first exhaling and then inhaling. Try it with a "T" by whispering "Tat! Tat! Tat!" (both inhaling and exhaling). Then try it with a "K" by whispering "Kak! Kak! Kak!"

To hear a repeated note and the scale in Tab 6-1 played first with "Tat" and then with "Kak" articulation, listen to Track 27 (0:27).

Double tonguing

When you're repeating a note quickly, your tongue may not be able to repeat "T" or "K" rapidly enough. *Double tonguing* is a technique for alternating between "T" and "K." Try whispering "Takatakatakataka" while playing a note (first exhaled, and then inhaled).

To hear exhaled and inhaled "taka" articulation followed by the scale from Tab 6-1 played with double tonguing on each note, listen to Track 27 (0:55).

An easier way to double tongue is to say "Di-Dl" (as in the word "diddle"). Try whispering "Di-dl-di-dl-di-dl" as you play exhaled and inhaled notes. This produces a different effect from T and K, smoother and less forceful. Cultivate all three, and then choose which one works best in any situation.

Tongue-blocked articulation

When you tongue block to play a single note (see Chapter 5), you place the tip of your tongue on the harp, so you don't have the ability to say "T" (though you can still say "K"). But you can still use the front of your tongue to articulate a note with a tongued P (it's called that because when you do it while speaking it sounds like a P).

Here's how you use a tongued P to articulate a note. When you're playing a tongue-blocked note, the front of your tongue is pressed against the harp, with an opening in your mouth at the right edge of the tongue to let air pass to the harmonica. By pressing your tongue slightly forward, you can widen it enough to block off the air passage completely. This lets you stop notes by blocking the passage to cut off the air flow, and start them by opening the passage to allow air through.

You can combine a K articulation with a tongued P for a double-tongued effect, but you may find it difficult to make the articulations cleanly. An easier solution is to alternate a glottal stop with a tongued P, like this: "!Ha-paHa-pa" An even crisper alternative is to switch to a pucker embouchure and use "Taka" or "Di-dl."

To hear a note starting and stopping with a single-tongued P articulation and then with a "!Ha-pa" double articulation, and to hear the scale in Tab 6-1 played with each of these articulations, listen to Track 28.

Pulsing a note

You can use your tongue to add pulsation to a note by whispering "yoyoyoyo" as you play. Try to get your tongue close to the roof of your mouth to intensify the effect. You may notice a small variation in the pitch of the note as you pulse it. You can pulse notes this way both when puckering and when tongue blocking.

You can hear tongue pulsation on Track 32, together with abdomen, throat, and hand pulsation.

Forming vowel sounds and coloring your tone

When you talk, you form vowels partly with your lips and partly with your tongue. However, when you play the harmonica, your lips aren't available, so your tongue does all the work.

For example, try saying "Ooh-Eee." When you say "Ooh," your tongue is pulled back with the tip pointed down. When you say "Eee," your tongue is elevated toward the roof of your mouth. Notice how the "Ooh" sounds dark and hollow, while the "Eee" sounds bright. You can say "Ooh" and "Eee" as separate syllables, or you can run them together into "Wee."

Try playing Tab 6-3 while you use your tongue to say "Ooh-Eee" and "Wee" as shown under the notes. The notes that are tied together should be played in one long breath. You can hear the lick on Track 29.

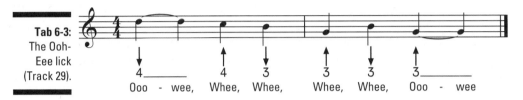

Tab 6-3:
The Ooh-
Eee lick
(Track 29).

Shaping Sound with Your Hands

Some performers use hand motion as a way to impress audiences. I've never seen a snake charmer use a harmonica, but the hypnotic effect of a player's hands may just work on a cobra — it certainly works on humans. But remember that hand moves are more than just display. They also have an impact on the sound of a harmonica.

In Chapter 4, I show you how to enclose the harmonica in a hand cup. If you need a refresher, take a look at that chapter. Otherwise, in the following sections, I show you how to use the cup to shape the sounds you make with your harp.

Tone color and vowel sounds

When you play with a completely closed hand cup, the tone is dark and distant-sounding, yet it's powerful and focused. When you play with an open cup, it's bright and immediate. To hear the difference between a closed cup and an open cup, listen to Track 29 (0:14).

When you close your cup while playing a note, it makes a sound like "Ooo," and when you open your cup while playing a note, it can sound like "Whee," "Wee," or "Wah." These harmonica syllables are among the repertoire of vocal sounds that the harmonica can make to imitate speech.

You can combine hand vowels with tongue vowels. For example, tongue "Ooo" goes with a closed cup, and tongue "Eee" goes with an open cup. To hear hand-cupped "Ooh-Wah" followed by combined cup and tongue vowels, listen to Track 29 (0:26).

You can also combine hand vowels with note bending for a vocal (and bluesy) sound. The bent note goes with the closed cup and the unbent note goes with the open cup. (See Chapters 8 and 12 for more information on bending notes.)

Try cupping a coffee mug in your hands along with the harp; make sure the mouth of the cup is pointed at the harp. When you play with your hands closed around the mug and the harp, it sounds distant and hollow, and the vowel sounds you get when you open your cup are strongly exaggerated. Some players have used the coffee cup technique to great effect. To hear it, check out the brief demonstration on Track 30 and also the song "Saint James Infirmary" on Track 96.

Pulsing notes

By opening and closing the edge opening of your hands at the front of the harp, you can create a note pulsation called *hand vibrato* (or *hand tremolo*). This pulsation can be strongly pronounced if you move your entire right hand, using your thumbs as a hinge. Or it can be subtle if you just move your pinky finger.

To hear both pronounced and subtle hand vibrato on Tab 6-1, listen to Track 31.

You can also fan the sound of the harmonica by rapidly sweeping your entire cupping hand past the harp by moving your entire forearm in a semicircle, pivoting at the elbow. You start with your arm pointed down to the floor, then sweep your forearm up, drawing your cupping hand past the harmonica until your hand and forearm are pointing straight up, then swing them back down past the harp again and repeat the entire motion several times. Each time your hand passes the harmonica, it produces a disturbance in the note you play. Sonny Terry used this fanning motion to great effect.

This fanning creates a unique sound that you can hear applied to a long note on Track 31 (0:30).

Adding Vibrato to Your Playing

Earlier in this chapter, I show you how to use your diaphragm, throat, tongue, and hands to pulsate your sound. In this section, I focus on using those same techniques to make a long note pulsate at a steady rate. This steady pulsation is called *vibrato*, though the term *tremolo* is also used.

Vibrato can impart expression and beauty to long notes, and it can also add a subtle rhythmic layer to your playing. When you listen to a singer, guitarist, violinist, or any wind instrument, always listen for the pulsation of vibrato and its expressive qualities, and try to incorporate some of what you hear into your playing.

To hear each type of pulsation in sequence on a long note, listen to Track 32.

Throat vibrato is the most widely favored by harmonica players. However, hand vibrato runs a close second. Abdominal vibrato is a mystery to most harp players, but a few are beginning to catch on. Tongue vibrato can be heard from a few jazz-oriented players like Howard Levy and Chris Michalek.

Timing your vibrato to the beat is an important concept that can make your playing stand out. Every beat divides into something smaller, usually either two or three divisions of equal duration. (For more on dividing beats, see Chapter 3.)

To get an idea of the flavor and pulsation that timed vibrato can give to music, listen to Track 33 on the CD. This track contains two brief grooves played by a backup band. In the first one, I divide the beat into three pulsations. In the second one, I divide the beat into four pulsations.

Chapter 7

Enhancing Your Sound with Your Tongue on the Harp

. . . .

. . . .

*U*sing your tongue on the front of the harmonica gives you a powerful tool to select and combine harmonica notes. You can give individual notes body and sizzle, you can play rhythms that make your playing catchier, and you can even play your own accompaniment by adding chords while you play a melody. The more you use *tongue blocking* — putting your tongue on the holes of the harp — the more you'll love the sounds you can create. And the more you'll notice that many of the greatest harmonica players rely on tongue blocking to give their sound that extra edge.

In this chapter, I take you through the most widely used tongue blocking techniques. For each technique I tell you the musical effect it creates, and then I illustrate the sequence of tongue actions on the harp. Finally, I give you a tune or lick you can play using that technique.

The tongue techniques in this chapter are skills that harmonica players traditionally learn by ear, and so no standard method exists to write them down. Consequently, every author comes up with a different way to name and notate these effects. In this book, I use simple symbols and names that are descriptive and conform with (or at least don't misuse) standard musical terms. However, you may find that other authors — and players — use different terms to describe the same effects and techniques.

Using Your Tongue to Combine Chords and Melodies

The diatonic harmonica was designed to play both *melody* (single notes played one after the other) and *chords* (several notes played at once). Any melody note you play sounds good in a chord with notes in the neighboring holes. (The only exception is the *dissonance,* or harsh sound, that's made by the combination of Draw 6 and Draw 7.) Your tongue plays a powerful role in combining melody and chords to add body and rhythm to your melodies.

Knowing the chords on your harp

When you use tongue techniques, you often play several notes at once, resulting in a *chord,* or a group of notes that sound good together and reinforce one another. A harmonica in the key of C provides the notes of the C major scale and arranges them so that when you play several neighboring holes, you get some of the most important chords that work with C major. Here are the three main chords:

- ✔ **The blow notes form the C major chord.** As you can imagine, the C major chord is the most important chord on a harmonica that's in the key of C. After all, it is the home chord.

- ✔ **The draw notes in Holes 1 through 4 form a G major chord, which is the second most important chord in C.** When you play the harmonica in second position, this chord is the home chord (see Chapter 9 for more on positions).

- ✔ **The draw notes in Holes 4, 5, and 6 and again in Draw 8, 9, and 10 form a D minor chord.** This chord blends easily with the G chord lower down and acts as an extension that adds richness and color to the G chord. However, when you play a C-harmonica in third position, D minor is the home chord.

Try playing each of these chords to get familiar with its sound and location on the harp. After you get familiar with each new tongue technique, try applying it to each of the chords.

Accompanying melodies with chords

If you place your mouth on several holes of the harmonica and then breathe, you activate the notes in those holes. However, you also can place your tongue on the harp to block some of the holes, as shown in Figure 7-1a.

When you do this, you're using a technique called *tongue blocking*. With your tongue on the harp, only one hole is open; and when you breathe, you play only the note in that hole. (For more on how to form a tongue block, see Chapter 5.)

You could just keep your tongue on the harp and play a melody consisting of a sequence of single notes. However, at certain points during the tune, you can lift your tongue off the harp — simply retract your tongue slightly into your mouth. When you do this, you expose several holes, as shown in Figure 7-1b. The exposed holes will respond to your breath and sound a chord. Harmonica players use this tongue lifting technique to add accompaniment to some melodies. The added chord notes make the melody sound fuller, and if you add chords to melody with a regular rhythm, you're supporting the melody with rhythm as well.

When you first try tongue blocking, try to widen your mouth to cover several holes, but stay within your range of comfort. At first you may not be able to tell how many holes are in your mouth. Try to have your mouth open wide enough so you have room to put your tongue on the harp and still leave one hole open on the right. Playing three to four holes is good, but for now, don't sweat it. If you can get a single note with your tongue on the harp, and you hear more notes when you lift your tongue, you'll be fine.

Figure 7-1:
Blocking holes to produce a melody note and exposing holes to produce a chord that's added to a melody note.

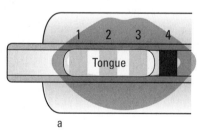
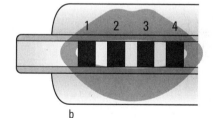

Tab 7-1 shows the tune "Mary Had a Little Lamb." You can make this tune groove by adding chords rhythmically. To prepare, learn to play the tune in single notes with a tongue block embouchure (see Chapter 5 for the basics of tongue-blocked melody). After you've mastered the tune, try lifting your tongue whenever you see an asterisk (*) in the tab. When you add chords, you don't change the length of any of the notes. In other words, the chord happens at the same time as the melody notes.

Here are the guidelines for following the asterisks:

- ✔ **When the asterisk comes after a note, start that note as a single note, and then, while you're playing the note, lift your tongue off the harp to add the chord.** For example, you start the first note of the tune in Tab 7-1 as a single note. Then you lift your tongue to add a chord. When you play the next note, you put your tongue on the harp and play that note as a single note.

- ✔ **When the asterisk is directly below a note, lift your tongue off the harp just before you play the note.** Instead of the single note, you play a chord, with the melody note as the top note. For example, the fourth note in Tab 7-1 has an asterisk directly below the tab. You would lift your tongue just as you start to play this note. Leave your tongue lifted for the duration of the note, and then put your tongue back on the harp to play the next note.

Lifting your tongue while playing a melody is a skill that harmonica players pick up by ear, and they apply this skill at their own discretion. No standard method exists to write down this effect. Consequently, every author comes up with a different way to write it down. I use the asterisk because it's quick and easy, but other authors may use different symbols.

In this chapter, you'll notice letters above the notation, such as C and G7. These are the names of chords that other instruments can play to accompany you while you play the tunes. If you have friends who play guitar or piano, they could play the chords while you play the melody.

You can hear a groovin' version of the childhood tune in Tab 7-1 on Track 34 of the CD.

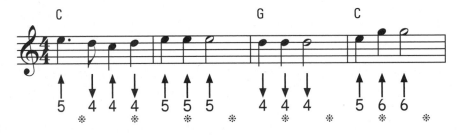

Tab 7-1: "Mary Had a Groovin' Little Lamb" (Track 34).

Chasing the beat with a chord

In "Mary Had a Groovin' Little Lamb" (refer to Tab 7-1), you lift your tongue on the second and fourth beats of each measure. However, you can also place chords in between the beats of a tune.

If you listen to blues and swing bands, you often hear the bass-playing note on every beat while it "walks" up or down the scale. This approach to bass playing is called a *walking bass* because it gives the impression of someone walking at a steady pace in a particular direction. You can accompany a *walking bass line* — any melody where the notes fall on each beat — by *chasing the beat*, or lifting your tongue to play a chord after each beat. (You often hear pianists and guitarists chasing the beat with chords. However, they usually use their fingers and not their tongues.)

Tab 7-2 shows "Chasin' the Beat," a tune you can use to try out the technique of chasing the beat. In the tab, each asterisk shows where you should lift your tongue to play a chord. (As none of the chords fall on the beat, I've moved the asterisks up beside the tab for easier reading.) To hear "Chasin' the Beat," listen to Track 35.

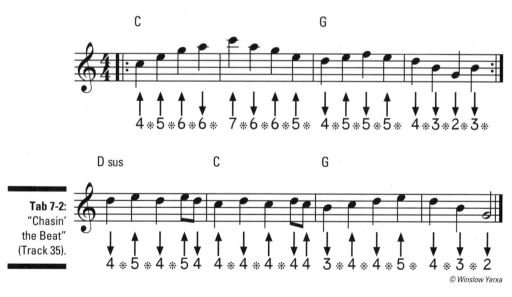

Tab 7-2:
"Chasin'
the Beat"
(Track 35).

© Winslow Yerxa

You may experience a problem playing the last notes of "Chasin' the Beat" (Tab 7-2) and "Slappin' the Blues" (Tab 7-3). Both tunes end with Draw 2, and when you play Holes 1 or 2 with a tongue block, you may find that the harp no longer covers the left half of your mouth, which is sort of hanging in the wind and leaking air between your lips and tongue. (I've heard of air guitar, but air harmonica is something you want to avoid!) However, you can easily seal off any air leaks by letting your lips collapse onto your tongue, as shown in

Figure 7-2. When the harmonica is inserted in your mouth, it tends to push your lips away from your tongue. As you slide the harp to the right, be aware of your upper and lower lips. As the harp moves out from between your lips, let your lips move in to take up the space left open by the harmonica so that your lips contact your tongue and seal off any leaks.

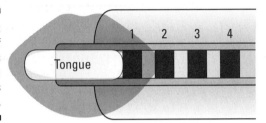

Figure 7-2:
Sealing off
air leaks
when you
play Holes
1 and 2.

Reinforcing Melody Notes with Your Tongue

Every instrument has a way of making melody notes sound bigger and more interesting. On the harmonica, the most powerful and natural way to reinforce a single note is by lifting your tongue selectively to add notes from the neighboring holes. Because all these notes are part of a chord, they reinforce each other and make the whole sound bigger than its parts.

The following sections introduce you to several techniques to reinforce melody notes. Each technique creates its own effect. After you learn these effects, you can use your own taste and judgment in applying them to melodies. You also can get ideas on ways of using these techniques by listening to how they're employed by professionals.

Applying the tongue slap

A *tongue slap* is a way of making a melody note sound bigger by starting it as part of a chord and then immediately isolating only the melody note. Here's how to do it:

1. **Start with a chord that has the melody note at the right side of your mouth.**

   Figure 7-3a shows how you start the slap by playing a chord with the melody note on the right.

2. **Perform the slap by covering the other holes with your tongue, leaving only the melody note.**

   Figure 7-3b shows your tongue on the harp after the slap, isolating the hole that plays the melody note.

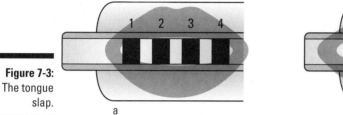
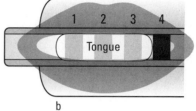

Figure 7-3:
The tongue slap.

a

b

Tab 7-3 shows a tune called "Slappin' the Blues." When playing this tune, you start each note with a slap. The asterisk just *before* a note indicates that you start that note with a slap. You can hear "Slappin' the Blues" on Track 36 of the CD.

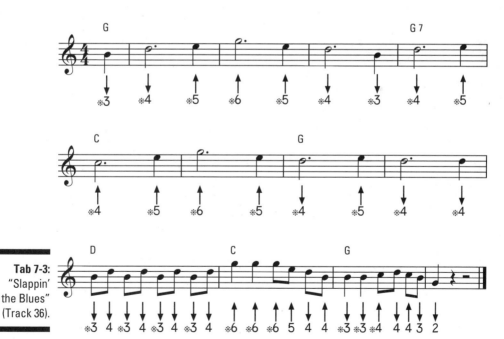

Tab 7-3:
"Slappin' the Blues"
(Track 36).

Combining widely spaced notes with a tongue split

You can reinforce a melody note with another note that's several holes to the left, played as a harmony. But how do you keep the holes in between from sounding? You block them out with your tongue, and leave space at the left and right corners of your mouth to direct air to the holes you want to play (as shown in Figure 7-4). Because you're taking a chord and splitting it apart into two harmony notes, harmonica players often call this a *tongue split* (at least when they're in polite company).

To get the hang of playing a tongue split, start with a chord that covers four holes. Then place your tongue on the harp so you hear the notes on the left and right sides together. Check out Figure 7-4 to see how your tongue should be positioned.

To hear what this technique sounds like for the blow and draw notes in Holes 1 and 4, listen to Track 37.

As you begin to master split intervals, you'll find that you can spread your tongue for widely spaced intervals and narrow it for closer ones.

Figure 7-4:
The tongue split (Track 37).

When you form a tongue split, you can keep it "locked" in formation, and then you can move it along with the melody as you play. This technique is referred to as the *locked split*. As you change breath direction and move from hole to hole, you play melody from the right side of your locked split, and the left side automatically supplies a lower harmony note.

Figure 7-5a shows a locked split that plays Hole 4, accompanied by Hole 1. In Figure 7-5b, the split is moved one hole to the right to play Hole 5 accompanied by Hole 2. When you play a locked split, you don't move your lips or your tongue. They stay locked in formation, and you just slide the harp when you move to a different hole. Try playing the demonstration line in Tab 7-4 with a locked split.

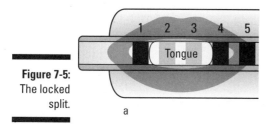 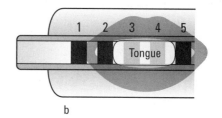

Figure 7-5:
The locked
split.

a   b

Creating Chord Textures with Your Tongue

When you play a chord, you can use your tongue to add texture — sort of like a guitar player does when he plays a fancy strum pattern instead of just hitting the notes of a chord once. In the following sections, I explore several different chord textures, including the chord rake, the chord hammer, the hammered split, and the shimmer.

On Track 38, you can hear each of the chord textures together with the locked split. I use the riff shown in Tab 7-4 and apply each texture in turn.

Tab 7-4:
A demon-
stration line
for tongue
textures
(Track 38).

Alternating tongue placements to produce the chord rake

When you play a *chord rake,* you rake your tongue from side to side across the holes of the harp while you play a chord. At any given time during the rake, some of the notes will sound and others will be blocked by your tongue. This constantly changing combination of notes creates a texture sort of like an up-and-down strum on a guitar.

Here's how you can produce a chord rake:

1. **Start with a chord of three or more holes.**

2. **Place your tongue on the harp to one side so that some holes are covered and some are open.**

3. **As you play, slide your tongue from side to side on the harmonica.**

Make sure that the edges of your tongue tap against the corners of your mouth to be sure that your tongue is travelling as far as possible to the right and left. Doing so allows you to get the maximum effect from the technique. Figures 7-6a and 7-6b show the left and right extremes of tongue placement when you play a rake.

Try playing a chord rake, and then apply it to the demonstration line in Tab 7-4. You can hear the chord rake applied to the demonstration line on Track 38 (0:15) on the CD.

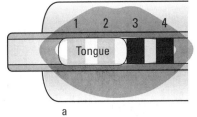
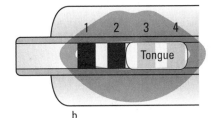

Figure 7-6: The chord rake (Track 38, 0:15).

Lifting and replacing your tongue to play a chord hammer

While you're playing a melody note, you can add an effect called the *chord hammer.* A chord hammer is a rapid-fire series of repeated chords that you play while the melody note continues to sound. A chord hammer sounds impressive (it's a favorite effect of blues harmonica players), but it's simple to play. Start with your tongue covering enough holes to play one note, as in Figure 7-7a. Then rapidly lift your tongue off the harp (see Figure 7-7b) and replace it. When you do this, you get a vigorous undulating sound — your tongue acts like a soft hammer delivering a rapid series of blows.

When you play a chord hammer, you don't have to move at lightning speed. The effect sounds twice as fast as you're actually moving, so don't sweat trying to move your tongue faster than you can control.

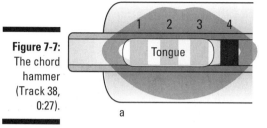
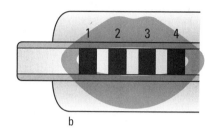

Figure 7-7:
The chord hammer (Track 38, 0:27).

a   b

Try playing a chord hammer, and then apply it to the demonstration line in Tab 7-4, which you can hear on Track 38 (0:27).

A *hammered split* is just like a chord hammer except for one detail: Instead of starting with a single note, you start with a tongue split. Whenever your tongue is on the harp, holes are open on both sides of your tongue, as shown in Figure 7-8a. Then, just like with a chord hammer, you rapidly lift your tongue off the harp (see Figure 7-8b) and replace it again.

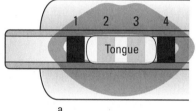
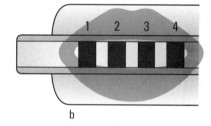

Figure 7-8:
The hammered split (Track 38, 0:40.

a   b

Try playing a hammered split, and then apply it to the demonstration line in Tab 7-4, which you can hear on Track 38 (0:40).

Rapidly alternating widely spaced notes with the shimmer

A *shimmer* is a little like a chord rake (see the earlier section, "Alternating tongue placements to produce the chord rake"). However, instead of playing all the notes in your mouth, the shimmer alternates between the note on the left side and the note on the right. And instead of sliding the tip of your tongue from side to side, you keep it in place on the harp. You initiate the wagging motion from farther back on your tongue so the tip of your tongue rocks in place. As it rocks from side to side, it alternately covers the holes on the left and right. Figures 7-9a and 7-9b show the left and right extremes of tongue placement when you play a shimmer.

Playing a shimmer allows you to eliminate chord notes that may not fit with what a guitar or piano player is playing. It also produces a more subtle effect than a chord rake or chord hammer.

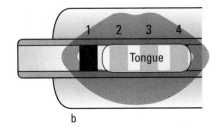

Figure 7-9:
The shimmer (Track 38, 0:53).

a   b

After you master the shimmer, try it on the demonstration line in Tab 7-4; you can hear it on Track 38 (0:53).

Playing Wide Leaps with Corner Switching

When you're playing a note on the harmonica and you want to jump to another note several holes away, you may have trouble landing in the right hole when you jump. You may also find that as you pass over the holes in between, those notes sound when you don't want them to. Fortunately, you can play wide leaps cleanly and accurately with *corner switching*.

When you use corner switching, you just switch between the note in the right corner of your mouth and the note in the left corner. You do this by simply sliding your tongue to the left or to the right — simple, eh?

Here's how you perform a corner switch:

1. **Position your mouth so that the left and right corners are placed over the first and second notes of the leap.**

2. **Place your tongue on the harp so that the hole containing the first note of the leap is open and all the other holes are blocked.**

   Figure 7-10a shows the first note of the leap as Hole 4.

3. **Shift your tongue so that the first hole is blocked and the note containing the second hole is now open at the other corner of your mouth, as shown in Figure 7-10b.**

You may notice that Figure 7-10 looks identical to Figure 7-9. And it should, because a corner switch uses the same tongue technique as a shimmer. However, you play a corner switch in a deliberate way — and usually only once, instead of the quick, repeated tongue motion of a shimmer.

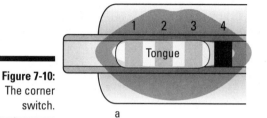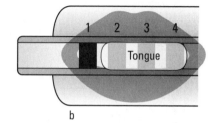

Figure 7-10:
The corner switch.

a   b

Tab 7-5 shows a line you can try to practice corner switching. The "R" and "L" above the notes stand for "right" and "left." These indicate whether you're playing a note from the right corner or the left corner of your mouth. The following is a breakdown of the moves you make:

1. **Start by playing Draw 4 on the right side of your tongue.**

2. **As you inhale, slide your tongue to the right to block off Hole 4 and uncover Hole 1.**

   You should hear Draw 1 on the left side.

3. **Slide your tongue to the left again to return to Draw 4 (right side).**

4. **Play the next few notes on the right side until you get to Blow 6.**

5. **Play Blow 6, and then slide your tongue to the right to block off Hole 6 and uncover Hole 3.**

   Now you're playing Blow 3 on the left side.

6. **Slide your tongue to the left again to return to Blow 6 (right side).**

7. **Play the next few notes.**

   The last notes lead you back to where you can begin the cycle again to practice your new skill.

Tab 7-5:
A line to
practice
corner
switching
(Track 39).

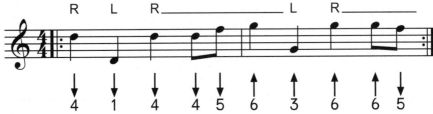

Play this very slowly at first. The hardest part is making sure you have the correct note on the left side of your mouth. That's why the first leap goes to Hole 1 — if there's no note to the left, you can tell you're on Hole 1. After you have Hole 1 on the left side, try to lock your mouth position so that the left side stays in formation with the right as you move to different places on the harp.

You can hear Tab 7-5 on Track 39 of the CD.

Chapter 8

Unlocking a Hidden Treasure: Bending Notes Down

*R*elax! When I talk about *bending a note,* I don't mean that you need to twist your harmonica with pliers. What I'm referring to is taking one of the notes that's built into the harmonica and playing it so that it changes to another note, usually one that's not built into the harmonica. You can bend some notes down to a lower note and others up to a higher note.

Bending can be very expressive, and it plays a big part in the harmonica sound you hear in recordings, advertising, and live music. When you use bending to slide a note down — or to bring it back up — the harmonica starts to sound like a human voice. For instance, when you bend a note while you open and close your hands around the harp or pulse your breath with your throat, you get crying sounds, moaning sounds, purring sounds, and slinky sounds — many of the expressive sounds that are so characteristic of the harmonica.

Bending to get these characteristic sounds is great, but bending is important for another reason as well: It supplies notes that are missing on the most popular type of harmonica, the *diatonic* harmonica. Diatonic means that the harmonica is designed to play in only one key, such as C, G, or A, and has only the notes of that key. A *chromatic* instrument, by contrast, has all the notes to play in every key, nearly twice as many as a diatonic instrument. Chromatic harmonicas exist (see Chapter 2 for a full description), but the diatonic is by far the most popular.

Even with notes missing, you can play a lot of music on a diatonic harmonica. However, blues, rock, and country music styles all use those missing notes, and that's where bending comes in. You can get about two-thirds of the missing notes by bending notes down, and you can get the remaining ones by bending notes up. Cool, eh?

To hear what expressive bending sounds like, as well as what bending for missing notes sounds like, listen to Track 53 and 40 on the CD.

In this chapter, I explain how you bend notes down so you can get most of the missing notes and add the characteristic blues harp sound to your playing. Bending notes up is a bit more challenging; I help you master that technique in Chapter 12.

Reaching back in time: A brief history of bending

Early in the 19th century, builders in Germany and Austria developed the harmonica to play songs and dance tunes popular in the German-speaking parts of Europe. They never dreamed that Americans in the rural South would find ways to make the harmonica slur, cry, and wail with bent notes.

Harmonicas became widely available in North America in the 1870s, and soon harmonica instruction books were being published in Chicago and other northern cities. None of them mentioned bending. By the early 1920s, harmonica players in the South, both black and white, were making records using bent notes with an artistry and technical sophistication that suggests bending had already been around for a long time.

Nobody knows who bent the first note (they forgot to have it bronzed), but the sliding pitches and deliberately lowered "blue notes" of African-American music suggest that note bending on the harmonica was an imitation of these vocal styles. Rural harmonica styles, complete with note bending used to imitate steam trains and fox hunts, came to country music through De Ford Bailey's Grand Ole Opry broadcasts from Nashville in the 1920s and '30s. The sound of bending notes came to urban folk music in New York in the 1940s and '50s through the playing of North Carolina harmonica wizard Sonny Terry and Oklahoma protest singer Woody Guthrie.

When rural harmonica styles arrived in cities like Memphis and Chicago, they started adapting to the urban environment. Rural mimicry took a back seat to topics like sex and drugs (rock-and-roll would soon follow). In the early 1960s, urban harmonica artists like Little Walter and Sonny Boy Williamson II visited the British Isles and made a strong impression on British rockers such as the Rolling Stones and the Beatles. When the British rock invasion reached American shores in 1964, British rockers with harmonicas introduced many young Americans to a sound their parents had either forgotten or never known.

Meanwhile, American folk-influenced artists like Bob Dylan began making hit records with squalling harmonica inspired by Woody Guthrie. In Nashville, country music had become a big business and had lost much of its folksiness until a young blues-inspired harmonica player named Charlie McCoy reintroduced the sound of bent notes where De Ford Bailey had left off decades earlier. Since then, note bending in rock, country, folk, and blues has become a permanent part of the sound of harmonica playing in popular music worldwide.

Getting Your First Bends

Getting your first bend is a rite of passage for harmonica players. Luckily, your initiation doesn't involve dumb stunts of bravado, such as riding a bicycle off a cliff into the ocean and living to tell about it. It's more like solving a mystery in total darkness. And the darkness is inside your mouth, so a flashlight won't help. What does help is paying attention to the subtle sensations inside your mouth as you breathe and move your tongue. This may not sound like the stuff of Indiana Jones, but once all the clues click into place and you get a bend, you may feel like a hidden cavern has opened up to reveal a dazzling treasure.

When you bend a note, you do two things:

✔ You activate the bend by narrowing the airflow between your tongue and the roof of your mouth. The place where you narrow the flow is called the *K-spot,* which I discuss next.

✔ You tune your mouth to a note that's a little lower than the note you're bending by moving the K-spot backward or forward in your mouth. I explain what I mean a little later in this section.

You can't tell if you've tuned your mouth to a bent note unless you activate the bend, so learning to activate comes first. Then you can practice tuning your mouth so that with experience you can tune your mouth *before* you activate the bend.

Starting off on the right foot with the basics

To get the most out of your first bending experience, make sure you can say "Yes" to all the following statements (signing in blood is optional):

✔ **You can direct all your breath through your mouth and shut off the airflow through your nose.** For instance, when you say "my nose," it should sound like "by doze," as if you have a cold. (Yeah, you can play harp with your nose, but let's not go there.) One way to master this technique is to inhale while you imagine that you're sipping liquid through a straw. If you can't yet direct all your breath through your mouth, spend some time with Chapter 4.

✔ **With your lips, you can form a relaxed, flexible seal around the harp, with no telltale hiss of air escaping from the corners of your mouth when you play.** To get a good seal, try the grin exercise: Open your mouth into a wide grin and insert the harp so that it touches the corners of your mouth. Then relax your lips so that the moist, inner parts of your lips form an airtight seal with the harp. When you inhale or exhale you should hear several notes playing at once, but you shouldn't hear any air hiss. If you need additional pointers on forming a good seal, flip to Chapter 4.

✔ **You can play a clear single note without putting your tongue on the harp.** To do this, you pucker your lips like you're going to kiss someone on the cheek (for some unknown reason, harp players call this way of getting a single note a *pucker*). To get a clear single note with a pucker, start with the grin exercise that you use to form a seal around your harp. To isolate a single hole, push your lips out a little — sort of like you're pouting — while you inhale or exhale through the harp. When you hear a clear single note, you're good to go. If you need more help playing a single note, check out Chapter 5.

✔ **You never swear or have an impure thought while playing.**

Just kidding about that last one. But don't forget that as you attempt your first bend, frustration may drive you to let loose with a few pithy words. Don't worry, though. The harmonica may be demanding, but it's also very forgiving.

The K-spot: Your link to activating a bend

When you bend a note, you activate the bend by narrowing the airflow in your mouth with your tongue. The way you do this is similar to the way you make the sound of the letter "K." You don't actually say "K" with the K-spot; you just approach "K" closely enough to create a suction-filled tunnel. If you were to take the harp away and look into a player's mouth, you'd see the tongue and roof of the mouth creating that tunnel, something like Figure 8-1.

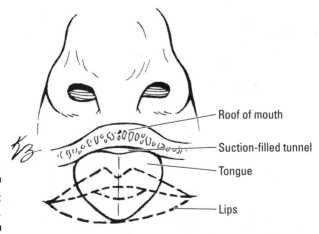

— Roof of mouth

— Suction-filled tunnel

— Tongue

Figure 8-1:
The K-spot.

— Lips

Creating a K-spot without a harmonica

To help yourself get ready to create a K-spot, try these steps to get the feeling of what you do with your tongue. Perform these steps without a harmonica so you can concentrate on your tongue and the airflow in your mouth:

1. **Open your mouth slightly, just enough so you can place a finger between your lips.**

   At this point, your tongue should be lying relaxed on the floor of your mouth.

2. **Take away your finger (if it's still there), drop your jaw slightly, and gently inhale some air through your mouth.**

   As you inhale, feel the area below your rib cage expand. When you breathe gently from this deep place you supply the power behind the bend.

3. **Whisper "Kayoooooooo" as you inhale.**

   Don't move your lips; let your tongue do all the work. Notice how you pull your tongue backward to make the "O" sound at the end of "Kayooooo."

4. **Add "K" to the end of the whispered word: "Kayoooook!"**

   Take your time getting to that final "K." As you slowly raise your tongue to the roof of your mouth, pay attention to the suction forming as the air passage narrows. This narrow passageway filled with suction is the K-spot.

Now, with the following steps, try creating the K-spot all by itself:

1. **With your tongue relaxed, slowly inhale and raise your tongue to the roof of your mouth, as if to say "K."**

   Feel the suction as you inhale.

2. **Sustain the suction for several seconds and feel it pulling your tongue upward.**

   You have to exert a small amount of control to keep your tongue from being pulled flat against the roof of your mouth.

Now you have a sustained K-spot. With these next steps, you add the K-spot back to the "Kayoo" sound to make a bend:

1. **Make the first "K" sound, and then drop your tongue slightly to form the "AY" sound.**

2. **Make the final "OOOO" sound by sliding your tongue backward while you form a K-spot.**

   With the K-spot engaged, you should feel suction while you're sliding your tongue back. While you do this, breathe gently but firmly. Making this final sound doesn't require force.

Using your K-spot to bend a note

Now it's time to pick up a harmonica. Your first job is to play a clean single note with no air leaking from the corners of your mouth. It's easier to get started with bending if you can play a single note without putting your tongue on the harp. Later I describe bending with your tongue on the harp.

Now look at the harmonica and find Hole 4 — the hole with the number 4 above it. Play Draw 4 — that is, inhale in Hole 4 so that you hear a note playing. As you play the note, form a K-spot and say "Kayooooo," drawing your tongue back on the "oooo" part while maintaining suction like you did in the previous section without the harp.

Not sure what the bend should sound like? Listen to Track 41 on the CD to hear the sound of Draw 4 bending down.

As you work on bending Draw 4, a few different things may happen:

- ✔ **The note doesn't change.** Check to make sure that you're feeling suction in the narrow tunnel between your tongue and the roof of your mouth. After you get suction at the K-spot, try sliding the K-spot slowly backward and forward in your mouth until you find the right place for the note to bend.

- ✔ **You get no sound at all.** You may not think so, but no sound is good — it means that you're almost there. Try increasing your air intake slightly until you get a sound. Also, try sliding your K-spot slowly forward and backward in your mouth.

- ✔ **You get a metallic squealing sound.** This squealing sounds bad, but again it's actually good because you're very close. Try moving the K-spot slightly forward in your mouth.

- ✔ **You bend the note down.** Congratulations! You've succeeded in bending your first note!

If at first you don't succeed: Practicing persistence

Getting the hang of bending down can be frustrating, but if you keep at it you'll be wailing with ease and wondering why it seemed so elusive. Here are some things to remember as you work on your first bend:

- ✔ **Your first bend may not happen right away, so be patient and keep trying.** It may take a few days before the feeling clicks into place. Even then, the bend may be elusive — you'll get it a few times and then lose it again. Eventually, with practice and patience, you'll be able to get it every time.

✔ **Don't use force when you get frustrated.** If you don't get the note right away, you may be tempted to use force. But if you suck real hard, you'll do just that: suck real hard! And that won't work very well. It will probably sound bad, and it can damage the harmonica. If you're frustrated, call the harmonica terrible names (I promise it won't hurt the harp). Then take a deep breath and work on forming your K-spot, feeling the slight suction in the tunnel, and moving the K-spot around until you find the bend.

✔ **Use the power of the pause.** As you work on getting the bend, it may go well at first. But after a while you may feel like you're putting in effort and not getting anywhere. That's a good time to go away and do something else before resuming. This pause has a way of helping things fall into place in the background. The important thing is to come back after the pause. Keep at it, and after a while the bend will come consistently, and you'll start to develop control.

After you get your first bend in Hole 4, try bending Draw 5 and 6. These notes are higher than Draw 4, so for each of these bends you need to place the K-spot a little farther forward. Moving the K-spot helps tune your mouth to those bends.

Tuning your mouth to different notes

In just ten holes, a harmonica covers a wide range — the bright, piercing notes in Hole 10 vibrate eight times as fast as the deep, dark notes in Hole 1. A guitar string needs to be as long as your leg to cover this range, but your mouth bends notes across the entire range of the harp using an area about the length of your hand. This short stretch runs from the back of your teeth to approximately where you swallow, and it's the prime real estate of bending. To help you master bending, this section takes you on a tour of all the major landmarks.

When you bend a note down, you tune your *mouth chamber* — the space inside your mouth — to a note slightly lower than the one that normally sounds in that hole on the harp. You tune your mouth chamber by changing its size.

You change the size of your mouth chamber by moving the K-spot. For high notes, you need a small chamber, so you move the K-spot forward in your mouth (see Figure 8-2). For low notes, you need a large chamber, so you move the K-spot farther back in your mouth (see Figure 8-3).

If the K-spot is too far forward or too far back, you won't hear a bend. If it's just behind the bend, the sound may stop entirely. When you get the K-spot into the right place, you'll hear the note bend.

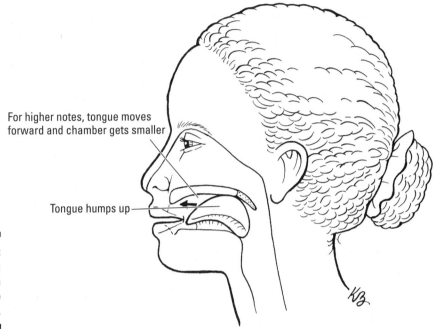

For higher notes, tongue moves forward and chamber gets smaller

Tongue humps up

Figure 8-2:
Tuning your mouth chamber to a high note.

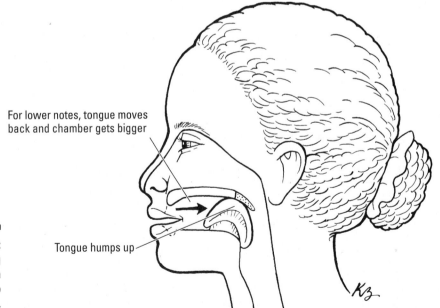

For lower notes, tongue moves back and chamber gets bigger

Tongue humps up

Figure 8-3:
Tuning your mouth chamber to a low note.

Rolling the K-spot along your tongue

So far in this chapter, I've described the K-spot as the tongue being humped up in the place where you say "K." It's true that you can simply move your tongue forward and back in your mouth to move the hump. But it gets better. You can also move that hump to different places on your tongue. Your tongue stays put and the hump rolls along it like a wave.

To better understand what I mean, imagine a rug that has one edge against a wall. And imagine that a foot from the wall, there's a raised crease in the carpet, humped up in a line that runs parallel to the wall. You can push the crease closer to the wall or farther away from it. The rug itself doesn't move, but you can move the crease to any point along the length of the carpet. Your tongue is like the rug and the crease is like your K-spot.

To get the feeling of creating a K-spot at a different place on your tongue, follow these steps:

1. **Say "Zzzzzzz."**

   Now, in the next step, I want you to try doing something a little different with this "Zzzzzzz" sound.

2. **Lower the tip of your tongue from the roof of your mouth and aim the buzzing sound directly at your front teeth.**

   To intensify the buzzing, bring the tip of your tongue closer to the roof of your mouth without touching it. (It may not sound exactly like "Zzzz" anymore — that's okay as long as it makes a strong buzzing sound.)

3. **Stop using your voice and just breathe through this tongue position, keeping your tongue pressed close to the roof of your mouth.**

   You should hear air rushing. Near the tip of your tongue you'll feel pressure as you exhale. When you inhale, you'll feel suction. That's a K-spot.

Now that you can form a K-spot at the front of your tongue, try making your tongue do the wave by rolling the K-spot back along your tongue (see Figure 8-4 for an illustration of the K-spot moving back along the tongue):

1. **Start by forming a K-spot near the tip of your tongue, and then begin to inhale.**

   As you do this, you'll begin to feel the suction.

2. **Keep the suction going and lower the tip of your tongue so that it points downward.**

Notice that the suction moves backward even though your tongue is moving down. As you peel your tongue away from the roof of your mouth, the front edge of the tunnel is receding back into your mouth.

3. **Keep lowering more of your tongue, from the tip on backward.**

   The front of the suction point will move backward along with it.

4. **Keep lowering more of your tongue until the K-spot reaches the area where you normally say "K."**

   Try to move the K-spot back past this spot without moving the front of your tongue. If you feel uncomfortable, stop.

5. **Now that you've slid the K-spot from front to back, try sliding it from the back all the way to the front.**

6. **Try rolling the K-spot while exhaling as well.**

   Instead of suction, you'll feel pressure at the K-spot as you move it backward and forward.

 As you roll the K-spot forward and back along your tongue, listen for the sound of the rushing air. As you move the K-spot forward, the sound will go up in pitch like a note getting higher. As you move the K-spot back, the sound will fall to a deeper pitch.

Finding the K-spot in the deep bending chamber

So far, you've traveled about three-fourths the length of your mouth chamber. For some notes you need that extra bit of length at the very back of your mouth. To get there, you need to make friends with your *soft palate,* the back part of the roof of your mouth. Until now you've been sliding your tongue against the *hard palate* — the rigid front part of the roof of your mouth (see Figure 8-5 for a look at the hard and soft palates).

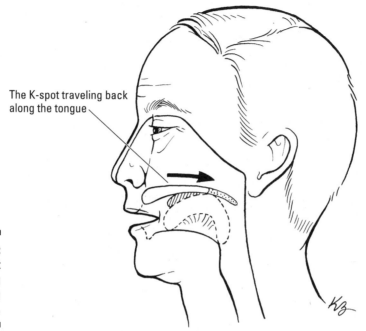

The K-spot traveling back along the tongue

Figure 8-4:
The K-spot traveling back along the tongue.

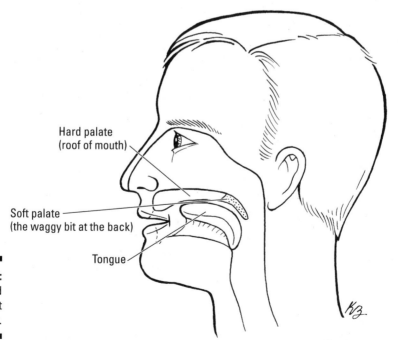

Hard palate (roof of mouth)

Soft palate (the waggy bit at the back)

Tongue

Figure 8-5:
The hard and soft palates.

As the name implies, the soft palate is, well, soft. Like the tongue, it's also capable of movement. Normally the soft palate just hangs there as air rushes past through the nose above and the mouth below. But you can actually wag the soft palate up to block air from going through your nose (see Figure 8-6). You can also wag the soft palate down to block air from going through your mouth (see Figure 8-7).

When you blow out a candle or suck liquid through a straw, you wag your soft palate up to close off the nose and concentrate air power in your mouth. That's why, all through this book, I tell you to close off your nose so all the air goes through your mouth.

Now I'm going to ask you to ignore that advice for a few minutes. Instead of wagging your soft palate up to close off your nose, I want you to wag it down to close off your mouth. This way you can explore the *deep bending chamber,* the area where your soft palate and tongue conspire in the dark to bend the really low notes.

Getting your soft palate and tongue to do the slide may feel a little funny at first, but it's as easy as making a few silly (but perfectly normal) sounds. Simply use these steps:

1. **Say the sound "Unggggggggg," holding the "ngggg" part like you're singing a note.**

   When you make this sound, your tongue and soft palate are touching, forcing air to exit through the nasal passages. Later, this contact point will form your K-spot in the deep bending chamber.

2. **While you're saying "Ngggggggg," lower your jaw.**

   Notice how your tongue slides against the soft palate. As the tongue drops, it also moves forward slightly and the contact point travels farther back on your tongue.

3. **Try moving your tongue forward, but this time without moving your jaw.**

   The tip of your tongue will point downward and the area in front of the soft palate will hump up. The contact with the soft palate will move backward on the tongue.

Now try going for the really deep K-spot. Know how your throat opens really wide when you yawn? That's how you get the deepest K-spot for the low bends. To go deep, follow these instructions:

1. **Make contact between your soft palate and your tongue as if to say "Ngggg."**

2. **Point the tip of your tongue down and hump the middle of the tongue forward.**

3. **Now open your throat like you're yawning. Feel the K-spot move even farther back on your tongue.**

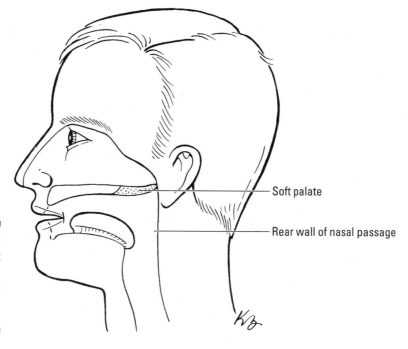

Figure 8-6:
The soft
palate
blocking
the nasal
passages.

Soft palate

Rear wall of nasal passage

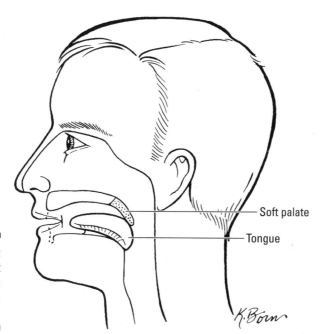

Figure 8-7:
The soft
palate
blocking
the mouth.

Soft palate

Tongue

For the deepest bends, you need to feel just how far back you can go with the contact between your tongue and soft palate. To feel the approximate limit of the deep bending chamber, try whispering, "Uh-Uh" (as in, "No way!") as softly as you can. Your throat closes momentarily at the beginning of each "Uh." You don't really close your throat for bending, but it's a useful marker. When you're going for those really deep bends with your throat open, you can slide your K-spot back nearly as far as the place where you cough.

Now it's time to reinstate the "no nose rule." Say "Nggggggg," and sustain the sound. (Are people starting to give you weird looks? Never mind — true art involves suffering.) Keep your soft palate and your tongue together, and wag your soft palate up to close off the nasal passages. Now you aren't making any sound at all because your soft palate is blocking your nose, and your tongue on your soft palate is blocking off your mouth.

May I ask you to disturb that beautiful silence by opening up a K-spot? Lower your tongue a tiny amount so that you have a narrow passage between your tongue and soft palate. As you open up that passage you may hear air. If you're exhaling you'll feel pressure, and if you're inhaling you'll feel suction. Later in this chapter, I show you ways to use the deep bending chamber when you bend notes.

Bending with your tongue on the harp

Until now, I've shown you how to bend notes with your tongue off the harp because it's the easiest way to start. But eventually you'll want to combine bending with the special techniques and effects available when you use *tongue blocking* — playing with your tongue on the harp and blocking some of the holes. (For more on tongue blocking, see Chapter 7.)

If you've already tried tongue blocking, you may have noticed that when the front of your tongue is on the harp, you can't slide your tongue forward or backward in your mouth. But as I show you earlier in this chapter, you can roll your K-spot along your tongue like a wave. The key here is that the whole tongue doesn't need to move forward or back; it can pretty much stay in the same place.

Location of the K-spot isn't everything. The K-spot activates the bend, but it also changes the total volume of your mouth cavity. For bending, the volume of your mouth cavity is more important than its length. If you can't change the volume by moving a wall, you can change it by moving the floor. In other words, if you can't change the volume by sliding the entire tongue forward or back, you can change it by moving the tongue up and down. By raising the level of your tongue in the area between the K-spot and your front teeth, you can narrow the space between your tongue and the roof of your mouth.

When you bend with a pucker (without your tongue on the harp), finding the right location for the K-spot and the right chamber size are usually the same thing. With tongue blocking, on the other hand, locating the K-spot and sizing the chamber are two independent operations. This is what makes bending with a tongue block a little trickier than bending with a pucker.

Try out your first tongue-blocked bend. If you aren't familiar with playing a single note with a tongue block, take some time to go over Chapter 7. The following instructions show you the basic action of bending with a tongue block:

1. **Place the tip of your tongue between your lips so that both lips are touching your tongue.**

   Make sure that the left edge of your tongue is touching the left corner of your lips (where upper and lower lips meet) and that you have an opening between the right edge of your tongue and the right corner of your lips.

2. **Turn the tip of your tongue slightly downward so that it touches the edge of your bottom teeth and your tongue gently bulges out between your lips.**

   This way, when you put your tongue on the harp, it doesn't poke into the holes.

3. **Now inhale gently through the opening at the right side of your tongue.**

   Feel the air traveling past your right cheek, but pay special attention to feeling it move over the surface of your tongue and the roof of your mouth.

4. **As you inhale, form a K-spot at the place where you say "K."**

   You'll feel the suction as you form the K-spot.

5. **Now pick up a harmonica and play Holes 1, 2, 3, and 4 together with an inhaled breath.**

6. **Place your tongue on the holes to block out everything but Hole 4. Now you have a single tongue-blocked note.**

   Your tongue should stay off Hole 4 itself; air should be free to pass through that hole.

   Going from four notes (see Figure 8-8a) to just Hole 4 (see Figure 8-8b) should sound like Track 42 You can visualize it by looking at Figure 8-8.

Figure 8-8: From a chord to a tongue-blocked single note in Hole 4.

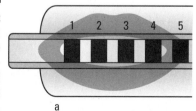
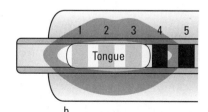

7. **After you have a clear single draw (inhaled) note in Hole 4, engage your K-spot at the place you normally say "K."**

   To get the bend, you may have to roll the K-spot forward a little. It may help to raise the surface of your tongue just in front of the K-spot.

Surveying the Bendable Notes

There are bends in every hole of the harp, and at first every one of them seems completely different from the rest. Will you spend the rest of your life mastering them all? No. It gets easier. Here are two things to keep in mind:

✔ As you develop your bending skill, the similarities between different bends come into focus and the differences start to melt away.

✔ Bending is governed by three simple principles. If you apply them carefully when you bend, you'll find bending much easier to achieve:

   • **Bending Principle No. 1:** You need a small mouth chamber to bend a high note and a large mouth chamber to bend a low note.

   • **Bending Principle No. 2:** Each hole of a diatonic harmonica has two notes, and one of them is pitched higher than the other. The higher note is the one that bends down.

   • **Bending Principle No. 3:** In each hole of the diatonic you can bend the higher note down to just above the lower note. The farther apart these notes are in the scale, the farther you can bend the higher note. The next section goes into more detail about this principle.

Finding the bending depth in each hole

If you're going to bend notes, you need to know which notes bend and which ones don't. After you choose a note to bend, you need to know how deeply it will bend so that you know what you can expect when you try to bend it. Figure 8-9 shows the layout of blow and draw notes on a diatonic harmonica in the key of C (the key used throughout this book).

Notice the following:

✔ The lowest notes are in Hole 1 and the highest notes are in Hole 10.

✔ In each hole, the *draw notes* (the notes played by inhaling) are shown on top and the *blow notes* (played by exhaling) are shown on the bottom.

✔ In Holes 1 through 6, the draw note in each hole is higher than the blow note. The draw note is the one that bends down.

✔ In Holes 7 through 10, the blow note in each hole is higher than the draw note. The blow note is the one that bends down.

Figure 8-9:
The note
layout of
a diatonic
harmonica
in C.

	1	2	3	4	5	6	7	8	9	10
Draw	D	G	B	D	F	A	B	D	F	A
Blow	C	E	G	C	E	G	C	E	G	C

Here's how to figure out how far a note will bend in any hole. Take the blow and draw notes in that hole and find them on the piano keyboard in Figure 8-10 (they should be within a few notes of each other). Now look at the notes in between them. Those are the notes you can get by bending.

You count the depth of a bend in *whole tones* and *semitones*. A semitone is the distance between any note on the keyboard and its closest neighbor, black or white. For instance, C and C♯ are next to each other — they're a semitone apart. C♯ and D are a semitone apart as well. E and F have no black key between them, and they're direct neighbors, so they're also a semitone apart. When notes are two semitones apart, like C and D, or G and A, or E and F♯, they're considered to be a *whole tone* apart.

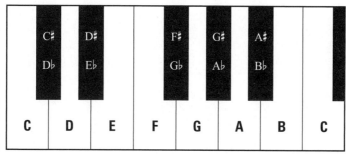

Figure 8-10:
A piano
keyboard.

Figure 8-11 shows the harmonica note layout again. But this time, I included the notes in between the blow and draw notes in each hole. These are the notes you can get by bending down.

In each hole, the note that bends down will bend by a certain number of semi-tones. For instance, Draw 4 bends down from D to C♯ — that's one semitone. Draw 3 bends down from B to A♯ to A to G♯, which is a total of three semitones.

If you bend notes on a harmonica in a different key, all the note names will be different. But the notes in each hole will still bend down by the same number of semitones. Also important to remember is that sometimes there won't be keyboard notes between the blow and draw notes, such as in Holes 5 and 7 in Figure 8-11. There are still expressive bends in those holes, but these bends cover a range of less than a semitone, so they're called *microtonal* bends.

Draw notes bend down

	1	2	3	4	5	6	7	8	9	10
Draw	D	G	B	D	F	A	B	D	F	A
Bends	Db	F#	Bb	Db	F~	Ab	C~	Eb	F#	Bb
		F	A							B
			Ab							
Blow	C	E	G	C	E	G	C	E	G	C

Blow notes bend down

Figure 8-11: The notes available by bending down.

The three bending ranges

The diatonic harmonica has three bending ranges — low, middle, and high — each with its own set of possibilities and challenges. If you hold a harp with the name and the hole numbers facing you, you can see what I mean:

- **The low range covers Holes 1, 2, and 3.** In this range, only the draw notes bend. Because the notes are low, you need a large mouth chamber to get these bends. You can bend Holes 2 and 3 farther than most other notes, but you need more practice to control them. Still, this is prime bending territory, and it's worth the effort.

- **The middle range covers Holes 4, 5, and 6.** Only the draw notes in this range bend down. And they only bend by small amounts. So the middle range is the easiest place for you to start.

- **The high range covers Holes 7, 8, 9, and 10.** In this high range, only the blow notes bend down. Because these notes are high-pitched, you need a very small mouth chamber to bend them. Miniscule differences in mouth size are critical in this range — a very slight change in size makes the difference between getting a bend and not getting it. It takes care and finesse to find exactly the right spot to make a high blow note bend down.

If you need a refresher on how to create the different-sized mouth chambers, refer to the section "Tuning your mouth to different notes," earlier in this chapter.

Exploring Bends on Your Harp

After you have the basic feel of bending, you can explore the bends in each of the three ranges of the harp, starting with the middle. In this section, I show you a series of simple *licks,* or short sequences of notes, for each hole in the range. Each lick gives you a specific challenge, such as one of the following:

✔ Starting or stopping the note while you're playing the bend

✔ Getting to or from the bent note from another breath or hole

✔ Playing a sequence of bends

As you work on these bends and licks, don't worry about rhythm or how long a note should last. Play these licks in the "timeless zone." In other words, while you play each note, give yourself time to think about where the next note is and how to get there. When you're ready, make your move. After you're more familiar with the moves involved, you can speed them up and play them with different rhythms.

Here are some things to keep in mind as you master these bends and licks:

✔ **Relax your lips, tongue, and jaw as much as you can while you play the bent note.** When you breathe through your K-spot, the airflow creates suction when you inhale and pressure when you exhale. You have to resist just enough to keep the bend stable, but you also want to avoid unnecessary muscle tension. You'll get better at finding this balance as you learn.

✔ **Play the bent note and the unbent note in one continuous breath, unless you're moving between a blow note and a draw note.** Just don't pause between notes unless you run out of breath.

✔ **Match the tone of the bent note to the tone of the unbent note as much as possible.** Stay on the bent note long enough to work on making it sound as full as the unbent note. Sometimes small movements of the K-spot or other parts of the tongue can make the note sound stronger. (You can see how to make these movements in the earlier section "Tuning your mouth to different notes.")

✔ **When you bend a note down all the way, it will be slightly out of tune.** The bottom of the bend goes slightly below normal pitch, so the note will be flat. As you learn to bend, make sure to compare your bent notes to a steady pitch reference, such as a keyboard, to ensure that you're playing your bent notes in tune.

✔ **Try adding flavor to bent notes by using your hands.** Try doing a hand "wah" on each note. To do so, start the note with your hands closed around the harp, and then open them quickly to produce a "wah" sound. Also, try closing your hands slowly as you bend a note down, and then open them again when you release the bend. (You can find out more about shaping sound with your hands in Chapter 6.)

Refer to Chapter 2 for a refresher on harmonica tablature (the arrows and numbers that tell you which hole to play and whether to blow or draw). Then you're ready to start bending!

Middle-range bends

The bends in the middle range — Holes 4, 5, and 6 — are shallow and not too difficult to control, so this is a good place to start. When you bend a note, you can isolate a single note either with a pucker (with your tongue off the harp) or with a tongue block (with your tongue on the harp).

Here's how to bend with a pucker:

1. **Form the K-spot and begin to inhale.**

2. **Slide your tongue backward in your mouth (if you aren't getting the bend, try moving it forward as well).**

3. **Drop the front of your tongue downward.**

4. **Listen for the vowel sounds as you play each bending lick.**

If you're having trouble with these steps, check out the earlier section, "Getting Your First Bends," for some help.

Here's how to bend with a tongue block:

1. **Form the K-spot and begin to inhale.**

2. **Roll the K-spot forward or backward while keeping your tongue on the harp.**

3. **Try raising your tongue toward the roof of your mouth in the area between the K-spot and your front teeth.**

4. **Listen for the vowel sounds as you play each bending lick.**

If you need a bit of extra guidance on these steps, refer to the earlier section "Bending with your tongue on the harp."

Each of the following licks has three versions — one for each of the draw bends in Holes 4, 5, and 6. Each lick helps you develop skill by placing the bend in the most important situations with the other notes. Play the notes of each lick as one fluid motion; avoid any pauses. Any time you have two or more draw notes in a row (including bends), play them on a single, uninterrupted breath.

For each lick, learn each version (Hole 4, 5, or 6) on its own. Then after you have mastered all three versions, you can play them all in a row as a continuous line.

ON THE CD

As you learn a lick from the tablature that follows, listen to the corresponding tracks on the CD, and try to play what you hear:

- **Yellow Bird lick** (Tab 8-1, Track 43): This lick starts with an unbent draw note. Bend the note down, hold it for a moment, and then release it back to an unbent note. Think "Eee-ooo-eee." *Tip:* For a crying sound, try closing your hands around the harp as you bend down, and then open your hands as you release the bend.

- **Bendus Interruptus lick** (Tab 8-2, Track 43, 0:16): This lick interrupts the bend so you can practice stopping and starting on a bent note. First, you go down to the note and stop your breath with the note still bent. Think, "Eee-ooh!" Hold your mouth in the bent position, and start your breath again so that you start the note already bent. Then let it rise back to the unbent note. Think, "Ooo-eee."

- **Close Your Eyes lick** (Tab 8-3, Track 43, 0:35): You play this lick in two different holes. Play a draw note and bend it down. Then move one hole to the left as you release the bend. You'll get a different unbent note from the one you started with. Now retrace your steps by shifting back to your starting hole as you start another bent note. Then release the bend. Think, "Eee-ooo-(shift to the left)-eee-(shift to the right)-ooo-eee."

- **Shark Fin lick** (Tab 8-4, Track 43, 0:55): This lick goes from blow to bent draw, and then back to blow. Don't let the unbent note creep in between the bent note and the blow note. Think "Hee-Ooh-Hee."

Tab 8-1:
The Yellow Bird lick in the middle range (Track 43).

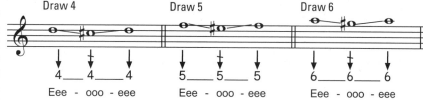

Tab 8-2:
The Bendus Interruptus lick in the middle range (Track 43, 0:16.

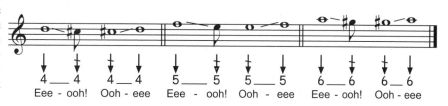

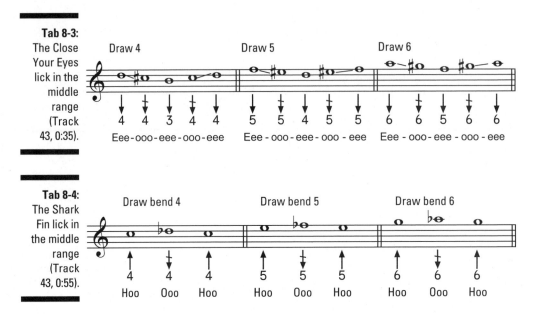

Tab 8-3: The Close Your Eyes lick in the middle range (Track 43, 0:35).

Tab 8-4: The Shark Fin lick in the middle range (Track 43, 0:55).

Low-range bends — heart of the harp

The deep draw bends in Holes 1, 2, and 3 are the power bends at the heart of modern harmonica playing. These bends are rewarding, but each has its own challenges. Hole 1 only bends one semitone, for example, but it challenges you because it's so low. Hole 3 is the highest of the three, but it bends the farthest — three semitones. Finding all three bent notes in Hole 3 takes a lot of control, so I save it for last. Hole 2 is in the middle of the range. It isn't too low, and it bends two semitones, which is a nice challenge (why do I feel like Goldilocks choosing bowls of porridge?). Hole 2 is also your home base for a lot of playing, so that's why I start with it.

Here's a summary of the techniques you can use to bend in this range:

✔ **You can bend with a pucker (tongue is off the harp):** To use this technique, form a K-spot, slide your tongue backward in your mouth, and then drop the front of your tongue downward. It may help to drop your jaw as well.

✔ **You can bend with a tongue block (tongue is on the harp):** Form a K-spot, and then roll it back in your mouth along your tongue. Make sure you can feel suction at the K-spot. You may need to move the K-spot back so that your tongue contacts the soft palate. For the lowest bends, you may need to open your throat area like you're yawning. (You can read about moving your K-spot in the earlier section "Tuning your mouth to different notes.")

Deep bends of two and three semitones may seem daunting, but bends are funny — they want to go down all the way to the bottom! The bottom of the bend is the part that actually vibrates most vigorously, so go for it! If the intermediate bends come more easily, start there.

Hole 2

The draw note in Hole 2 bends down either one semitone for a shallow bend or two semitones for a deep bend. On your first attempt, you could get either of these bends. Try the Yellow Bird lick, as shown in Tab 8-5. Then listen to Track 44 to find out whether you're getting the shallow bend or the deep bend. Focus on strengthening the one you get first, and then work on getting the other.

Tab 8-5:
Draw 2
bends with
the Yellow
Bird lick
(Track 44).

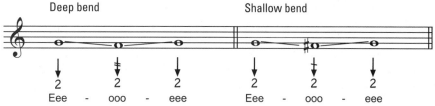

To find the bend, move your K-spot slowly backward. It helps to concentrate on breathing gently from your abdomen. If you aren't able to find the deep bend, try making an especially strong "ee-YOO" and drop your jaw. If you're tongue blocking, try rolling your K-spot back to ride on the soft palate. Like your first bend, finding this one could take awhile, so be patient. Work on finding the bend while you're doing something undemanding, like watching television. The distraction can help, strangely enough.

After you can reliably get either a shallow or a deep bend, extend your control by playing the shallow and deep versions of the following licks:

✔ **Bendus Interruptus lick** (Tab 8-6, Track 44, 0:15): Slide down to the bent note, and then stop your breath with the note still bent. Hold your mouth in the bent position, and start your breath again so that you start the note already bent. Finally, let it rise back to the unbent note. Think "Eee-ooh! Ooo-eee." *Remember:* Don't let the note creep back up when you stop your breath. Stop and start again with the note bent down.

✔ **Modified Shark Fin lick** (Tab 8-7, Track 44, 0:28): Start with the unbent note, bend it down, and then go to the blow note. Then head back to the bend, and end with the blow note. Don't let the unbent note creep in between the bent note and the blow note. Think, "Eee-ooo Hoo Ooo Hoo."

✔ **Close Your Eyes lick** (Tab 8-8, Track 44, 0:44): Play a draw note and bend it down. Then release the bend as you go one hole to the left. You'll get a different unbent note from the one you started with. Think, "Eee-ooo (shift) eee (shift) ooo-eee."

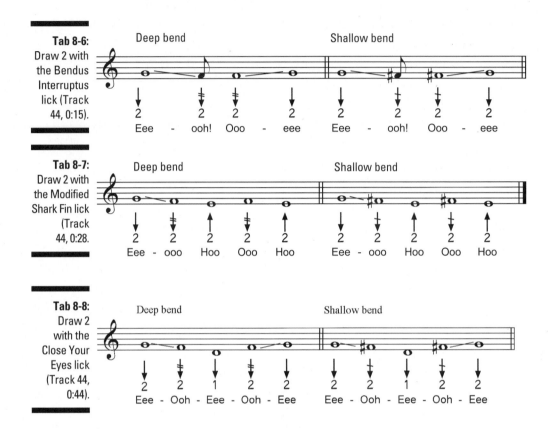

Tab 8-6: Draw 2 with the Bendus Interruptus lick (Track 44, 0:15).

Deep bend   Shallow bend

2 2 2 2   2 2 2 2
Eee - ooh! Ooo - eee   Eee - ooh! Ooo - eee

Tab 8-7: Draw 2 with the Modified Shark Fin lick (Track 44, 0:28.

Deep bend   Shallow bend

2 2 2 2 2   2 2 2 2 2
Eee - ooo Hoo Ooo Hoo   Eee - ooo Hoo Ooo Hoo

Tab 8-8: Draw 2 with the Close Your Eyes lick (Track 44, 0:44).

Deep bend   Shallow bend

2 2 1 2 2   2 2 1 2 2
Eee - Ooh - Eee - Ooh - Eee   Eee - Ooh - Eee - Ooh - Eee

Hole 1

Hole 1 is just like Hole 4, but deeper — it's an octave lower. Draw 1 has only one bent note. Focus on opening up the back of your throat and sliding your K-spot back to your soft palate. Try playing some licks in Hole 1 similar to what you've already done in this section. For the licks, see Tab 8-9 and listen to Track 45.

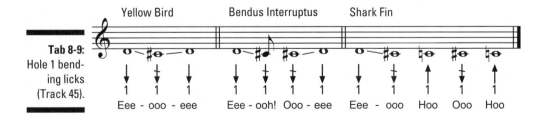

Tab 8-9: Hole 1 bending licks (Track 45).

Yellow Bird   Bendus Interruptus   Shark Fin

1 1 1   1 1 1 1   1 1 1 1 1
Eee - ooo - eee   Eee - ooh! Ooo - eee   Eee - ooo Hoo Ooo Hoo

Hole 3

Hole 3 has the biggest bending range, and it's the biggest challenge. To begin, try the Yellow Bird lick as shown in Tab 8-10 to see which bend you get first — shallow, intermediate, or deep. Try playing Draw 3, bending it down, and then releasing it. Try it a few times, and then listen to Track 46 to identify which bend you're getting (or getting close to).

Tab 8-10: Shallow, intermediate, and deep bends in Hole 3 (Track 66).

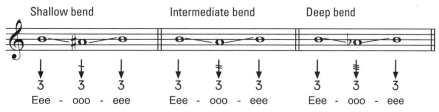

There's a good chance that the bend you get won't be predictable at first. One time it'll be deep, another time shallow, and another time intermediate. Mastering Hole 3 bends can take a long time, but finding them is well worth the effort.

Try these bending licks, which you can listen to on the CD:

- **Bendus Interruptus lick** (Tab 8-11, Track 46, 0:18): Slide down to the bent note, hold it for a moment, and then stop your breath with the note still bent. Hold your mouth in the bent position, and start your breath again so that you start the note that's already bent. Finally, let the bent note rise back to the unbent note.

- **Close Your Eyes lick** (Tab 8-12, Track 46, 0:35): This lick starts the note unbent, then bends it down, then moves one hole to the left for an unbent draw note. Finally, it retraces its steps. Try it with all three bends. *Tip:* The intermediate bend version of the Close Your Eyes lick is by far the most useful. Work on playing it with the intermediate bend in good tune.

- **Shark Fin lick** (Tab 8-13, Track 46, 0:56): This lick will develop your control of alternating Hole 3 bends with Hole 3 blow. Don't let the unbent note creep in between the bent note and the blow note. Think, "Hoo Ooo Hoo."

- **Cool Juke lick** (Tab 8-14, Track 46, 1:16): The Cool Juke lick is a useful one. It never uses the unbent Draw 3. It starts on the shallow bend, goes to the intermediate bend, and then heads to Draw 2. *Tip:* Don't use Blow 3 for this lick (even though it's the same note as Draw 2). Draw 2 sounds better and will connect better with other bending licks and lines in the low range.

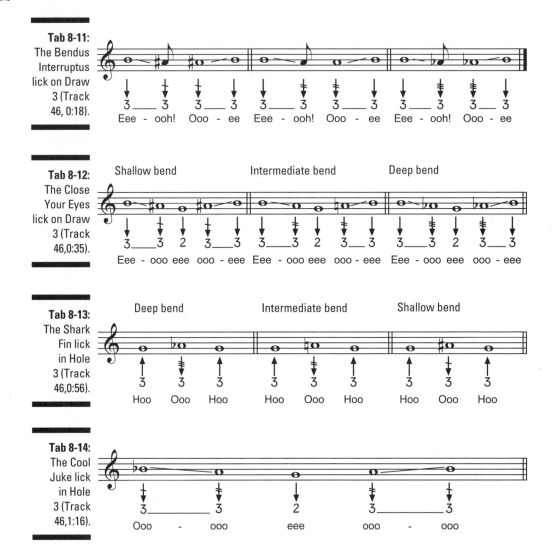

Tab 8-11: The Bendus Interruptus lick on Draw 3 (Track 46, 0:18).

Tab 8-12: The Close Your Eyes lick on Draw 3 (Track 46, 0:35).

Tab 8-13: The Shark Fin lick in Hole 3 (Track 46, 0:56).

Tab 8-14: The Cool Juke lick in Hole 3 (Track 46, 1:16).

High-range bends

Holes 7, 8, 9, and 10 make up the high range of the harmonica. In each of these holes, the highest note is the blow note, so the blow notes are the ones that bend. The blow note in Hole 7 gives a microtonal bend, while Blow 8 and Blow 9 each bend one semitone. (If you forget what these terms mean, refer to the earlier section "Finding the bending depth in each hole.") Blow 10 bends two full semitones, but it's at the high extreme. At first you may be able to find the full two-semitone bend but not the one-semitone bend. Don't worry, though. Most of the licks in this section are written for the full bend.

When bending the highest notes, the basic technique is the same as for the lower notes. However, be aware of one important difference: You need to tune your mouth to a much smaller size when working with the highest notes.

If you hear a momentary "thrum" in the note when you try to bend it, you're hearing your tongue rushing past the sweet spot. In other words, you went by too fast and missed the spot where you activate the bend. The difference between being on the sweet spot and missing it is really tiny, so take it slow.

Here are a few tips to keep in mind:

✔ Hole 8 is probably the easiest for your first high blow bend. Why? It's the lowest-pitched hole that bends a full semitone.

✔ High bends are easier to learn on a harp in a low key, such as G, Low F, Low E, or Low D. This tip is especially true if you're working on tongue-blocked high bends — in this situation, the lower the key of the harp, the better. (For more on different keys and ranges of harmonicas, see Chapter 2.)

✔ When puckering, try placing the K-spot just behind the tip of your tongue. Then move your tongue forward in your mouth in a bunching motion.

After you find the bend on a blow note, you may notice pressure pushing against the front of your tongue. Work that pressure — push forward against it or retreat from it. It can help guide you as you control the bend.

✔ For tongue blocking, form a K-spot approximately where you say "K." Then pay special attention to the area near the front of your tongue. This area consists of a series of important points that are one behind the other:

 • The tip of your tongue is pointed down.

 • Just behind the tip of the tongue is the area that touches the harp.

 • Behind the area that touches the harp is an area that you can press forward against the roof of your mouth and the backs of your upper teeth. Play around with pressing in this area.

 • Just behind that area, you should feel some air pressure as you breathe. It may feel like a little air pocket caught between your K-spot and the area pressed against the roof of your mouth. Squeeze the air pocket from the front and the back to find the bend.

Make sure your tongue doesn't block the edge of the hole you're playing, so that you don't interfere with the airflow from your mouth to the harp.

By the way, if you're reading the music notation above the tab, all the examples for the high-range bends are written an octave lower than they sound.

The following bending licks, which you can hear on the CD, can help you master bending in the high range:

- **Yellow Bird lick** (Tab 8-15, Track 47): This lick starts with an unbent blow note. Bend the note down, hold it for a moment, and then release it back to an unbent note. Think, "Eee-ooo-eee."

- **Bendus Interruptus lick** (Tab 8-16, Track 47, 0:21): This lick goes down to the bent note and stops there. Hold the bend, and then stop your breath while holding your mouth in the bend position. Finally, start breathing again so that you begin with a bent note. Think, "Eee-ooh! Ooo-eee."

- **Close Your Eyes lick** (Tab 8-17, Track 47, 0:40): This lick goes from unbent to bent, and then it shifts one hole to the left for an unbent blow note. It ends by retracing its steps. Think, "Eee-ooo (shift) eee (shift) ooo-eee."

- **Shark Fin lick** (Tab 8-18, Track 47, 1:05): This lick goes from blow to bent draw, and then back to blow. Don't let the unbent note creep in between the bent blow note and the draw note. Think, "Ooo Hee Ooo."

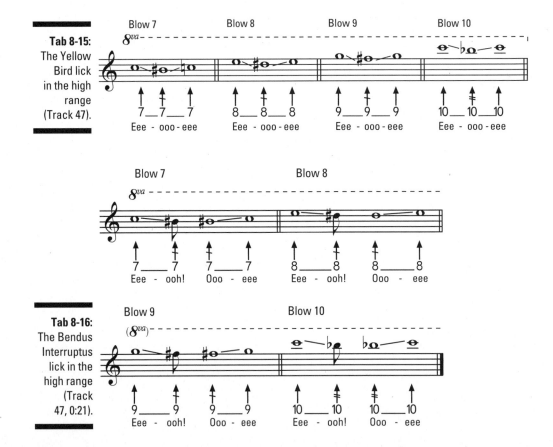

Tab 8-15: The Yellow Bird lick in the high range (Track 47).

Tab 8-16: The Bendus Interruptus lick in the high range (Track 47, 0:21).

Tab 8-17: The Close Your Eyes lick in the high range (Track 47, 0:40).

Tab 8-18: The Shark Fin lick in the high range (Track 47, 1:05).

Bending on Different Types of Harmonicas

Most harmonicas have some kind of bending ability. The ones you're most likely to encounter include chromatic harmonicas and double reed harmonicas. I explain bending techniques for each in the following sections. (Characteristics of both these harps are described in detail in Chapter 2.)

Chromatic harps

Chromatic players bend mostly for expression, because they don't actually need to bend for missing notes — the chromatic harmonica has all the notes for every key. Listen to players like Stevie Wonder and Larry Adler — they bend notes on the chromatic and it sounds great! But bending on this harp is different from bending on the diatonic in several ways.

Here are the main differences in bending on chromatics:

- Both the blow notes and the draw notes bend down, except in the top few holes. In those holes, only the draw notes bend.

- There's no fixed bending range for most of the notes on the chromatic (the top three holes bend like Holes 5, 6, and 7 on a diatonic). Many of them will bend much farther than the same notes on a diatonic.

- The tone of bent notes on chromatics tends to be less rich and dynamic.

- Bending on the chromatic can't be attacked the same way that it can be on the diatonic. It takes a gentler initiation.

- Sustaining a bent note on the chromatic isn't as easy as on a diatonic. However, that's all right, because on the chromatic you don't need to bend for specific notes; it's mostly for expression.

Double reed harps

Double reed harmonicas, such as tremolo and octave harmonicas, have two reeds for each note and two rows of holes. These double reeds reinforce and color the sound. When you play a double reed harp, you normally play both the bottom and the top row together, so you're always playing two blow reeds or two draw reeds — one on the bottom row and one on the top.

Two draw reeds played together or two blow reeds played together will not bend predictably, even if they're the same note. To bend a note with this type of harp, you have to isolate either the top row or the bottom row so you have only one reed per note. With some experimentation, you may find that you can bend both blow and draw notes down.

Double reed harps actually offer more variety of bending potential than diatonic or chromatic harmonicas. However, going into the details would take a separate chapter. So all I'll say at this point is this: If you have a double reed harp lying around, try isolating the top row of holes and see if you can get some bends out of it.

Part III
Growing Beyond the Basics

The 5th Wave   By Rich Tennant

...and on harmonica
is Vic Strangelove
who learned his instrument
sitting in his dad's recliner.

In this part . . .

After you have some basics under your belt, you're ready to stretch your skills a little. In this part, you find out how to get the authentic harmonica sound by playing it in a few different keys. Then you discover how songs work and how to further develop your melodic abilities. You can also check out how to bend notes up instead of down.

Chapter 9

Positions: Playing One Harp in Many Keys

In This Chapter

▶ Discovering why to use positions

▶ Figuring out what harp to use for a position

▶ Gaining experience playing in six popular positions

*I*f you watch a harmonica player in action, she probably won't stand on her head while she plays or reach her arm around the back of her neck to bring the harmonica up to her mouth. But afterward she may make a remark like, "I played that tune in third position, but during the solo I switched to second position." Is she doing some sort of invisible yoga?

Actually, harmonica positions are nothing mysterious or exotic. A *position* is just the relationship between the key of the harp and the key of the tune you play on it.

In this chapter, I explain how positions work, and then I help you get familiar with and explore the six most popular positions.

Understanding How Positions Help Your Playing

If you always used a C-harmonica to play in all 12 keys, you wouldn't need to talk about positions. You'd just play that C-harp in C, G, B♭, or whatever. Likewise, if you always used a key of harmonica that matched the key of the music, such as a G-harmonica to play in G or a B♭-harmonica to play in B♭, again there would be no point in talking about positions. The idea of positions is useful when you play more than one key of harp, and you play each harp in more than one key.

I hear you asking, "If there are 12 keys of harmonica, why play in positions at all? Just get 12 harmonicas and play each one in the key it's designed for." This approach sounds reasonable, but consider the following facts:

- ✔ Harmonicas are tuned to major scales, and positions allow you to play music that uses other scales, including the minor scales. (I discuss scales in this chapter and in Chapter 10.)

- ✔ Every position has its own cool set of possibilities. (I take you through some of them in this chapter.) In each position, the harmonies, chords, and bendable notes on the harmonica sound different because they have a different reference point.

- ✔ For a lot of music, second position sounds way cooler than first position, so it's used far more often than first.

- ✔ Many harmonica players tend to be cheap, so they want to get as much as they can out of a single instrument. (I'd like to say I'm kidding, but I'm not.)

So, as you can see, playing a diatonic harmonica in different keys is a good idea. But you may still be wondering why harp players bother to talk about positions. After all, why not just say, "I'm playing in G on a C-harp," or, "I'm playing in A on a D-harp?" You could do that, but then you'd have 144 different combinations (12 keys of harp times 12 keys of music), each with a different set of note names. The idea of positions reduces those combinations to only 12 by focusing on the similarities instead of the differences.

The key to the position concept is this: On different keys of harmonicas, the same actions produce the same results. The system of positions gives you a simple, consistent method to transfer what you know on one key of harp to a harp in any other key.

For example, you could pick up a C-harmonica and play "Mary Had a Little Lamb," starting on Blow 4. The tune would come out in the key of C. If you were to pick up an F♯-harp and play the same sequence of blow and draw notes in the same holes, you'd still get "Mary Had a Little Lamb," but in the key of F♯. All the note names would be different, but you would recognize the tune because the pattern of notes would remain the same. On both harps, the same actions produced the same results. In this instance, because the key of the tune matches the key of the harp, you'd be playing in first position.

Anything you can do on one key of harp has an exact correspondence on all keys of harmonicas. You don't need to know what the note names are; you just need to be familiar with the sequence of moves that produces a pattern of notes. Thinking about positions frees you to concentrate on what different keys have in common — instead of details — and then you can get down to making music.

I'll illustrate my point by way of a story. Say that you're a harmonica player who has gained some experience playing different positions. You know how to make the moves, and because you've played those moves, you know what they sound like (think of it: this is you in a few months, with a little practice). So, you're in the audience listening to another harmonica player onstage who is playing an incredible solo. Now, you don't know what key the song is in, and you don't know what key of harp the soloist is playing (gee, 144 different possibilities!). But that doesn't matter. Because you know your positions, you can tell just by listening exactly how the harp player onstage is playing all those cool licks. You can walk away and play a lot of those licks yourself (provided you can remember them all and have acquired the skills).

Figuring Out a Position

Positions on a harmonica are numbered 1 through 12. Each time you count up five scale steps from the key of the harp, you've reached the next position. The *blow chord* (C on a C-harmonica) is designed to be the home chord of the harmonica. When players use the blow chord as home base, they call it *straight harp,* or first position.

The *draw chord* in Holes 1, 2, 3, and 4 (G on a C-harmonica) also makes a great home base for playing. Players discovered this position early on and called it *cross harp,* or second position. The G draw chord happens to be five scale steps up from the C blow chord. And five steps up from the G chord is a D minor chord (the draw chord in Holes 4, 5, and 6), and that's a great launchpad for playing. This is third position (it never had a nickname that really stuck).

Eventually, players agreed that simply adding a number to a position each time you go up five steps is a consistent way to name positions. However, some early books use different systems.

With 12 keys of music, 12 keys of harmonica, and 12 possible positions, you may wonder how you can keep all the relationships from getting tangled up. Harmonica players use a simple diagram borrowed from music theory, called the *circle of fifths.* This circle, which is shown in Figure 9-1, lets you figure out the relationship between key of harp, key of tune, and position.

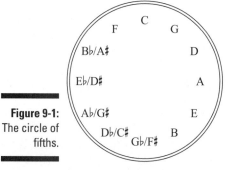

Figure 9-1:
The circle of fifths.

With the circle of fifths, as long as you know two elements, you can figure out the third. Here's how:

- **If you know the key of the tune and the position, and you want to find the key of harmonica to use, follow these steps:**

    1. Start with the key of the tune and call that "1."

    2. Move counterclockwise until you reach the position number, and then use the corresponding key of harp.

    For example, say you're going to play a tune that works in third position, and you know that the tune is in A. What harp should you use? Start with A (the key of the tune), which you can call "1." Then count to 3 counterclockwise (A-D-G). So to play in the key of A in third position, you need to use a G-harmonica.

- **If you know the key of the harp and the key of the tune, and you want to know what position that is, follow these steps:**

    1. Start at either the key of the harp or the key you're playing in (it doesn't matter which one).

    2. Count the shortest distance from one to the other. (It doesn't matter if it's clockwise or counterclockwise, as long as it's the shortest way.)

    Say, for example, you're playing a C-harmonica and you figure out that you're playing in E. What position is that? You can start at C (the key of the harp) and count to E (the key of the tune). Or you can start at E and count to C. As long as you go the shortest distance (either E-A-D-G-C or C-G-D-A-E), you'll discover that you're playing in fifth position.

- **If you know the key of the harp and the position, and you want to know the key of the tune, follow these steps:**

    1. Start with the key of the harp and call that "1."

    2. Count clockwise until you come to the position number; when you hit the position number, you've found the key.

    For example, imagine that you're grooving in second position on an A♭-harmonica. You want to know what key you're grooving in. You start at A♭ (the key of the harp) and call that "1." The next stop clockwise is second position. So, as you can see, you're stylin' in E♭ — crazy, baby!

Relating Positions, Modes, and Avoid Notes

When you use a C major scale to play a tune in D, the result doesn't sound like C major (after all, you're in D). But it doesn't sound like D major or D minor either. In this situation, you're using something called a *mode,* or a *modal scale.* You get a mode when you center a scale on one of the notes of the scale. Even using the C major scale to play in C is one of the modes of that scale.

By playing a harmonica in a position that's centered on one of the notes in the scale, you automatically get a modal scale (though you can alter it by bending notes up or down). In each modal scale, some of the notes may be lower or higher than they are in the major scale, giving the new scale a unique character. Many folk tunes, jazz tunes, and even some popular and rock tunes use the special characteristics of modal scales.

Harmonica players often play in a position that doesn't fully match the scale of the tune. They do this because something about that position sounds really cool and is fun to play — whether it's the chords, the bends, or the licks and riffs.

A note in the position you're playing may not match the scale of the tune, and it will sound sour unless you treat it with care. This type of note is referred to as an *avoid note.* You avoid playing that note and play something else instead. You may be able to bend up or down to a note that would better match the tune, or you can substitute another note in the modal scale.

Of the twelve positions, seven are based on notes built into the harp and have modal scales. However, five of the positions are *bent positions* — they're based on bent notes that aren't built into the harp and don't correspond to a mode of the major scale. I don't have enough space to cover bent positions in this book, but they're worth checking out after you get the hang of the more popular positions.

Rocking with Six Popular Positions

In this section, I take you on a tour of the six most widely used positions: first, second, third, fourth, fifth, and twelfth. I note important things about each of them. In each position you get to try out licks that help you become familiar with that position and with its unique musical qualities.

For each position, I tab a dozen licks that cover all three registers of the harp — high, low, and middle. The first few licks are in the register where players spend the most time in that position. After that, the licks move on so you can explore the other registers.

Repeat each lick as many times as you like, and play along with the corresponding CD track. Doing this will keep you grounded on the home note of the position. If you find that a lick is too difficult for you or uses bending skills that you haven't quite mastered yet, skip that lick for now and play the ones that come to you more easily. You can also use the CD track for each position simply to explore and experiment with playing in that position. The backing track provides the home chord, which helps keep you anchored in the position.

Above some of the music you'll see "8va" followed by a dotted line. This has no effect on the tab you play. It's just a way of telling anyone reading the notation that the music under the dotted line (but not the tab) is played one octave higher than written. (If the notes were written where they really sound, they might climb five or six added lines above the staff, making them hard to read.)

You don't have to play these licks correctly! They aren't laws chiseled on a stone tablet; they're just paths for exploring. If you accidentally play different notes and come up with something cool, that's great. If you want to jazz up the rhythm or bend a note for effect, go for it!

For each position in the following sections, I include a note layout chart showing how each unbent note on the harp corresponds to the scale in that position. Here's how to decipher the charts:

- ✔ The notes of the scale are numbered, starting with the home note, which is 1. When notes of the scale are numbered, they're called *scale degrees*.
- ✔ The home note that players often use as the home base for playing is in a black box.
- ✔ The notes of the home chord are 1, 3, and 5. They're in gray boxes.
- ✔ Wherever a note in the scale is lower than it would be in a major scale, it has a flat symbol (♭) in front of the number.
- ✔ Wherever a note in the scale is higher than it would be in a major scale, it has a sharp symbol (♯) in front of the number.

First position (C on a C-harp)

The harmonica was designed to play melodies in first position. The scale in first position is the major scale, which is also called the *Ionian mode.* You can hear first position used in all sorts of music, including fiddle tunes, campfire songs, and songs by popular singer-songwriters, such as Bob Dylan, Neil Young, Alanis Morissette, and Billy Joel, often played in a rack around the player's neck. While most blues is played in second position, blues harmonica players often use first position as well (check out Jimmy Reed's wonderful high-register work).

To explore first position, try the licks shown in Tab 9-1. You can hear the licks on Track 48 of the CD.

Avoid notes are rare when you play a major scale tune in first position, because the scales match. However, you sometimes encounter avoid notes when you play blues in first position (more on that in Chapter 13).

Home note and home chord

The blow note in Hole 4 of a harmonica is the home note that's most often used as a home base. The home chord consists of all the blow notes, as shown in Figure 9-2.

Tab 9-1: First-position licks (Track 48).

In the low register (Holes 1 through 4), the 4th and 5th notes of the scale are missing. You can create the 4th degree by bending Draw 2 down, and you can create the 6th degree by bending Draw 3 down.

Figure 9-2:
The home note and home chord in first position.

Hole	1	2	3	4	5	6	7	8	9	10
Draw	2	5	7	2	4	6	7	2	4	6
Blow	1	3	5	1	3	5	1	3	5	1

Draw bends

Blow bends

Bendable notes

The most important bendable notes in any position are the notes of the home chord. In first position, the home chord consists of the blow notes, and Blow 7, 8, 9, and 10 are the only ones that bend down.

However, one blow note, Blow 3, is duplicated as a draw note, Draw 2, which also bends down (see Tab 9-1, Lick 11). Bending Draw 3 down gives some nice bluesy sounds, as shown in Licks 9, 10, and 12 in Tab 9-1. First position blues often jumps from the blow bends in the top register (Holes 7 through 10) down to the draw bends in the low register while skipping the middle register (Holes 4 through 7).

Related positions

The IV and V chords — the chords built on the 4th and 5th degrees of the scale — are the most important among the chords that are played in the background to accompany a tune (see Chapters 3 and 11 for more on chords and how they work in tunes). Twelfth position corresponds to the IV chord and second position corresponds to the V chord. Being able to play those positions well can help your first-position playing.

Second position (G on a C-harp)

Second position originated with blues, but it has spread out to many other styles of music. Even for major-key songs, second position is more popular than first position — probably because the notes of the home chord bend in the low and middle registers (Holes 1 through 6).

Try some of the second-position licks in Tab 9-2 to become familiar with playing in second position. You can hear the licks on Track 49.

Home note and home chord

For most playing, the main home note is Draw 2. However, the home note is also found in Blow 3, Blow 6, and Blow 9.

Tab 9-2:
Second-
position
licks
(Track 49).

The notes of the home chord (marked 1, 3, and 5) surround Draw 2, as shown in Figure 9-3. This makes for a nice big home chord in the draw notes of the low register (which is where most second-position playing takes place).

Notes of the home chord are also scattered through the middle and upper registers. You can extend the home chord and make it sound bluesier by adding the scale degrees marked 2 and 7.

Figure 9-3:
The home note and home chord in second position.

Draw bends

Hole	1	2	3	4	5	6	7	8	9	10
Draw	5	1	3	5	♭7	2	3	5	♭7	2
Blow	4	6	1	4	6	1	4	6	1	4

Blow bends

Modal scale and avoid notes

Second position uses a scale called the *Mixolydian mode*. It differs from a major scale by one note: The 7th degree is considered minor because it's a semitone lower than the major scale 7th degree. This note is characteristic of blues and often works in blues-based rock.

When you use second position to play major melodies that contain the major 7th degree, the minor 7th degree will clash — it becomes an avoid note. This situation comes up in country music, where players prefer second position but have to play a lot of tunes that have major scales.

You can avoid a clash easily in Holes 2 and 9 by bending the home note down one semitone to get the major 7th. But in the middle register, the only bending option is to overblow, and not all players have good overblow control, so they find other ways of avoiding a clashing note:

- ✔ You might play another note that harmonizes with the major 7th, such as Draw 4 or Draw 6.

- ✔ You might play Blow 6, which is the neighboring note in the scale.

- ✔ You might play a country-tuned harp (see Chapter 14 for more on country tuning).

When playing blues and rock, second position usually works well. However, many country and pop tunes have melodies that use the standard major scale.

Bendable notes

In any position, the most important notes are the notes of the home chord, and if they also are bendable notes, that's a big plus. In second position, the draw notes in Holes 1, 2, 3, and 4 are part of the home chord, and they all bend down. Blow 9 is the only other bendable note of the home chord, but it's sort of by itself in the top register without any other bendable home chord notes beside it.

Related positions

In second position, the important IV and V chords (built on the 4th and 5th degrees of the scale) correspond to first and third positions. Playing in those positions will give you more versatility in second position. (See Chapter 3 for more on chords built on scale degrees.)

Third position (D on a C-harp)

Third position is heard in blues and rock songs and sometimes in fiddle tunes. It also has a minor sound that goes well with tunes like "Scarborough Fair" and "Greensleeves." Third position plays fluidly in the middle and upper registers, and blues harpers often use the challenging deep bends in the low register as well.

Try out some of the third-position licks in Tab 9-3. Listen to the licks on Track 50.

Home note and home chord

Draw 4 is the home base for third position, and the home chord can be found in Draw 4, 5, and 6, and again in Draw 8, 9, and 10 (as shown in Figure 9-4). The draw notes in Holes 3 and 7 can be added to the chord to give it a haunting quality. For most playing, the main home note is Draw 2, though the home note is also found in Blow 3, Blow 6, and Blow 9.

You have to be careful about the draw chord in Holes 1 through 4. Even though Draw 1 and Draw 4 both play the home note in third position, when you play Draw 1 through 4 together as a chord, you get the home chord of second position. If you concentrate too much on that chord, or on Draw 2 as a single note, you can lose the feeling of playing in third position.

Modal scale and avoid notes

The scale in third position is known as the *Dorian mode.* It's a minor type of scale, but one note in the scale can sometimes clash with minor keys. This note is the 6th of the scale, which is found in Draw 3 and Draw 7.

If you find this note clashing, you can bend Draw 3 down but not Draw 7 (you can play a 6 overblow instead). Or you can just be careful and avoid the note if it clashes.

Bendable notes

The notes of the home chord in Draw 4, 5, and 6 all bend down and can really wail. The draw notes in Holes 2 and 3 aren't home chord notes, but you can bend them down from Draw 2 to the ♭3 scale degree and from Draw 3 to the 5 scale degree, both of which are home chord notes.

Figure 9-4:
The home note and home chord in third position.

Draw bends

Hole	1	2	3	4	5	6	7	8	9	10
Draw	1	4	6	1	♭3	5	6	1	♭3	5
Blow	♭7	2	4	♭7	2	4	♭7	2	4	♭7

Blow bends

If you have good control of these bends, they have a special tone quality that's worth cultivating. The high blow notes aren't part of the home chord, but when you bend them in third position, they can have an eerie, out-on-the-edge quality that can bring suspense to a solo.

Related positions

In third position, the IV chord (built on the 4th degree of the scale) corresponds to second position and the V chord (built on the 5th degree of the scale) corresponds to fourth position (see Chapter 3 for more on these chords). In the Dorian scale, the ♭VII chord (built on the 7th degree of the scale) is important in some Celtic and fiddle tunes. This chord corresponds to first position. Exploring these positions can give you additional ways to explore third position.

Fourth position (A on a C-harp)

Even though it's rarely used for blues, rock, or country, fourth position offers great flexibility in the high register for folk, klezmer, jazz, and even some classical melodies. However, some of these melodies require that you alter the fourth position scale with specific types of bent notes.

The licks in Tab 9-4 can help you explore fourth position with nothing but the scale that the harp gives you (except for a few expressive bends). You can hear the licks on Track 51.

Home note and home chord

For most fourth-position playing, the main home note is Draw 6. However, the home note is also found in Draw 10, as shown in Figure 9-5.

The home note doesn't have chord notes in the neighboring draw notes (the other notes of the home chord are blow notes). In fact, the draw notes that border the home note can create clashes with the home chord. But those draw notes can be combined beautifully in melodies.

Tab 9-4:
Fourth-
position
licks
(Track 51).

Figure 9-5:
The home
note and
home chord
in fourth
position.

Draw bends

Hole	1	2	3	4	5	6	7	8	9	10
Draw	4	♭7	2	4	♭6	1	2	4	♭6	1
Blow	♭3	5	♭7	♭3	5	♭7	♭3	5	♭7	♭3

Blow bends

The home note is missing in the low register. You can create it by bending Draw 3 down, as shown in Licks 9, 10, 11, and 12. (This can be a challenging bend, but the result is worth the reward.) Fourth position tends to work most fluidly in the high register.

Modal scale and avoid notes

Fourth position gives you a scale called the *Aeolian mode.* This scale is also known as the *natural minor;* it's considered the pure form of the minor scale. In some minor melodies, the 6th and 7th degrees of the scale are raised, so you may have to bend notes up or down to match them.

Bendable notes

Home note Draw 6 bends, as do the chord notes in Blow 7, 8, and 10. Blow 9 is the 7th degree of the scale, which sometimes works as an extension to the home chord, and it bends nicely too (see Tab 9-4, Lick 6).

In the low register, Draw 3 bends down to the home note (and to a note one semitone below the home note). In Hole 2, the draw note bends down from the 7th degree of the scale to the 6th degree, helping to fill out the scale.

Related positions

In fourth position, the IV chord (the chord built on the 4th degree of the scale) corresponds to third position, and the V chord corresponds to fifth position. (Refer to Chapter 3 for more on these chords.) Folk tunes in the Aeolian mode sometimes use the ♭VI and ♭VII chords. Twelfth position corresponds to the ♭VI, and second position corresponds to the ♭VII.

Fifth position (E on a C-harp)

Fifth position was recorded in blues as early as 1928 by William McCoy in the tune "Central Tracks Blues." Fifth position also has been used by country harmonica player Charlie McCoy (no relation to William McCoy). It's a minor-sounding position that makes great use of the bendable notes in the low register.

To explore some of the sounds, try the licks in Tab 9-5. They can be heard on Track 52 of the CD.

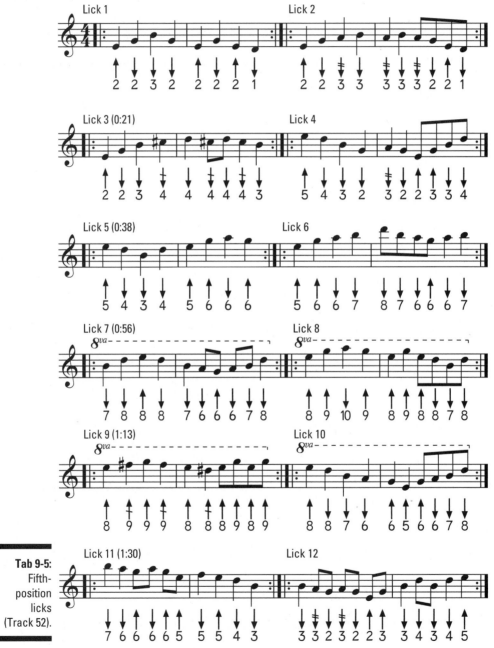

Tab 9-5:
Fifth-position licks (Track 52).

Home note and home chord

The home note for fifth position is found in Blow 2, 5, and 8 (refer to Figure 9-6). Blow 2 tends to be favored as the home note because of all the home chord notes in the vicinity. Blow 2 and 3 are home chord notes, and so are Draw 2 and 3. This combination lets you play blow-draw patterns entirely on the home chord, which is something that's unique to fifth position. In the middle and high registers, two of the home chord notes are blow notes and one is a draw note.

Figure 9-6:
The home note and home chord in fifth position.

Draw bends

Hole	1	2	3	4	5	6	7	8	9	10
Draw	♭7	♭3	5	♭7	♭2	4	5	♭7	♭2	4
Blow	♭6	1	♭3	♭6	1	♭3	♭6	1	♭3	♭6

Blow bends

Modal scale and avoid notes

The scale in fifth position is a minor type of scale called the *Phrygian mode*. The 2nd degree of the scale is a semitone lower than in most scales. It can give a Spanish or flamenco sound to music, but in most circumstances it will sound sour. I've included it in Tab 9-5, Lick 11 as a sort of blue note.

The ♭6 degree is always one hole to the left of the home note in fifth position. Avoid playing this note in a chord with the home note unless you know that it belongs in the chord. Otherwise, it may clash with the background chord.

Bendable notes

As in several other positions, the most important bendable notes in fifth position are the notes of the home chord. In fifth position, the draw notes in Holes 2 and 3 are part of the home chord, and you can have a lot of fun playing expressive bends on these notes.

Draw 2 and 4 is the 7th degree of the scale, but it works as a sort of extension to the home chord. And it bends nicely, as shown in Lick 3 (refer to Tab 9-5). Draw 6 is the 4th degree of the scale, and it gives a wailing sound when you bend it. Blow 8 and 9 are also home chord notes that bend nicely (see Lick 9 in Tab 9-5).

Related positions

In fifth position, the IV chord (the chord built on the 4th degree of the scale) corresponds to fourth position. The V chord corresponds to sixth position, but I don't cover that here. If you want to explore the flamenco possibilities of fifth position, the characteristic ♭II chord corresponds to twelfth position. (Be sure to rinse the sangria out of your mouth before playing, and note that grabbing a rose in your teeth may interfere with your harp playing.)

Twelfth position (F on a C-harp)

Twelfth position has gained popularity only in recent years, although it was used effectively by Daddy Stovepipe on his 1931 record "Greenville Strut." It isn't a very bluesy position, but it can be great for major-scale melodies. However, there is one avoid note (see the later section, "Modal scale and avoid notes").

To explore twelfth position, check out the licks in Tab 9-6. Listen to the licks on Track 53.

Home note and home chord

For most playing, the main home note for twelfth position is Draw 5 in the middle register, though the home note is also found in Draw 9 in the high register (as shown in Figure 9-7). In the low register, you can create the home note by bending Draw 2 down.

The 1st and 3rd notes of the home chord are both draw notes and can be played together, but the 5th is a blow note. You can often include the 6th degree in the chord — your ear has to be the judge. The 6th note is always one hole to the left of the home note.

Modal scale and avoid notes

The scale in twelfth position is a type of major scale called the *Lydian mode*. The only avoid note is the raised 4th degree of the scale, which sometimes sounds okay if you follow it with the 5th degree of the scale. You can bend down the raised 4th to the regular 4th in Draw 3, and you can create the regular 4th degree by bending Blow 10 down.

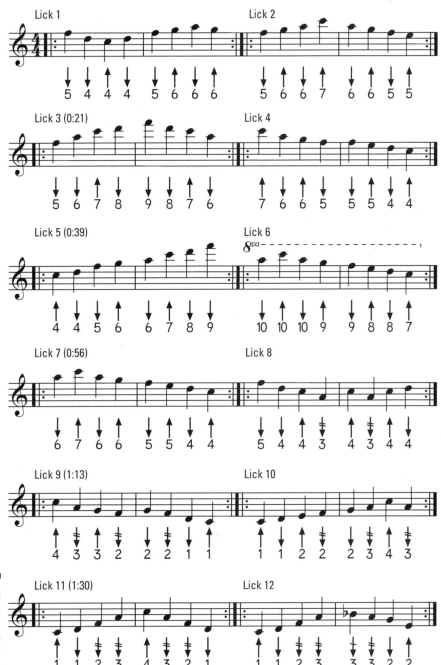

Tab 9-6:
Twelfth-
position
licks
(Track 53).

Draw bends

Hole	1	2	3	4	5	6	7	8	9	10
Draw	6	2	♯4	6	1	3	♯4	6	1	3
Blow	5	7	2	5	7	2	5	7	2	5

Blow bends

Bendable notes

Bendable home chord notes are spotty in twelfth position. In the middle register, Draw 5 and 6 are home chord notes, and they bend. In the high register, Blow 10 is a chord note, and it, too, bends. In the low register, Draw 2 and 3 bend down to reach the home chord note and the 3rd degree.

Related positions

In twelfth position, the V chord (built on the 5th degree of the scale) corresponds with first position. The IV chord corresponds with eleventh position, which isn't covered here. (Check out Chapter 3 for more on these chords.)

Chapter 10

Fancy Playing: Developing Flair and Speed

In This Chapter

▶ Relating scales to chords

▶ Decorating the melody with ornaments

▶ Getting faster in your harp playing

*W*hen you can play with speed and flair, you've likely internalized where all the notes are (or at least the notes you need in order to play what you want to play), what those notes sound like, and how to play them. When you're still in the early stages of playing the harmonica, your mind plays a big part. It helps you understand the names of the notes and how they fit together as well as how the musical structures work. Your mind also helps you go through the step-by-step process of learning all the moves — moves that you'll eventually master.

However, after a while, your mind can bow out and leave the details to your ear and muscle memory. The more you play the harmonica, the more your ear and your muscle memory allow you to just think of a series of notes and play it. When you can play what you want without thinking about the mechanics, you're free to be playful — to have flair.

To get the most out of this chapter, you need to be able to play single notes (see Chapter 5). Being able to bend notes down is helpful but not essential. Reading about some of the theory concepts in Chapter 3 may deepen your understanding of the materials in this chapter. However, if you simply play the tabbed patterns in this chapter, you'll improve your familiarity with the harmonica and your ability to move around on it.

Some of the melodic patterns in this chapter may take you months to work through. Don't feel like you need to master them immediately, or that you need to master all of them. Listen to them on the CD and decide whether they take you where you want to go. Check out the other chapters as you determine what inspires you to play.

Your choice of harmonicas plays a part in your strategy for becoming fluent in a way that suits you. You may decide to employ any of the following strategies, each of which is pursued by at least one professional player:

- Play standard-tuned harmonicas only, in two or three positions, and use as many keys of harmonica as you need. (This is what most players do.)

- Play harmonicas in one position only, use alternate tunings for different scales (minor, major, blues), and use as many keys of harmonica as you need.

- Play some mixture of positions and tunings.

- Play standard harmonicas in all 12 keys in all types of scales, using all 12 keys of harmonica. (Only a few players master this approach.)

- Play one C-harmonica (or one alternate-tuned harmonica) in all 12 keys. (Even fewer players take this approach.)

Mastering Melody from the Ground Up

Most music you play either goes from one note in the scale to its immediate neighbor (*stepwise* movement) or leaps to a note farther away. However, most of the leaps go from one chord note to another. In other words, if the chord being played in the background by guitar or piano is C, and the notes of a C chord are C, E, and G, the melody will often leap from C to E, E to G, or G to C. When you play the notes of a chord one by one, you're playing an *arpeggio*.

If you practice scales, arpeggios, and scale-based patterns, you'll get familiar with patterns that you'll later find in lots of songs and instrumental tunes. As Don Les of The Harmonicats once told me, "If you've been everywhere, you always know where you are."

Seeing the scale

The harmonica was designed to play the major scale. Everything else is based on that scale. When you develop your mastery of the major scale, you're erecting one of the main pillars of your harmonica fluency.

The scale is played differently in each register. In the top register, the draw notes shift one hole to the right, and you have to bend for one note in Hole 10. In the bottom register, you have to bend for two of the notes, which are missing, and one note is duplicated (Draw 3 and Blow 3 play the same note).

If your bending isn't yet developed to the point of including bent notes, play these exercises anyway and just leave out the bent notes. Substitute the note before or after for the missing bent note.

Tab 10-1 shows the major scale played up and then down, in all three registers. You can hear the scale being played on Track 54 of the CD.

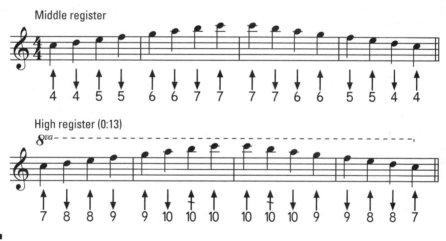

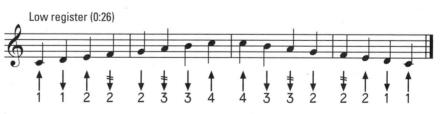

Tab 10-1: The major scale in three registers (Track 54).

Recognizing scale patterns

When you play a scale, you can play one note in the scale, followed by the next, and so on. However, instead of going up or down a plain old scale, you can decorate it by applying a short melodic pattern to each note in the scale. Many elaborate-sounding melodies use this simple principle, and they often use one of only a few standard patterns. After you pick up these patterns, you can play (and recognize) many complex melodies.

The patterns that you play on scale notes are usually described by counting from one note to the next. You start with the scale note that starts the pattern and call that "1." Then you count up or down to the next note in the pattern, give that a number, and on to the next. You do this on each note of the scale to which the pattern is applied. The sequence of numbers you get when you count out the pattern becomes the name of the pattern.

For example, in Tab 10-2, you start with the first note of the scale. Then you count up 1-2-3 and play the note you find on 3. So you play a 1-3 pattern. In this pattern, you don't play the 2, just the 1 and the 3. On the next note of the scale, you do the same thing. To make it easier to play, when you come back down the scale, the pattern is reversed to a 3-1 pattern and goes down instead of up. You can hear this scale on Track 55.

Even though a pattern in the scale may be consistent, the sequence of physical actions on the harmonica isn't. If you can't decipher musical notation, you still can see how the notes form consistent patterns and shapes — but when you try playing the harmonica tab, you find that the patterns of action aren't consistent. For example, in Tab 10-2, some of the 1-3 patterns are both blow, some are both draw, and a couple of them mix blow and draw notes. Memorizing the shifts in the action patterns on the harmonica is a big part of integrating your muscle memory with musical logic and with what your ear is asking to hear.

Check out the following patterns on the CD:

- ✔ Tab 10-3 (Track 56) shows the scale with a 1-2-3 pattern on each scale note. Coming down the scale, the pattern reverses to 3-2-1.

- ✔ Tab 10-4 (Track 57) shows the scale with a 1-2-3-5 pattern. The pattern reverses to 5-3-2-1 coming down the scale.

- ✔ Tab 10-5 (Track 58) shows the scale with a 1-2-3-4 pattern. The pattern reverses to 4-3-2-1 coming down the scale.

Tab 10-2:
A scale with
a 1-3 pattern
(Track 55).

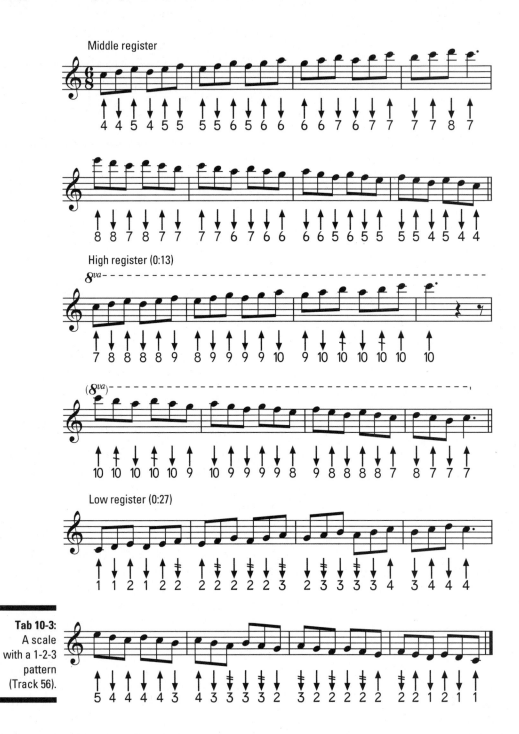

Tab 10-3: A scale with a 1-2-3 pattern (Track 56).

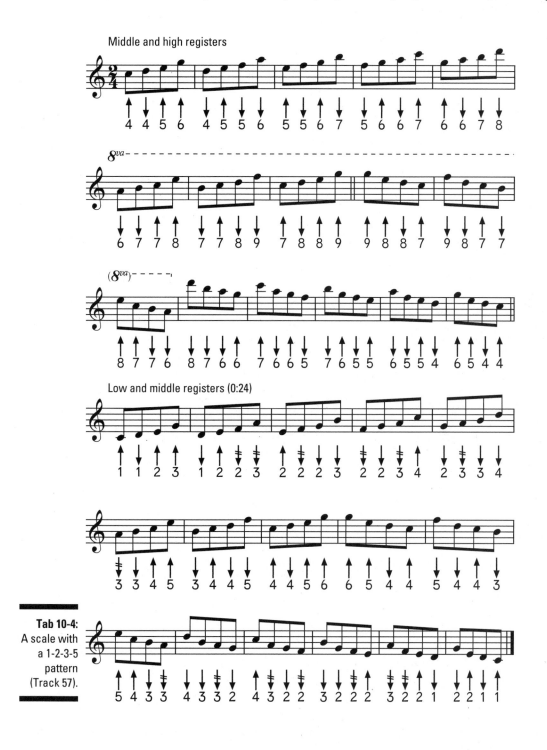

Middle and high registers

Low and middle registers (0:24)

Tab 10-4: A scale with a 1-2-3-5 pattern (Track 57).

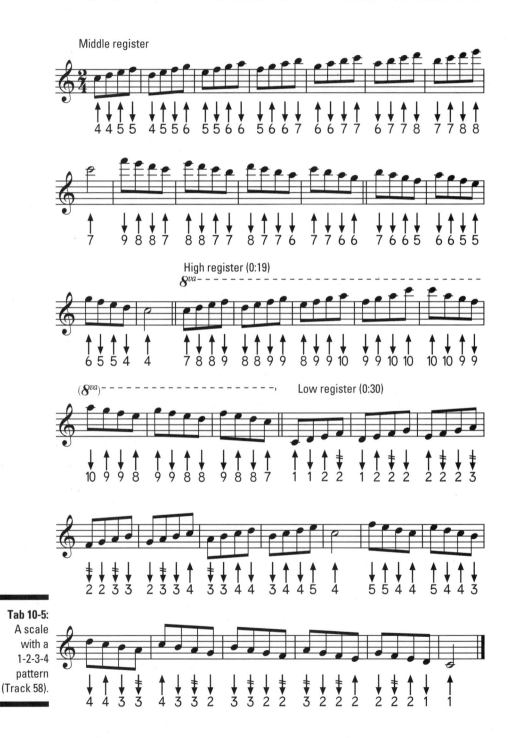

Tab 10-5:
A scale
with a
1-2-3-4
pattern
(Track 58).

All these patterns play a part in both song melodies and improvisation. But instead of playing patterns going from one note in the scale to its immediate neighbor, you can also play patterns that jump to different notes in the scale.

In Tab 10-6 (Track 59), the notes don't go C, D, E, F, G, A, B, C, and back down. Instead, they go C, F, B, E, A, D, G, C. Each new note either jumps up four notes in the scale or moves down five. If you built a chord on each of these notes, you'd get a sequence of chords, called a *chord progression*. You've likely heard chord progressions in songs before. If you number these chords in the key of C, they're I, IV, VII, III, VI, II, V, I, as shown in Tab 10-6. Instead of repeating the same melodic pattern through this progression, two different patterns are alternated. Popular songs often repeat or alternate melodic patterns through a chord progression.

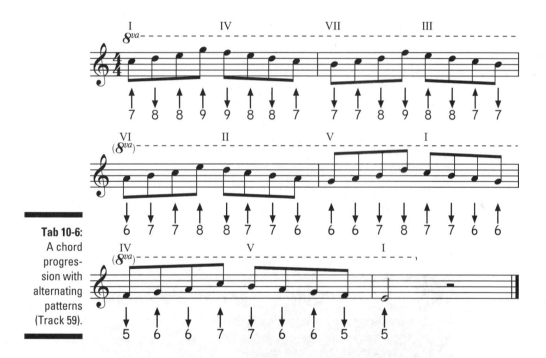

Tab 10-6: A chord progression with alternating patterns (Track 59).

Anchoring melodies on chord notes

Most melodies either move directly from one chord note to another or pass through one or two *non-chord tones* (notes that aren't part of the scale) along the way.

If most of the chord notes are played on the beat, you hear the chord, even though the notes don't all sound at once. Chord notes work together to reinforce the root note of the chord — a powerful phenomenon. When you hear the notes of the chord, you hear equilibrium and rest — or, in musical terms, *resolution*.

If a few of the notes played on the beat aren't chord tones, you hear a disturbance of the chord, or *musical tension*. Soon after, you hear chord notes on the beat. Moving from resolution to tension and back to resolution creates interest.

Figure 10-1 shows the note layout of a harmonica in first position (see Chapter 9 for more about positions). Hole 4 Blow is the home note, which is numbered 1. All the other notes in the scale going up from 1 are numbered as well. If you build a chord on 1, the notes of the chord are 1, 3, and 5. All the blow notes are part of the chord, so they're all 1, 3, and 5.

Figure 10-1:
A harmonica with the notes of the scale numbered in first position.

Hole	1	2	3	4	5	6	7	8	9	10
Draw	2	5	7	2	4	6	7	2	4	6
Blow	1	3	5	1	3	5	1	3	5	1

The chord may be a resting place, but not all notes in the chord are equally restful:

- ✔ The 1, or root of the chord, is the place of absolute rest.

- ✔ The 5 is the next strongest resting place in the chord.

- ✔ The 3 is the weakest resting place of the three. This note sort of sounds like it's asking a question that wants to be answered.

All the other notes — 2, 4, 6, and 7 — are non-chord tones.

Tab 10-7 shows the scale starting on the 1st degree of the scale, in Hole 4 Blow. The notes are grouped into pairs of eighth notes (♪). The first note in the pair is played on the beat, and the second note comes between the beats. Listen to Tab 10-7 being played on Track 60 on the CD.

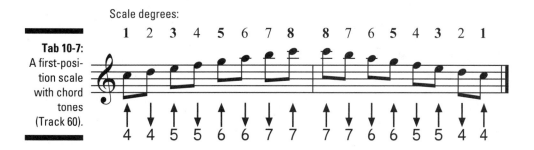

Tab 10-7: A first-position scale with chord tones (Track 60).

Scale degrees:

When you play the scale in Tab 10-7 ascending, the chord notes are on the beat except at the end of the scale — you get a little turbulence before you land. When you come down the scale, most of the chord notes are between the beats, so the notes that land on the beat create tension, until finally you land on the 1 again, on the beat, and reach resolution.

Tab 10-8 shows a melody that alternates between resolution and tension. You can hear the melody on Track 60 (0:15).

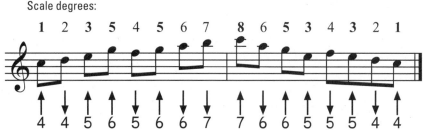

Tab 10-8: A melody alternating between resolution and tension (Track 60, 0:15).

Scale degrees:

Simplifying the scale to five notes

The major scale has seven notes. But a lot of music is played with a simplified scale that has only five notes, called the *pentatonic scale.* The pentatonic scale includes the three chord tones — 1, 3, and 5 — and two other notes. Consider the following:

- ✔ **The major pentatonic scale includes 1, 2, 3, 5, and 6.** You can use this scale for the major home chords in first, second, and twelfth positions.

- ✔ **The minor pentatonic scale includes 1, 3, 4, 5, and 7.** You can use this scale for the minor home chords in second, fourth, and fifth positions.

Take some time to listen to and play through the pentatonic scales in the following tab. They show up in a huge amount of the music you hear, and they're fun to play around with.

 ✔ Tab 10-9 (Track 61) shows the major pentatonic scale in first position in all three registers. Try playing it going up as shown. Then experiment with playing the scale going down, and playing just a few neighboring notes of the scale.

 ✔ Tab 10-10 (Track 61, 0:18) shows the minor pentatonic scale in fourth position. If you compare the notes of the scale, you'll find that they're the same notes as the major pentatonic scale in first position. However, the different home note makes this scale sound very different.

 ✔ Tab 10-11 (Track 62) shows the major pentatonic scale in second position, while Tab 10-12 (Track 62, 0:18) shows the minor pentatonic scale in fifth position. These two scales use the same notes, but they sound very different.

 ✔ Tab 10-13 (Track 63) shows the major pentatonic scale in twelfth position, and Tab 10-14 (Track 63, 0:18) shows the minor pentatonic scale in third position. These two scales use the same notes to produce different results.

Tab 10-9:
The major pentatonic scale in first position (Track 61).

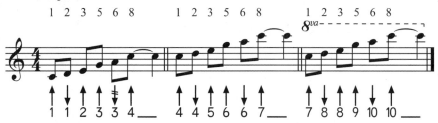

Tab 10-10:
The minor pentatonic scale in fourth position (Track 61, 0:18).

Tab 10-11: The major pentatonic scale in second position (Track 62).

Tab 10-12: The minor pentatonic scale in fifth position (Track 62, 0:18).

Tab 10-13: The major pentatonic scale in twelfth position (Track 63).

Tab 10-14: The minor pentatonic scale in third position (Track 63, 0:18).

Adding Ornaments to the Melody

Ornaments are decorations you add to a melody. Sometimes you use ornaments to emphasize certain notes and outline the melody more clearly. Sometimes you use ornaments to make a simple line more elaborate and create interesting patterns. And sometimes you use ornaments simply for special effects.

On most instruments, you create ornaments by briefly playing additional notes before or after a melody note. However, some of the tongue-blocking effects described in Chapter 7 (such as slaps, hammers, rakes, and shimmers) serve the same functions as ornaments, so you can consider using them as such.

Shakes

When you do a *shake,* you rapidly alternate notes in two neighboring holes. The two notes in a shake will both be either blow notes or draw notes. Instead of a plain harmony, you get a texture created by the rate of alternation. Shakes are used a lot in blues and have spread from blues to rock and country music.

Some players do shakes by holding the harp still and moving their head from side to side. Other players do it by using their hands to move the harp. Moving the harp gives you more control and is less likely to give you neck pains or make you dizzy.

When you do a shake, you usually treat the hole on the left as the main note and the hole on the right as the added note. Use your right wrist to rock your hands and the harp one hole to the left; then let your hands spring back to their original position. You can play a shake so that the two notes are distinct, or you can blend them together for a sort of textured chord sound.

Tab 10-15 shows a simple melody line that you can play with shakes on each note in the line. In the tab, the little stack of diagonal lines next to the hole number indicates a shake. You can hear what the melody sounds like with shakes on Track 64 of the CD.

Tab 10-15: A melodic line with shakes (Track 64).

Rips, boings, and fall-offs

You can approach a note by sliding into it from several holes to the left or right. When you do that, you hear a cascade of notes that makes a sort of ripping sound leading up to your landing note; this move is called a *rip*.

You can also play a note, and then rip away from it in a way that doesn't lead to another note; it just trails off. When you rip away from a note by moving to the right, the pitch goes up, which gives an impression a bit like a ball bouncing; this move is called a *boing*. When you rip away from a note by moving to the left, the pitch of the trailing notes falls. So, naturally, this move is called a *fall-off*.

Rips, boings, and fall-offs, shown in Tab 10-16, are used in jazz and sometimes in blues, rock, and popular music. You can hear these ornaments on Track 65.

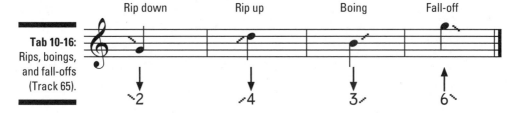

Tab 10-16: Rips, boings, and fall-offs (Track 65).

Grace notes

You can emphasize a note in the melody by starting with a different note — the *grace note* — in a neighboring hole just before it's time to play the note you're going for. You play the grace note for just a split second, and then you hit the main note. The quick motion from grace note to main note creates a percussive texture that emphasizes the main note. Tab 10-17 shows a descending scale with two grace notes. You can hear the grace notes on Track 66.

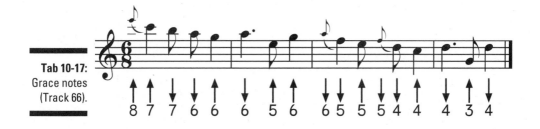

Tab 10-17: Grace notes (Track 66).

In Celtic music, several types of grace notes are played on instruments like fiddle and flute. Most of these grace notes are played using the neighboring note in the scale because that's the easiest note to use. On harmonica, playing the note in the neighboring hole is the fastest, smoothest way to produce a grace note, even though the notes involved aren't usually neighboring notes in the scale.

Developing Your Speed

Learning to play the harmonica fast is a little like learning to talk. First you learn to mouth sounds. Then you learn to shape the sounds into words, connect the words into simple sentences, and have conversations. At that point, you become fluent — your language can flow.

When you learn to play the harp fluently, you start with individual notes. You learn to connect the notes to form short phrases (like words). Then the short phrases turn into longer ones until you can play in a way that flows. In other words, you become fluent.

Becoming fluent on the harmonica is also like cutting a pathway through thick brush. Cutting brush, shifting logs, and moving rocks is hard work. But after you've done the heavy labor, you have a quick, easy way to pass through the forest.

On harmonica, you're cutting new neural pathways in your brain. The well-traveled ones get stronger, while the seldom-traveled ones get overgrown with brush. Repetition is the key to developing fluency because it keeps those neural pathways open and clear.

Here are my tips for getting faster on the harp:

✔ **Start slow and know each individual move.** When you move from one note to another, you need to know three things:

- Where you're at on the harmonica. In other words, you need to know what hole you're playing.

- What actions you take to get to the next note. For example, you may have to change holes to the left or right, change breath direction, or bend up or down.

- What the new note will sound like when you get there. After all, how will you know you're in the right place if you don't know what the right place is?

To make your move, you need time to think about what you're going to do, and then you need time to do it. Playing slowly gives you that time. The newer a move is, the more time you need to play it.

Most musical actions involve several notes played in a sequence. Some moves are more complex or may be less familiar to you than some other moves. The new, complex moves take the most time to plan and execute, so you need to play the *whole* sequence slowly. Don't rush through the easy parts and then slam on the brakes for the hard parts. Always set a *tempo* (the speed of the beat) with a metronome that's slow enough to perform the trickiest move, and then play the whole sequence at that tempo.

✔ **Learn in small chunks.** When you're learning moves that are unfamiliar, break up long sequences into shorter segments of two, three, or four notes. Practice each short chunk. If the moves are really unfamiliar, you may have to practice that short chunk over and over at a very slow tempo until it becomes familiar. Then you can move on to the next chunk.

If you come across a longer sequence that's mostly easy, play through it, identify any problem areas, and then isolate and practice just those bits through slow repetition. Before you put them back in the context of a longer sequence, try adding only the notes that come just before and just after the segment. As you reintegrate the problem area, play the entire passage at a tempo that allows you to play through the problem area with confidence.

✔ **Speed it up — slowly.** When you can play a new or difficult passage at a slow, steady tempo, try to speed it up by a very small amount. If you increase the tempo too much too soon, you may find yourself gliding and faking your way through the difficult bits, pretending to play them instead of playing them cleanly, accurately, and with confidence. Slowly increasing the tempo and being sure you can play through each new increase builds your confidence and your ability.

✔ **Think and play in larger units.** Notes are like individual sounds, and short sequences of notes are like words. As you get familiar with scales, arpeggios, and characteristic licks and riffs in your chosen style of music, you can play them without having to think about individual notes or sequences of notes. You'll be able to string together longer and longer sequences made up of shorter ones.

Chapter 11

Mastering New Songs

How do you learn new music? You can either pick it up by ear or read it. Nowadays, there are some great software tools for ear learning. Harmonica tab can help when it's available as well. And then there's reading — either chord charts or actual notation. These are all great ways to learn new music. But you can strengthen your learning abilities if you also know how songs are put together. In this chapter, I fill you in.

Understanding How Songs Work

Both songs and jam tunes made up on the spot have certain organizing principles. If you understand a little about those principles, you understand the playing field and the rules of the game that you're playing. I explain the most important principles in the following sections.

The container: Structuring time

Songs are made up of structures that repeat and alternate, and each structure is made up of the following smaller components:

✔ **Beats and measures:** Time in music is measured in *beats,* and beats are grouped into twos or threes or fours (mostly fours) called *bars* or *measures* (these two terms are used interchangeably). When I talk about the length of one part of a tune, I mean the number of measures. You count out measures as they go by saying, "One-two-three-four, Two-two-three-four, Three-two-three-four," and so on.

Always identify how many beats are in a bar when you first hear a piece of music. That way you know how to count the measures.

✔ **Phrases:** Most music is made up of phrases that combine to make a complete statement, almost like phrases in a sentence that follow logically, or like a question followed by an answer. If you count the measures, you'll find that most phrases are 4 measures long.

✔ **Parts:** A part is made up of two or more 4-bar phrases that add up to a total length of 8, 12, or 16 measures. A song may have just one part, such as a verse that simply repeats, like most blues songs. Or a verse may be followed by a different part, such as a chorus, and then another verse and another chorus, and so on. Some songs also have a *bridge,* which is a part that may shift the song temporarily to a different key.

Usually, all the parts are equal in length, but something makes each part different — such as the words, the melody, and the *chord progression* (the sequence of chords that accompanies the melody; see the following section for more details).

✔ **Form:** The *form* of a song is just the sequence of parts. You may hear a verse and then a chorus. If you hear that same sequence repeating, that's the form. Some sophisticated tunes may go off on a departure from the form, but most songs set up a form and stick to it.

Listen for the overall form the first time you hear a song. Then, when you start to play it, you'll always have an idea where you are in the song and what comes next.

Figure 11-1 shows a chord chart for an imaginary song. This chart doesn't include the melody. Instead, the chart shows the form of the song and the chord progression, using diagonal slashes to represent the beats in each measure. Chord charts are used by bass players, guitarists, and pianists, who just need to know the chords and the form of a tune so they can make up an accompaniment for the song.

The song has two repeated parts — you repeat whatever is within the repeat signs (⫿: repeat this :⫿). Each part is 8 measures long but plays twice, for 16 measures. The whole form of the tune is 32 measures long.

The shifting backdrop: Chord changes

Songs are usually accompanied by a *chord progression,* a series of chords that change at certain points in the tune. Chords to a tune may be written over a melody, over lyrics, or on a chord chart (refer to Figure 11-1). In the later section, "Choosing the Right Harp," I show you how to relate the chords in a tune to your choice of harmonica.

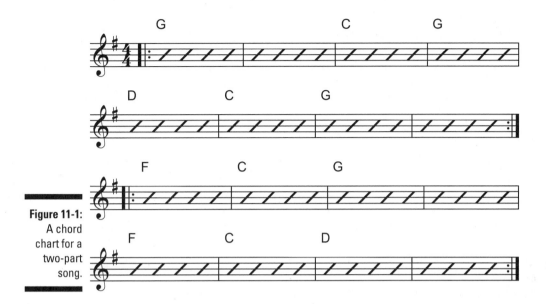

Figure 11-1: A chord chart for a two-part song.

The chords may move away from the key note of the tune and then come back at certain key points, such as the ends of phrases. Knowing the chord progression can help you know where you are in the tune, even if no one is playing the melody. It also can help you express the melody or give you the basis for making up a solo or accompanying part, because what you do needs to fit with the chords and the form of the song.

The chords in Figure 11-1 have a story to tell. The tune is in G (you can tell by the key signature; see the section "What are the notes in the scale?" later in this chapter). The first part of the tune begins and ends on G. The second part of the tune is a bit more adventurous. It brings new energy by starting with F, a new chord that hasn't appeared before. Instead of ending back home on a G chord, it leaves you in suspense by ending on D, just waiting for G to come back when you return to the first part of the tune.

The foreground: Melody

The melody is the heart of a tune. This may be all you care about, but knowing the form, the phrase structure, and even the chord changes of a tune can help you be clear about the melody — when it repeats, when it changes, and when it goes into a variation. The more you understand about the structure of a melody, the easier it is to learn and the easier it is to keep from getting lost while you're playing. The more secure you are in knowing a melody and its context, the more you can focus on interpreting it artistically.

Choosing the Right Harp

When you learn a new tune, what key of harp do you use? The key of the tune is just the beginning, because the scale may not be the major scale. The first thing to figure out is the key of the tune. This may be written down some-where: "This tune is in the key of Z demented." You may have to look at a piece of sheet music or a chord chart. Or you may have to just listen and try to identify the key note intuitively and try to match that note to Blow 1 on a harmonica to identify the name of the key note.

What are the notes in the scale?

If you have written music for a song, look at the very beginning of the tune to see the *key signature,* a group of sharps or flats clustered together at the beginning of each line. The key signature tells you which notes need to be played always sharp or always flat so that the scale will have the right notes for the key of the song. Even if you don't read music, you can deduce the key of the song from the key signature by comparing the number of sharps or flats with Table 11-1.

Table 11-1	**Key Signatures**	
Number of Sharps or Flats	*Major Key*	*Minor Key*
None	C major	A minor
1 sharp	G major	E minor
2 sharps	D major	B minor
3 sharps	A major	F♯ minor
4 sharps	E major	C♯ minor
5 sharps	B major	G♯ minor
6 sharps	F♯ major	D♯ minor
1 flat	F major	D minor
2 flats	B♭ major	G minor
3 flats	E♭ major	C minor
4 flats	A♭ major	F minor
5 flats	D♭ major	B♭ minor
6 flats	G♭ major	E♭ minor

Each key signature can indicate either a major key or a minor key. Because these keys use the same key signature, they're considered family. For instance, C major is the *relative major* of A minor, and A minor is the *relative minor* of C major.

 How can you tell whether the key signature indicates a minor or major key? Look at the beginning and ending chord names written above the piece. These are probably the *tonic chord,* the chord of the key note of the piece. If the opening and closing chords are minor, the tune is probably in the relative minor key. If the chords are major, the tune is probably in the relative major key.

If the tune is in a major key, choose a key of harmonica that will give you first or second position. If the tune is in a minor key, choose a key of harmonica that will be in third or fourth position relative to the key of the tune. (For more on positions, see Chapter 9.)

What are the notes in the chords?

Say you're having trouble choosing a harp for the chord chart in Figure 11-1. The tune is in the key of G (you can tell from the one sharp in the key signature), but when you try a G-harp, some of the notes on the harp don't seem to fit with some of the chords. Here's one way to arrive at a good harp choice:

1. **Find out the chord progression of the tune.**

   The chords may be written above the notated music or printed lyrics or on a chord chart.

2. **Figure out what notes are in each chord.**

   You need to learn a little theory or look it up in a theory book or a book of guitar chords.

3. **Take all the notes of all the chords and put them in alphabetical order, like a scale.**

4. **Find a harp that has that scale or one that's very close to it.**

   See Appendix A for note layouts. If the harp has some of those chords built in, that's even better.

For example, the tune in Figure 11-1 has the chords G, C, D, and F. Here's a breakdown of the notes in those chords:

- **Notes in a G major chord:** G B D
- **Notes in a C major chord:** C E G
- **Notes in a D major chord:** D F♯ A
- **Notes in an F major chord:** F A C

When you put the chords in alphabetical order, they look like this:

A B C D E F F♯ G

This scale *almost* matches the scales of a G-harmonica and a C-harmonica. The G-harp has F♯ but not F, and the C-harp has F but not F♯. At least now you know that the F chord and F note are causing the problems with the G-harp. Where a note on the harp doesn't fit, maybe you can bend a note to fit or just avoid that note.

When you look at the available chords on the two harps, the G-harp has G and D chords and can outline the notes of C, but not F. The C-harp has a G chord and a C chord, and it can outline the notes of an F chord. It also has a D-minor chord (while the tune uses a G-major chord). If you look at the chord chart, though, the first chord is G, followed by C. Those chords are available on the C-harp, so maybe the C-harp is a better choice.

When you can't completely match a key of harmonica to a scale or the notes of a chord progression, you have a few ways to evaluate possible keys of harp to use. Ask these questions:

✔ **Do the bent notes available on the harp help you match important notes in the scale or melody?** If the notes that you need aren't built into the harp, you may be able to create those notes by bending existing notes either down or up in pitch. (See Chapter 8 for more on bending notes down, and Chapter 12 for bending notes up.)

✔ **Can you match most of the notes in the chords on one harp?** If so, maybe you can leave out some of the notes.

✔ **Are some chords more important than others?** Some are just *passing chords* — chords that pass by quickly while helping one chord transition to another. You may be able to ignore these chords.

✔ **Can you switch harps, playing one harp for one part of the tune and a different harp to match the chords in another part of the tune?** Switching harps can be a great stage gimmick in addition to helping you out musically.

Making It Up versus Playing It Straight

When you learn a song, do you just want to know what the melody is, and how to play it? Or do you want to *jam* — noodle around and find a part by ear and maybe find a little rhythm groove or *lick* (short melodic fragment) that fits? Most people use a little of each approach, depending on the situation. The two approaches, which I explain in the following sections, reinforce each other — you don't have to choose one or the other.

Learning melodies . . .

You can learn melodies by several different methods, as I discuss in this section. You may prefer one method to the others, but each method has unique strengths, and I suggest you try them all.

. . . From written music

Learning melodies from written music gives you a huge amount of music to choose from. You can learn from written music quickly because you don't have to spend a lot of time deciphering what you hear and trying to find it on the harmonica. People make a big deal out of learning to read music, but it's just another skill. If you get a good book (such as *Music Theory For Dummies,* by Michael Pilhofer and Holly Day [Wiley]) or take a course, it's really not that difficult. And the more you do it, the easier it gets.

. . . From tab

Relatively little music is tabbed out for harmonica, and even less is done professionally, so you don't know how accurate it is. However, you can generate your own tab.

The easy way to get tab is to use a tab-generating computer program that will take a *MIDI file* (an electronic file that computers and synthesizers can turn into music) and give you harmonica tab for the key of harmonica and even any special harmonica tuning you want to use. One such program is Harping MIDI Player (www.harpingmidi.com).

You can also generate your own tab by hand. You take sheet music, figure out what key it's in and what harp to use (using the tools in this chapter), and then tab out each note for that harp, writing the tab under the notes. Hand-tabbing music takes time, but you can learn a lot about where the notes are on the harp, and you may learn to read music while you're doing it!

. . . By ear

No matter what else you learn, you should always cultivate your ability to learn music by ear. Start by figuring out what key the music is in and whether it sounds like it's major or minor. Then choose a harp. You may have to noodle around with the music, trying different harps.

When you have the key and a harmonica, start by figuring out just the first two or three notes and finding them on the harmonica. Listen to the tune and determine where one phrase ends and the next one begins.

Music tends to divide into phrases that often follow one another in a sort of question-and-answer format. Pairs of phrases may add up to a complete statement, sort of like a sentence. The musical sentences add up to paragraphs. Paragraphs correspond to sections of a tune, like a verse and a chorus.

Learn the first phrase, and then the second one. Note where a phrase repeats or comes back after intervening material. If you've already learned it, you're ahead of the game. Work your way through the first section of the tune, and review it. Then move on to the next part of the tune. If you're learning from a recording, note the time in the tune where each phrase and section begins, so you can easily find that point again.

Popular programs for learning melodies and licks by ear include the Amazing Slow Downer (www.ronimusic.com) and SlowGold (www.slowgold.com). They slow down digital audio so you can pick out the individual notes. Both manufacturers offer free trial versions.

Jamming on a tune

When you play music, you don't always play a set melody or even a set part. Sometimes you jam on the tune — you make things up within a framework that includes

- ✓ **Key and scale:** The first thing you should do is identify the key of the song and whether it has a minor or major feel. You may or may not have information on the chord structure to help you choose a harp. If not, choose a harp in a position that's comfortable (unless you're feeling adventurous and want to try something unlikely).

- ✓ **Chord progression:** Maybe the tune is just a one-chord jam. But if the bass note changes or the guitar chord sounds different, the chord has probably changed. When that happens and you play something you tried before, the effect will be different because of the new context. Notes that fit before may not fit now, and notes that sounded wrong before may sound right. Listen closely for the effect of chord changes.

You can try playing through changes intuitively, or you can find out the chords and try to match your harmonica notes closely to them. Either approach is useful, but try also to develop a sense of the form of the tune as you play it so you can anticipate when a chord change will happen.

- ✔ **Licks, riffs, and bits of melody:** Often a tune has characteristic licks or *riffs* (repeated melodic lines, often backing the melody) that are played by bass guitar, saxophone, or maybe everyone together. Try to figure these out and join in on them when they're played.

- ✔ **Rhythmic feel:** Usually rhythmic feel is just that — a feel that you adapt to intuitively. Sometimes, though, there may be rhythms that are characteristic of a style of music, such as specific Latin rhythms. Or the tune may develop its own rhythmic identity. Try to remain aware of the overall rhythm, and play things that either copy that rhythm or fit with it.

Don't overplay when you're jamming with other players. One of the biggest sins when jamming is to hog all the playing time. When you're experimenting and trying to find your way, it's natural to try out different possibilities. But when you're playing a high-pitched melody instrument like harmonica, you may not leave room for anyone else's ideas if you play all the time. One way to deal with this is to play quietly, into your hands, without a mic, when it's not your turn to be in the spotlight.

Trial and Error: Playing Along with Random Music

You can learn a lot and gain confidence by playing along with music you've never played, and maybe never even heard before. You don't have to play without mistakes, and you don't even have to sound good. The point is to make mistakes, stumble, fumble, and find your way without fear or expectations.

Find music that just keeps coming automatically, such as music you hear on the radio, on television, or on podcasts. If the choice of music isn't under your control, that's even better; it forces you to adapt. Songs that are tuneful and simple may be the easiest to play along with. When trying out this exercise, stick with tunes that you've never played before. And it's fine if you've never heard the tunes before, either.

Here's what to do:

1. **Try to find the home note of the key on your harp.**

2. **Try to either play the melody of the tune or just notes that sound like they kind of fit.**

   If some notes don't fit, that's okay. But do keep them in mind.

3. **If you feel like trying to figure out what position you're in (see Chapter 9 for more on positions), look at the key of the harp.**

   Figure out which note on the harp is the main note of the key by using the note layout charts in Appendix A. Then compare the key note of the tune with the key of the harp, either with the circle of fifths in Chapter 9 or with the position chart on the Cheat Sheet in the front of this book.

4. **If you don't feel like the harp is matched well to the tune, figure out which note on the harp is the key note of the song by using the note layout charts in Appendix A.**

   This way you can use that note to find a key of harp that plays that key in first, second, or maybe third position.

I'm not suggesting that you play along with random music in public (unless you think you can make money at it). After all, few others will be able to stand your playing. But for you, the practice can be engrossing and can help you a lot in learning to play.

Chapter 12

Behind the Hidden Treasure: Bending Notes Up

*Y*ou may already know about bending notes down (see Chapter 8), but did you know you also can bend a note *up* to a higher note than the one it normally sounds? If bending notes down is the hidden treasure for harmonica players, then bending notes up is the treasure *behind* the hidden treasure.

Bending notes up is called *overbending*. When you bend a note up, the note you get is higher than — or, over — the note you started from (which is why it's called an overbend). You get some overbends by exhaling and others by inhaling, so players often talk about *overblows* and *overdraws*. Whatever you choose to call it, the overbending technique has revolutionized diatonic harmonica playing in recent years. Overbending can give you complete freedom to play any note or scale on a single diatonic harmonica.

When you bend a note up, you use the same basic technique as when you bend a note down, but the results come out backward. When you bend a note up, it doesn't slide up smoothly from your starting note the way a bent-down note slides down. Instead, an overbend just pops into existence without any apparent connection to the other notes in the same hole, almost like a mirage appearing mysteriously out of nowhere. But as I show you in this chapter, bent-up notes are no mirage. They happen in a logical, predictable way — which means you can master them and use them in your own music.

In order to bend a note up, you need to have a good command of bending notes down. After all, bending notes up is just a different application of the bending-down technique. So, if you haven't yet grasped the concept of bending notes down, spend some time with Chapter 8 before you try getting a note to bend up.

Considering the Coolness of Overbends

Bending notes down supplies some — but not all — of the missing notes of the harmonica. Bending notes up fills in the last missing gaps and gives you a new expressive tool for blues, country, jazz, or nearly any style of music.

Playing more licks, riffs, and scales

In Holes 1 through 6, you can bend draw notes down to get some of the cool notes, often called *blue notes*. But above Hole 6, the draw notes won't bend down. The blow notes bend down, but not to the notes you're looking to duplicate. Not having those notes can cramp your style. However, overbends come to the rescue by giving you a way to add the missing notes.

For example, let's say that you have a *lick* (a short sequence of notes) like the first five notes in Tab 12-1. The lick includes Draw 3 bent down from B to B♭. If you try to play that lick an octave higher, you find that B in Draw 7 doesn't bend down. But you can get that B♭ another way: by playing an overblow in Hole 6. Tab 12-1 shows that five-note lick extended into a longer line by playing it first in the lower part of the harp with a draw bend, and then in the higher part with an overblow. You can hear this lick on Track 67 of the CD.

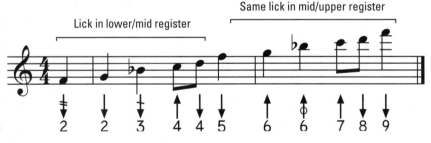

Tab 12-1:
A blues line using a bent note and an overblow (Track 67).

In harmonica tab, an overblow or overdraw is indicated by a little circle through the shaft of the breath arrow. Think of it as an "O" for "overbend."

Say you want to make that line even bluesier by adding D♭ to the lick. The lick in Tab 12-2 bends Draw 4 from D down to D♭. But when you try to play it an octave higher, D in Hole 8 doesn't bend down. Here's where an overdraw comes to the rescue. Hole 7 Overdraw is a D♭, giving you a way to extend this lick into a long line. You can listen to Tab 12-2 on Track 67.

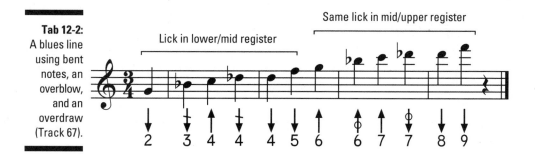

Tab 12-2: A blues line using bent notes, an overblow, and an overdraw (Track 67).

The overblow and overdraw that I show you in this section are simple, blues-based examples of what overbends can do for you. With overblows and over-draws, all blues licks, all jazz riffs, and even some heavy-metal guitar lines become possible on the diatonic harmonica.

Playing in more keys

If you have all 12 notes of the chromatic scale, you have the potential to play any melody in any key on one diatonic harmonica. However, some scales and some keys require a lot of bent notes. Moving back and forth among blows, draws, bent-down blows and draws, overblows, and overdraws — and keeping them all in tune — can be a lot of work. At a certain point, you may find that it's easier to use a different key of harp that works more easily for the tune and the key it's played in (or even to use a chromatic harmonica). How you get your results is a matter of personal choice. Overbends are just another tool to use.

Exploring the Things to Know Before You Start

Bending notes up is a normal part of harmonica playing, not a superhuman feat of strength. But to do it you need a suitable harmonica, and it helps to understand how overblows and overdraws behave. I cover both of these in the following sections.

How to choose a suitable harmonica

Some harmonicas — like Suzuki Fire Breath and Pure Breath models — come from the factory specifically adjusted for both overblows and overdraws. However, these models are fairly expensive.

Some mid-priced models respond favorably to overbending, but they work much better with reed adjustment. (See Chapter 18 for more on setting reed action.) Most mid-priced models from Hering, Hohner, and Seydel are good candidates.

Harmonicas from Japanese manufacturers such as Lee Oskar, Tombo, or Suzuki (except the models I mention earlier) are generally of high quality, but the reeds have a tendency to squeal when bending notes up. You can reduce squealing with some of the fixes described in Chapter 18.

Cheap harps usually won't work because they leak too much air and the reeds are poorly adjusted. But if you're into fixer-upper projects, you may be able to make a cheap harp airtight and responsive enough for overbends.

Any harp that's described as being "valved" will not work for overbending. This includes the Suzuki Valved Promaster and the Hohner XB-40.

Determining which notes overblow and overdraw

Overblows and overdraws are played in different places on the harp. Table 12-1 outlines the differences.

Table 12-1	Overblows versus Overdraws
Overblows	*Overdraws*
You can play overblows in Holes 1 through 6.	You can play overdraws in Holes 7 through 10.
An overblow is always one semitone higher than the draw note in the hole where you play it.	An overdraw is always one semitone higher than the blow note in the same hole.

A *semitone* is the smallest distance between two neighboring notes, even if one of the notes isn't part of the scale (see Chapter 3 for more on semitones).

Figure 12-1 shows the tuning layout of a C-harmonica with all the overblows and overdraws, together with the bent-down notes.

	1	2	3	4	5	6	7	8	9	10
Overblow	E♭	A♭	C	E♭	G♭	B♭				
Draw	D	G	B	D	F	A	B	D	F	A
Bends	D♭	F♯ / F	B♭ / A / A♭	D♭	F~	A♭	C~	E♭	F♯	B♭ / B
Blow	C	E	G	C	E	G	C	E	G	C
Overdraw								D♭	F	A♭	D♭

Figure 12-1: A harmonica note layout showing overblows and overdraws.

Draw notes bend down   Blow notes bend down

Preparing your mind, body, and ears

Here are a few tips to consider as you learn to overblow and overdraw:

- **Always hear your target note in your mind when going for an overbend.** The CD tracks that accompany this chapter allow you to hear the note you're going for.

- **Pay attention to your tongue placement and the air you inhale or exhale.** As with bending notes down, bending notes up is all about placing your tongue to set up the right conditions, coupled with a small amount of air pressure or suction.

- **At least in the beginning, overbends are easier to learn with a pucker than with a tongue block.** Tongue blocking and overbending do mix, but you'll probably experience success quicker if you start with a pucker. (See Chapter 5 for more on puckering and tongue blocking.)

- **Make sure to be physically relaxed.** Check on your abdomen, shoulders, arms, hands, and especially your jaw, cheeks, and lips to make sure they aren't tensed up. Don't press the harp hard into your face either. Tension and pressure just tire you out, and they won't help you achieve an overblow or overdraw.

- **Remember that the "over" part of "overbend" doesn't refer to excessive force or pressure.** You can play overbends very softly, and you can control them better with finesse than you can with force.

How overbends work

Reeds are the tiny strips of springy brass in a harmonica that vibrate to sound the notes. They're sort of like a series of tiny doors mounted in a wall, each with its own specially fitted doorway. The wall is a metal plate called a *reedplate,* and the doorways are slots cut in the reedplate that let the reeds swing freely as they vibrate.

Half the reeds — the blow reeds — are designed to play when you exhale; the other half — the draw reeds — play when you inhale. When you play normally, your breath pushes or pulls the reed into its slot, and then the reed springs back. The reed moving into its slot is like a door closing, so it's called a *closing reed* (see the following figure).

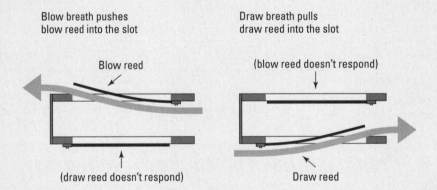

However, you can also make a reed move away from its slot before it springs back, like a door opening. When a reed behaves this way, it's called an *opening reed.* When a reed opens, it sounds a note that's nearly a semitone higher than the note it sounds when closing. The following figure illustrates opening reed action when you overblow and overdraw.

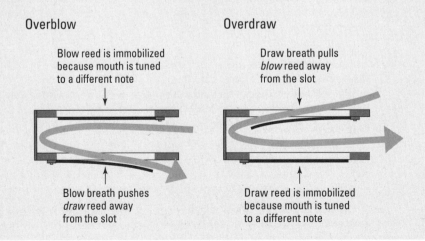

In Holes 1 through 6, when you play a regular draw bend, the draw reeds bend down as closing reeds, while the blow reeds bend up as opening reeds — each bent-down note is actually sounded by two reeds coupled into a dual-reed pair. And when you bend down the blow notes in Holes 7 through 10, the draw reeds open to support the blow bends.

In Holes 1 through 6, overblows come from the reeds designed to play draw notes. You shape your mouth to play a bend, and then you exhale. This produces two results:

✔ The blow reed can't respond to the bend, and it remains still.

✔ The draw reed opens a semitone higher than its closing pitch.

In Holes 7 through 10, overdraws come from the reeds designed to play blow notes. When you shape your mouth to play a bend, and then inhale:

✔ The draw reed can't respond.

✔ The blow reed opens a semitone higher than its normal pitch.

Getting Your First Overblows

With practice, you may be able to race up and down the harp, popping out overblows and overdraws with ease and abandon. But your first one will take some concentrated effort, and it probably will cause you some frustration. Just like learning to bend notes down, learning overblows takes patience.

A couple of approaches can help you get over that first hurdle. I call one of them the *push-through approach,* and the other I call the *springboard approach.* I cover them in the following sections.

The overblows in Holes 4, 5, and 6 are the most useful and the easiest to get. I suggest starting with Hole 6.

The push-through approach

To prepare, first play Blow 8, bend the note down, and hold the bend for a few seconds before releasing it. Note the feeling of your tongue, your K-spot (see Chapter 8), and the air pressure in your mouth. Then follow these steps:

1. **From Hole 8, move to Hole 7 and bend down Blow 7.**

   It doesn't bend far, and you can feel it resist a bit more than Blow 8 does. Bend it as far as it will go, and then hold it for a few seconds while you observe the sensations of your tongue, K-spot, and the air pressure in your mouth.

2. **Now move to Hole 6 and repeat what you just did in Holes 8 and 7.**

   This time the reed really resists bending down. Still, you may be able to get it to go down a tiny bit. Increase the air pressure slightly. You're trying to press deeply, pushing through to the overbent note.

One of three things happens next:

✔ **The reed goes silent and you hear air rushing.** That's good — you're halfway there. Think about the note you're aiming to hear and try to focus your K-spot and the pressure buildup in front of your tongue.

✔ **You hear a weird mixture of squeals and conflicting sounds.** Try moving your K-spot forward slightly, and then slightly increase the volume of air.

✔ **A clear note, higher in pitch than the blow note, suddenly starts to play.** Congratulations! You have achieved your first overblow.

Tab 12-3 shows the push-through approach traveling from Blow 8 down through Hole 7 to Hole 6. Check out Track 68 on the CD to hear Tab 12-3.

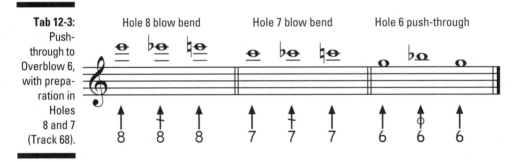

Tab 12-3: Push-through to Overblow 6, with preparation in Holes 8 and 7 (Track 68).

Hole 8 blow bend   Hole 7 blow bend   Hole 6 push-through

When you can get an overblow in Hole 6 by approaching it via Holes 8 and 7, try pushing through to Overblow 6 without playing Holes 8 or 7 first. Then try it in Holes 5 and 4, as shown in Tab 12-4. You can listen to Tab 12-4 on Track 68.

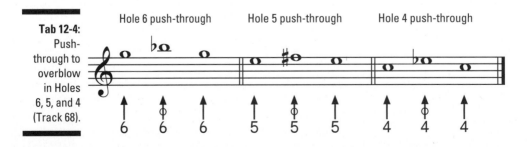

Tab 12-4: Push-through to overblow in Holes 6, 5, and 4 (Track 68).

Hole 6 push-through   Hole 5 push-through   Hole 4 push-through

The springboard approach

Because the overblow note comes from the draw reed, you can get a little assistance if the draw reed is already in motion when you start the overblow. Here's what to do when using the springboard approach to get your first overblow:

1. **Play a bendable draw note, such as Draw 6.**

2. **Bend the note down and hold it.**

   Be aware of what your tongue is doing, and note the feeling of the air flow and suction in your mouth.

3. **Switch your breath from inhaling to exhaling, but keep everything else the same.**

   Don't move anything inside your mouth — just switch breath direction. Any feeling of air suction around your K-spot will be replaced by a feeling of air pressure.

If you get the overblow note, congratulations! If you don't get the overblow, try one or more of the following:

- ✔ Move your K-spot forward or backward by a very small amount.
- ✔ Slightly increase your breath volume.
- ✔ Try a different hole in the harp.
- ✔ Try a different harp.

I suggest the last two because individual reed adjustment on any particular harp or hole in a harp may make that note responsive or unresponsive to overblows.

Tab 12-5 shows the springboard approach applied to Holes 6, 5, and 4. You can hear the tab played on Track 68.

Tab 12-5: The spring-board approach to overblows in Holes 6, 5, and 4 (Track 68).

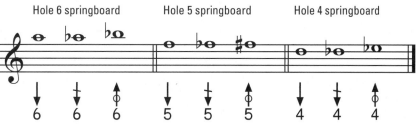

Achieving More Overblows

After Holes 4, 5, and 6, the only holes that overblow are 1, 2, and 3. Hole 1 Overblow is the most useful of the three, because it supplies a missing note. The overblows in Holes 2 and 3 duplicate other bent notes, but they can sometimes be put to good use.

Hole 1 Overblow is the lowest overblow on the harp. You may find that you can only get Overblow 1 to sound for a brief moment before Blow 1 takes over again. Reed adjustment can be a big help in making the Hole 1 Overblow accessible. However, to get Overblow 1 to sound, even on a well-adjusted harp, you need to treat it like a deep bend, as discussed in Chapter 8.

Perhaps the easiest approach to Overblow 1 is to go from the unbent draw note to the overblow. Going from the bent draw note to the overblow (the springboard approach) is slightly more difficult, and the most challenging approach is going from the blow note to the overblow (the push-through approach).

These approaches are shown in Tab 12-6, which you can hear on Track 69.

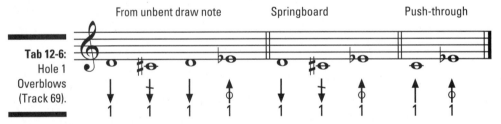

Tab 12-6:
Hole 1
Overblows
(Track 69).

Getting Your First Overdraw

Like high blow bends, overdraws are in the highest register of the harp, where tiny movements of your K-spot make the difference between getting the note and not getting it. Most harmonicas can benefit from reed adjustment so that overdraws can start easily and sound clearly (see Chapter 18 to find out how to adjust reeds). A few models, such as the Suzuki Fire Breath and Pure Breath, come pre-adjusted for overdraws.

The tabs and audio examples in this book are for a C-harmonica, but you may benefit from trying your first overdraws on a harp in a lower key, such as A or G, whose lower pitch may make the highest notes a little easier to bend.

Every harp is slightly different, but often the easiest overdraw to get is in Hole 8. It's too bad that this overdraw duplicates Draw 9, but it's nice to at least get an overdraw so you can feel what it's like.

For overdraws, the springboard approach is probably a little easier to start with than the push-through (see the sections "The push-through approach" and "The springboard approach," earlier in this chapter). When you switch from the blow bend to the overdraw, you'll notice a large amount of suction. Try to concentrate the suction in your mouth in the area in front of your tongue. If you feel the suction in your chest, you're letting it escape. If you keep your K-spot firm and you keep the suction in the front of your mouth, you'll have better success with overdraws.

Tab 12-7 shows the springboard approach to overdraws in Holes 7, 8, 9, and 10. Try them all, but start with Hole 8. You can hear Tab 12-7 on Track 70 of the CD.

Tab 12-7: The springboard approach to overdraws in Holes 7 through 10 (Track 70).

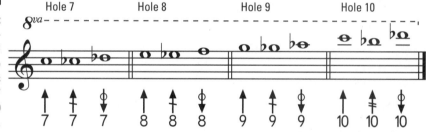

When you succeed in getting an overdraw in any of the holes with the springboard approach, see if you can go directly from the draw note to the overdraw, as shown in Tab 12-8, which you can hear on Track 70. Instead of a push-through, this is a pull-through.

Tab 12-8: The pull-through approach to overdraws in Holes 7 through 10 (Track 70).

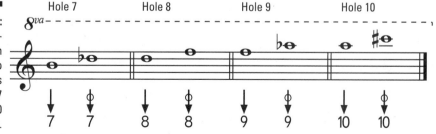

Raising the Pitch of an Overbend

The note you hear when you play an overbend seems to pop out of nowhere, with no slide up from another note. But when you start an overbent note, you can slide it up in pitch just as you can slide bent-down notes down in pitch.

Playing overbends in tune

When a reed opens, it plays a note that's a little flat, so it'll sound out of tune unless you bend it up slightly. By carefully moving your K-spot forward slightly, you can raise the pitch of the note until it's in tune.

On Track 71, you can hear Overblow 4 and Overdraw 7 played while a reference note sounds. First, the overbend is played at its lowest pitch; it sounds out of tune because it's a little below pitch. Then I raise the pitch of the overbent note slightly so that it's in tune with the reference note.

When you work on your overblows and overdraws, spend some time working with a reference note from a piano, synthesizer, guitar that's in tune, or other pitch reference. You always sound better when your playing is in tune, regardless of what techniques you're using.

Bending overbends up

You can slide an overbend up in pitch to another note. The technique is the same as raising an overbend to play it in tune; you're just pushing it a little farther. Some overblows can be pushed up several semitones before the note breaks up. You can help sustain the overblow if you carefully increase the volume of exhaled air as you move your K-spot forward to raise the pitch.

On Track 72, you can hear a tune called "Gussy Fit" (shown in Tab 12-9) that uses overblows in Holes 4, 5, and 6. If you listen closely, you can hear Overblow 5 moving smoothly up one semitone to Blow 6. I'm bending the overblow up enough to make a smooth transition. You can also hear me playing Overblow 6, quickly bending it up two semitones and bringing it back down.

Tab 12-9: "Gussy Fit," a tune with overblows (Track 72).

© *Winslow Yerxa*

Part IV
Developing Your Style

The 5th Wave   By Rich Tennant

"So you're attempting to learn how to play
harmonica, but your wife hates country music.
Go on..."

In this part . . .

Each style of music is unique, but there's a lot of borrowing back and forth as well. In this part, you get to try out some tunes in several different styles while discovering how the harmonica can play a role in each. Get down in the alley with blues and rock in Chapter 13; take a hayride with country music in Chapter 14; and feel the moss of the old country under your feet with folk and Celtic music in Chapter 15.

Chapter 13

Blues and Rock

....

....

Blues harmonica has to be one of the most forgiving musical activities you could engage in. You get to make up your music as you go, and it's difficult to play a note that sounds wrong. People respond positively to the expressive sound of a blues harp. And besides, wailing away on the blues harp is just plain fun!

You can start trying to play blues at any point in your harp development, but you'll get more out of it as you learn the core techniques of shaping your sound (Chapter 6), using your tongue (Chapter 7), and bending notes down (Chapter 8). If you're adventurous and want to add new sounds, you can add the skill of bending notes up (Chapter 12). Understanding positions (Chapter 9) is helpful for blues, because you usually use a harmonica in a different key from the key of the tune you're playing.

The more you work out with these techniques, the more you'll start hearing them in the playing of others — and the more you'll find ways to use them. But hey, don't let me load you down with all this stuff. These aren't requirements — they're just suggestions for ways to deepen your enjoyment of playing blues.

Most rock harmonica — such as that played by Steven Tyler, Mick Jagger, Huey Lewis, Magic Dick (the guy from J. Geils), and many others — is basically blues harmonica set to slightly different beats. Everything in this chapter applies to rock harmonica as well.

Feel free to adapt and spice up the simple rhythms used in the licks and riffs in this chapter. Blues rhythms feel natural when you hear them or play them, but when you go to write them down they can look fussy and complicated on the page. So I wrote the licks and rhythms in this chapter using simple rhythms that you don't need to puzzle out. After you get the hang of a lick, try adapting its rhythm to sound more like the rhythms you hear on good blues records.

The 12 Bars of Blues

Blues uses the underlying structure of a musical form called *12-bar blues,* which is like the verse of a song. This verse form is the container for blues songs and solos, and when you understand its features, you can easily find things to play within it.

The "bar" in *12-bar* is just a group of two, three, or four beats (usually four) with emphasis on the first beat. The 12-bar blues has — you guessed it — 12 of these bars. What's inside those bars? It could be any one of hundreds of different melodies, or thousands of different solos, all identifiable as 12-bar blues to anyone familiar with its form. So what gives 12-bar blues its distinct identity if it isn't melody? In the following sections, I fill you in.

Identifying the three chords of blues

Behind any blues melody or solo is a sequence of chords (which is referred to as a *chord progression*). *Chords* are groups of notes played at the same time, usually by backing musicians on guitar, piano, and bass. Each chord is based on a note in the scale, and the other notes in the chord reinforce that note. (See Chapter 3 for more on chords and Chapter 11 for more on how songs generally work.)

The most important chord is based on the key note of the scale. This chord is called the *I chord* (pronounced, "one chord," as in Roman numeral I). All the other chords in the scale also have Roman numerals that you can figure out by counting up the scale from the key note. The most important chords after the I chord are the IV chord and the V chord.

Why refer to chords as I, IV, and V instead of, say, C, F, and G? Because the relationships between the chords stay the same no matter what key the song is played in. When you gain experience listening to 12-bar blues, you can identify the I, IV, and V chords by ear without knowing what key the song is in. In other words, by listening for relationships, you can understand what's going on in a piece of music without having to know the specifics.

Making a statement: Tell it, brother!

A verse of 12-bar blues has three main parts, and you make a statement in each of those parts. The first two statements move from one to the next in a way that feels compelling and flows into a resounding third, final statement. It's a little like the way a good preacher sets up a premise and then brings home an important point while thrilling the congregation.

Figure 13-1 shows a 12-bar blues divided into its three parts. Each part is four bars long, and each bar has four beats, represented by diagonal slashes. The chords are written above the slashes as Roman numerals.

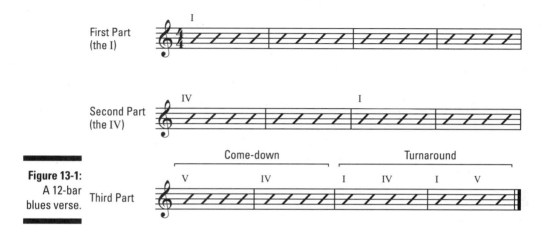

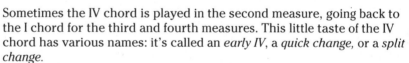

Figure 13-1:
A 12-bar blues verse.

Each part of the verse is defined by its place in the chord progression. Consider the following:

✔ **The first part of the verse is called the I because it starts on the I chord.** In the simplest version of 12-bar blues, the I chord lasts for four bars. You make your initial statement in the I part.

Sometimes the IV chord is played in the second measure, going back to the I chord for the third and fourth measures. This little taste of the IV chord has various names: it's called an *early IV*, a *quick change,* or a *split change.*

✔ **The second part of the verse is called the IV.** It starts with the IV chord, which lasts for two bars, followed by the I chord, which comes back for two more bars. In the IV part, you can repeat your initial statement, or you can make a new statement that elaborates on the first one.

✔ **The third part of the verse is where you deliver the final summation that answers the first two statements and prepares for the next verse.** The third part is the busiest part of the verse. It has two components:

• **The come-down:** The *come-down* introduces the V chord. The V chord is played for one measure, and then it comes down to the IV chord for one measure.

• **The turnaround:** The *turnaround* lands back on the I chord. In a simple blues tune, the last two bars of the tune may play nothing but the I chord. However, often the turnaround goes through a quick sequence of I-IV-I-V (refer to Figure 13-1).

Fitting the notes to the chords

Melodies always give a prominent place to the notes that make up the background chord. More time is spent on the chord notes than other notes, and chord notes are often played on the first and third beats, which get the strongest emphasis. Knowing which notes on the harmonica correspond with which chord in the 12-bar progression gives you a launching pad for everything you play.

Three Positions of the Blues

If you play a C-harp in the key of C, or a D-harp in the key of D, or any harp in its labeled key, that's *first position*. First position is always played the same way regardless of the key of the harmonica (as long as the key of the tune matches the key of the harmonica).

Second position is when you play a C-harp in G, or a D-harp in A. Again, second position always plays and sounds like second position, just in different keys. Second position is by far the most popular position, so I discuss it first and give it the fullest treatment. Blues harmonica players also spend some time playing in first position and in another position called *third position*. (I describe positions more fully in Chapter 9.)

I wrote this book so that you could play everything on a C-harmonica, so the second-position tunes will be in the key of G, while the first-position tunes will be in C, and the third-position tunes will be in D. In the following sections, I guide you through some of the basic elements of playing blues while allowing you to become familiar with second position. I show you a stockpile of second-position licks, and then I take you on a brief tour of some of the cool features of first and third positions.

Second-position blues

Most blues songs are played in second position. To orient second position to the three chords of blues, consider the following:

✔ **The I chord is formed by the draw notes, with Draw 1, 2, 3, and 4 being the main notes you use.** Draw 2 is the main home note of the I chord. Blow 6 and Blow 9 are auxiliary home notes higher up the harp.

✔ **The IV chord is formed by the blow notes.** Blow 4 is the main home note of the IV chord. Blow 1, Blow 7, and Blow 10 are supplementary home notes for the I chord. Draw 2 is the same note as Blow 3; this note belongs to both the I chord and the IV chord.

✔ **The V chord is formed by the draw notes in Holes 4 through 10.**
However, it's a minor chord (see Chapter 3 for more on chords). The
background chord is usually a major chord, but the clash between major
and minor is a characteristic element in the blues.

The main home note for the V chord is Draw 4. Draw 1 and Draw 8 are
auxiliary home notes for the V chord. Draw 1, Draw 4, and Draw 8 are
notes that belong to both the I chord and the V chord.

Some of the tabs in Chapters 7 and 12 use 12-bar blues tunes in second position to demonstrate specific techniques. These tabs include Tab 7-2 (chasing
the beat, or chording between the beats), Tab 7-3 (tongue slaps on melody
notes), and Tab 12-12 (a tune with overblows).

Exploring 12-bar blues using second position

In this section, I show you several elements of 12-bar blues, including playing
the root note of each chord in the 12-bar verse, playing rhythm chords over
the 12-bar verse, playing the same line over the three different parts of the
verse, and playing wailing notes. Each element is embodied in a tune that you
can play in second position.

Outline Blues

Outline Blues is shown in Tab 13-1, and it can be heard on Track 73 of the CD,
where I play it as the first of four verses. All you do is outline each chord by
playing its notes one at a time starting on the root, or main note, of the chord.
Try playing along with the CD — this will give you a sense of where each
chord comes in the verse. It's okay to play more than one hole at a time,
because the neighboring blow or draw notes are part of the chord.

When you get familiar with the main home note of each chord and the neighboring notes, try exploring some of the supplementary home notes instead.
For example, try playing Blow 4 for the IV chord and Draw 1 for the V chord.
Or you could travel up the harp and use Blow 6 for the I chord. You could
even go up to the top of the harp and play Blow 9 for the I chord, Blow 7 (or
even Blow 10) for the IV chord, and Draw 8 for the V chord.

Rhythm Chord Blues

Tab 13-2 shows a way to play rhythm chords over a 12-bar blues. Although the
tab shows the home note of the chord, you can play two, three, or even four
holes at the same time. You can hear Tab 13-2 being played during the second
of four verses on Track 73 (0:17).

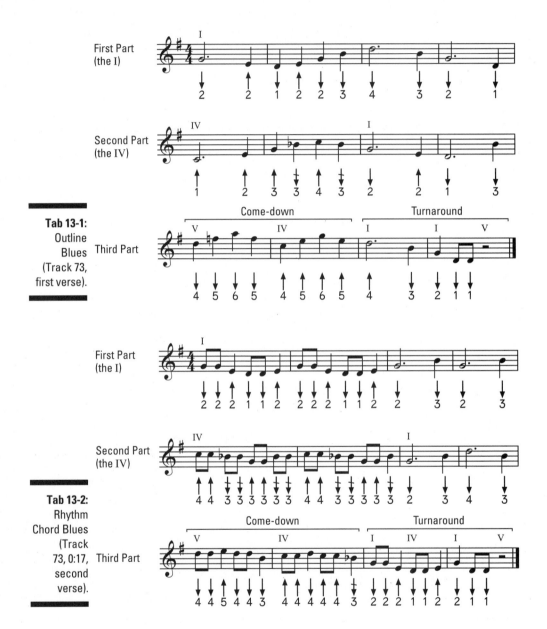

Tab 13-1: Outline Blues (Track 73, first verse).

Tab 13-2: Rhythm Chord Blues (Track 73, 0:17, second verse).

Red Sock Blues

Often in a blues song, the melody played over the I part is repeated over the IV part. It sounds a little different because the background of chords is different. It's sort of like the way a red sock creates one impression when you hold it up against a yellow background and another impression when you hold it up against a blue background — each background reacts differently with the color of the sock.

You can hear Red Sock Blues played as the third verse on Track 73 (0:32).

In many blues songs, the melody really only moves around during the first two bars of each four-bar phrase, as shown in Tab 13-3. If you were the singer singing this line, a harmonica or guitar might play a *fill* in the last two bars to fill up the space and comment on what you just sang.

Always bend Draw 3 down slightly when you play it over the IV chord, as shown in Tab 13-3. Bending Draw 3 down makes it fit better with the IV chord and sound a bit bluesier.

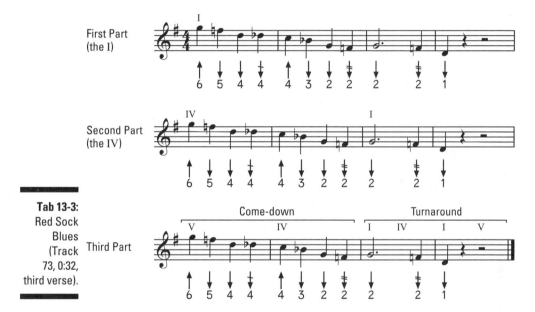

Tab 13-3: Red Sock Blues (Track 73, 0:32, third verse).

Wailing Note Blues

Wailing notes are notes that you can hold and bend down to get a wailing sound. The strongest wailing notes are Draw 4 and Draw 5. Draw 6 is also a strong wailing note, though it can be strident if you use it too much. Draw 3 bent down is a more subtle wailing note that works well over the IV chord. When you're wailing, you don't really need to make your notes match the underlying chords; though you still need to have a sense of where you are in the 12-bar blues verse. Tab 13-4, "Wailing Note Blues," uses all the wailing notes I just mentioned. Try playing it as written, and then explore these notes on your own and make up your own lines.

You can hear "Wailing Note Blues" as the fourth verse on Track 73 (0:46). The first three verses go at a faster tempo. Before launching into "Wailing Note Blues," the band hits four strong notes at the new tempo. Think of these notes as the "One, Two, Three, Four" counting off the beginning of the new tune.

TIP

"Wailing Note Blues" ends the four-verse blues on Track 73 by using a typical blues song ending. Over this ending, try playing some of the licks to end a tune shown in Tab 13-8.

First Part (the I)

Second Part (the IV)

Tab 13-4:
Wailing
Note Blues Third Part
(Track
73, 0:46).

A stockpile of second-position licks and riffs

One thing that makes experimenting with 12-bar blues easy is that a lick or riff that fits over one part of the tune may work elsewhere as well. However, note that some licks and riffs really only fit over the come-down or turnaround.

ON THE CD

In the following list, I tab out some "anywhere" licks that fit on any part of the verse — some that are meant to specifically fit over the second part of the verse, some that fit specifically over the come-down and the turnaround, and some you can use to end a tune. You can listen to these licks on the CD and learn how to play them from the tab as you play along. As you become familiar with them, try mixing and matching different licks to create your own blues verses.

✔ **Anywhere licks:** Tab 13-5 (Track 74) shows some anywhere licks. Remember to bend Draw 3 down if you play these over the IV chord.

✔ **Second-part licks:** Tab 13-6 (Track 75) shows a few second-part licks that fit over the IV chord. Use these to contrast with an anywhere lick that you play in the first part of the verse.

✔ **Come-down and turnaround licks:** Tab 13-7 (Track 76) shows some licks you can play over the come-down and the turnaround.

✔ **Licks to end a tune:** Tab 13-8 (Track 77) shows four common ways to end a tune. You play these over the turnaround, after the come-down. Note that when you end the tune, you stay on the I chord instead of ending with the V chord.

1st Anywhere Lick

2nd Anywhere Lick (0:12)

3rd Anywhere Lick (0:23)

Tab 13-5: Anywhere licks (Track 74).

1st Second-part Lick

2nd Second-part Lick (0:12)

3rd Second-part Lick (0:23)

Tab 13-6: Second-part licks (Track 75).

Tab 13-7: Come-down and turnaround licks (Track 76).

Tab 13-8: Licks to end a tune (Track 77).

Third-position blues

When you play in third position, you change the sound of blues harmonica and bring variety to your playing. Third position glides effortlessly through the middle and high registers because the draw notes in those registers form the home chord. Because the home chord is a minor chord, third position has a minor feel, but most third-position blues is played over major chords — the clash is part of the blues sound. Keep the following in mind:

- **The I chord is formed by the draw notes in Holes 4, 5, and 6, and in Holes 8, 9, and 10.** The main home note is Draw 4. Draw 1 and Draw 8 are auxiliary home notes. You can bend Draw 2 down a whole step and Draw 3 down a whole step to create additional chord notes in the bottom register.

- **The IV chord is formed by the draw notes in Holes 1, 2, 3, and 4.** You can use the draw notes above Hole 4 as part of the IV chord as well as part of the I chord. Draw 2 is the main home note of the IV chord. Blow 6 and Blow 9 are auxiliary home notes higher up the harp.

- **The V chord doesn't exist as a complete chord.** Draw 6 is the main home note of the V chord. Draw 10 and Draw 3 bent down two semitones are auxiliary home notes of the V chord. Blow 2 and Blow 3, Blow 5 and Blow 6, and Blow 8 and Blow 9 are part of the V chord. Blow 1, Blow 4, Blow 7, and Blow 10 aren't part of the V chord, but they work as *blue notes*, which are notes that clash with the chord notes but sound good anyway. You can bend Draw 1 or Draw 4 down a semitone to play one of the notes of the V chord.

Tab 13-9 shows a third-position blues verse in the top and middle registers, and Tab 13-10 shows a third-position blues verse in the low and middle registers. They're played one after the other on Track 78.

The little stack of diagonal lines next to Draw 5 and Draw 4 in the third part of the verse in Tab 13-9 means to do a *shake* — rapidly alternate the note you're playing with the note one hole to the right. (See Chapter 10 for more on shakes.)

Tab 13-9: Third-position blues in the top and middle registers (Track 78, first verse).

Tab 13-10: Third-position blues in the low and middle registers (Track 78, 0:36, second verse).

First-position blues

The really cool thing about first position is that the four highest blow notes bend down and they're the notes of the home chord. As you can imagine, a lot of first-position blues is played in the top register. However, the draw notes in the bottom register can be bent down to create bluesy sounding notes, so you often hear players leaping between the top and bottom registers.

Here's a thumbnail picture of the three chords of blues when you play in first position:

- ✔ **The I chord is formed by the blow notes throughout the range of the harmonica.** The main home note is Blow 4. Blow 1, Blow 7, and Blow 10 are auxiliary home notes. The notes of the home chord that bend down are all in the top register (except for Draw 2).

- ✔ **The IV chord doesn't exist as a complete chord.** Draw 5 and 6 form a fragment of the chord, while Draw 9 and 10 duplicate those notes higher up. If your bending skills are well developed, you can create these notes in the low register by bending Draw 2 or Draw 3 down two semitones. Blow 1, Blow 4, Blow 7, and Blow 10 (the home note of the key) are also part of this chord, but of course blow notes and draw notes can't be played at the same time. Draw 5 is the home note of the chord. Draw 2 bent down two semitones and Draw 9 are auxiliary home notes.

- ✔ **The V chord is formed by the draw notes in Holes 1, 2, 3, and 4.** These notes all bend and can be used to create missing scale notes and blue notes. The remaining draw notes also function as part of the extended V chord. Draw 2 is the main home note of the V chord. Blow 6 and Blow 9 are auxiliary home notes higher up the harp.

Tab 13-11 shows a verse of first-position 12-bar blues played in the top register. The bendable blow notes get most of the action. Those high notes really wail, but they can sound piercing, so there's lots of silence left between them. When you're playing in the top register, brevity can be very tasty. At the end of the verse, you tumble down through the middle register on the way to the bottom.

Tab 13-12 shows a verse of first-position 12-bar blues played in the bottom register. This verse really works the low-register bends to create a muscular sound, and it can help you work up your bending muscles as well.

Tab 13-11 and Tab 13-12 are played together as a two-verse tune on Track 79.

Tab 13-11: First-position blues in the top register (Track 79, first verse).

Tab 13-12: First-position blues in the bottom register (Track 79, 0:36, second verse).

Chapter 14

Headin' South with Some Country Tunes

In This Chapter

▶ Seeing how harps fit into country music

▶ Exploring some first position songs

▶ Taking on second position songs

Country music is a patchwork quilt of American musical styles. Rooted in the songs, fiddle tunes, and gospel music brought by early Scots-Irish settlers, country music weaves in scraps of blues and of Mexican and Cajun music. It even has a few gaudy swatches from the Tin Pan Alley pop songs of the Northern cities. Like blues, country has an improvisational aspect, but it also places strong emphasis on melody.

Country harmonica has one foot in blues and the other in major-scale melodies — and fiddle tunes are never far away. When you play country tunes on harmonica, it helps to have a little background in all three of these traditions.

This chapter helps you get started playing country tunes in first and second position. Chapter 13 covers the elements of playing blues, while Chapter 15 goes into fiddle tunes. For some suggested listening in all three styles, check out Chapter 21.

Choosing Harps for Country

Most of the time, country harmonica players use standard diatonic harmonicas, and they play them in second position. But they occasionally use first position as well (see Chapter 9 for more on positions). They favor second position because the notes of the home chords (Draw 1, 2, 3, and 4) are bendable and expressive. However, standard diatonic isn't your only choice. In this section, I discuss some other types of harmonica that you may hear when you listen to country records.

When they play in second position, country players can run into a problem: Draw 5 doesn't fit the major scale — it's flat. This flat note fits well when you play blues, and it also fits certain fiddle tunes. But in major-key melodies, you have to avoid it because it usually sounds sour. To solve this problem, you can play a harmonica in *Country Tuning*.

In a country-tuned harp, the note in Draw 5 is raised one semitone to fit the major scale. Country Tuning gives you all the advantages of second position while letting you easily play a major scale. You can buy some models of harmonica in Country Tuning, or you can retune Draw 5 yourself. (See Chapter 18 for information on how to tune harmonicas.)

The chromatic harmonica is rarely heard in country music, though Jimmie Riddle played chromatic on some of Roy Acuff's recordings in the 1940s, including "Tennessee Waltz" and "Freight Train Blues" and later on his own albums. The tremolo used to be rare in country music, but Mickey Raphael plays it to good effect in Willie Nelson's band (see Chapter 19 for information about chromatic and tremolo harmonicas).

Visitin' with Some Country Songs in First Position

First position — playing a harmonica in its labeled key — was once the favored way to play country music on harmonica. Second position has since become more popular, but first position is still the best way to play some traditional melodies.

When you play in first position, your home note is Blow 4. Your home chord is formed by all the blow notes. (Refer to Chapter 9 if you need a refresher on playing in first position.)

Most of the tunes in the following sections are old country favorites — you'll probably meet others who know how to play them on guitar. They aren't too difficult to play, so grab a harp and get started.

"Blue Eyed Angel"

"Blue Eyed Angel" (refer to Tab 14-1) is a tune that has been used (in slightly varied versions) for such famous country songs as "I Am Thinking Tonight of My Blue Eyes," "Great Speckled Bird," "Wild Side of Life," and "It Wasn't God Who Made Honky-Tonk Angels." You can hear this tune on Track 80 of the CD.

In the third measure, the note with an asterisk above it is played as Draw 5. In the most familiar version of this melody, you would instead play Draw 3 bent down two semitones, which is difficult to play in tune. However, you may want to try this challenge as you develop your bending skills. (Flip to Chapter 8 for details on bending notes down.)

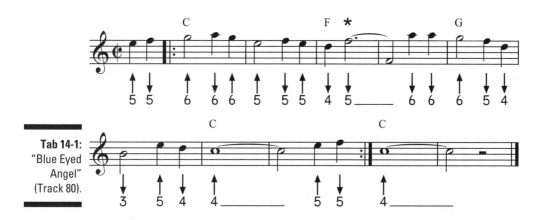

Tab 14-1: "Blue Eyed Angel" (Track 80).

"Wabash Cannonball"

"Wabash Cannonball," shown in Tab 14-2, is a popular country tune that originated as a hobo's ode to a mythical train. This lively tune gives you an opportunity to work on your country chops in the middle and upper registers of the harmonica. Listen to this tune on Track 81.

You can try this tune an octave lower, starting on Blow 3. When you do this, you can fatten up the sound of the lower notes in the tune with the notes of the draw chord in Holes 1, 2, and 3. But you also have to bend Draw 3 down for one of the notes.

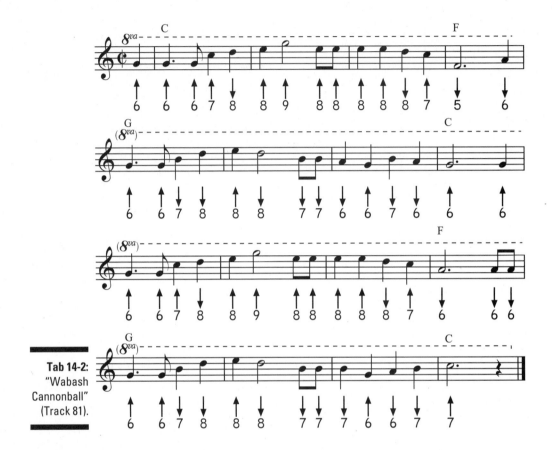

Getting Acquainted with a Few Second-Position Country Songs

Second position — playing the harmonica in the key of the draw chord, with Draw 2 as the home note — is the favored way to play country harmonica nowadays because you can bend all the notes of the home chord. In the following sections, I provide you with some tunes that lie well in second position. Grab a harp and try them out.

"Foggy Mountain Top"

"Foggy Mountain Top" (see Tab 14-3) is a traditional bluegrass tune that's fairly easy to play, so it's a good introduction to playing second position for country tunes. You can hear this tune on Track 82 of the CD.

See the swooping symbols that surround Draw 3? They tell you to approach and leave a note with expressive bends. To do this, follow these steps:

1. **Start the note slightly bent, and immediately release it to an unbent note.**

   You hear a little upward glide when you do this.

2. **Just before you leave the note, bend it down a little.**

   You hear a little downward glide just before you go to the next note.

Near the end of the tune, you have to bend down Draw 3 for real.

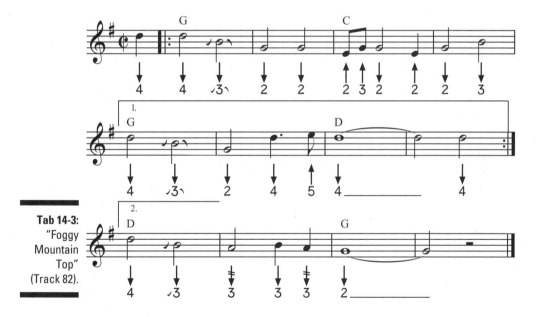

Tab 14-3: "Foggy Mountain Top" (Track 82).

"Since I Laid My Burden Down"

"Since I Laid My Burden Down," an African-American spiritual (see Tab 14-4), was the basis for the well-known country gospel tune "Will the Circle Be Unbroken?" This tune is widely known and loved, and it isn't difficult to play. When you play this song in second position, you can express the feeling of it by bending draw notes in Holes 2, 3, and 4. Hear this tune on Track 83.

One note in this tune requires you to bend Draw 3 down two semitones. If you're having trouble getting that bent note, just bend Draw 3 in an expressive way without trying to hit the note. (Refer to Chapter 8 for more on bending notes down.)

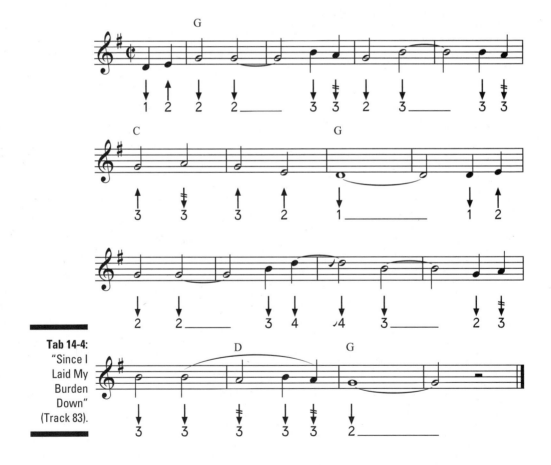

Tab 14-4: "Since I Laid My Burden Down" (Track 83).

"One Frosty Morn"

ON THE CD

I wrote "One Frosty Morn" (shown in Tab 14-5 and heard on Track 84) to play in second position while sounding similar to the "Blue Eyed Angel" tune earlier in this chapter. This tune is designed to let you work on two bent notes that supply missing notes in the major scale. Here are the bent notes:

- ✔ Draw 3 should be bent down two semitones, for the 2nd degree of the scale.

- ✔ Draw 2 should be bent down only one semitone, for the 7th degree of the scale.

    The bend in Draw 2 isn't the deep two-semitone blues bend. It takes a lighter touch and some finesse. Achieving it may require some work, but after you've mastered it, you'll have added a valuable note for playing major scale melodies.

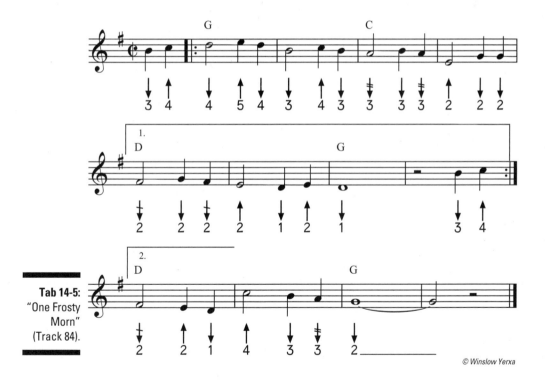

Tab 14-5: "One Frosty Morn" (Track 84).

© Winslow Yerxa

"Lonesome Whistle Waltz"

I composed the "Lonesome Whistle Waltz" to express the bluesy side of country music on the harmonica as shown in Tab 14-6. Here are a few special notes to keep in mind when you're playing this waltz:

✔ Near the end of the first line of tab, you play Holes 3 and 4 together, and then you play Hole 4 by itself. You can make this transition smoothly by narrowing your mouth opening slightly on the left to exclude Draw 3. Next, you hold Draw 4, and as you play it, add Draw 5. You make this transition by widening your mouth opening slightly on the right.

✔ In the middle of the second line of tab, you play a shake by rapidly alternating draw notes in Holes 5 and 6. The shake is indicated by that stack of diagonal lines in the tab. (Check out Chapter 10 for more on shakes and other ways to spice up your playing.)

You can hear "Lonesome Whistle Waltz" on Track 85 of the CD.

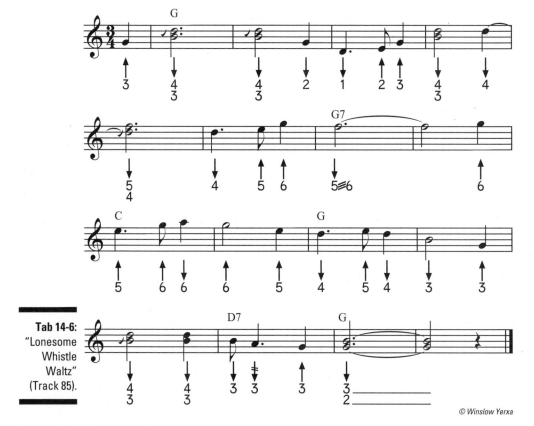

Tab 14-6: "Lonesome Whistle Waltz" (Track 85).

© Winslow Yerxa

"Muscle Car Boogie, Part 1"

The rockabilly side of country produced legends like Carl Perkins, Jerry Lee Lewis, Johnny Cash, Brenda Lee, Wanda Jackson, and Elvis Presley. Where would a cool cat be without a powerful car? I wrote "Muscle Car Boogie, Part 1," shown in Tab 14-7, to mimic the guitar lines often heard in rockabilly tunes and help you deliver the goods on an uptempo country tune. Check out Track 86 of the CD to hear this tune.

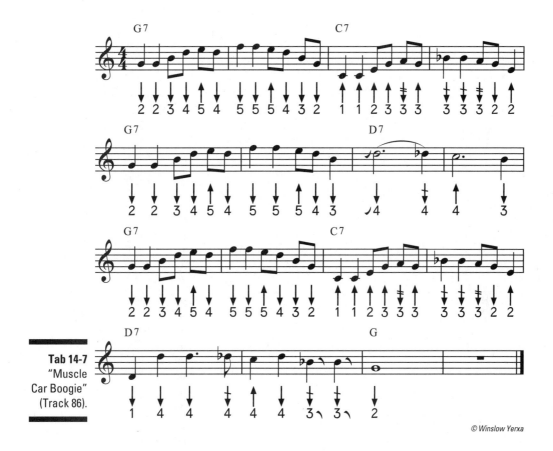

Tab 14-7
"Muscle Car Boogie" (Track 86).

© Winslow Yerxa

Chapter 15

Fiddlin' the Night Away with Folk and Celtic Songs and Dance Tunes

- -

In This Chapter

▶ Determining which harps to use for folk and Celtic tunes

▶ Exploring fast fiddle tunes

▶ Playing songs in five different harmonica positions

- -

Melody is the most important element of traditional music. The songs that transmit cultural values and stories are often set to haunting melodies that are handed down for several generations. Dance melodies often hark back to the days when a solo piper or fiddler playing without any accompaniment could propel a whole roomful of enthusiastic dancers into action, armed only with well-crafted dance melodies containing all the rhythmic cues needed to keep bodies in motion.

The traditions of England, together with the Celtic traditions of Scotland and Ireland, play a strong part in both the song and dance traditions of much of the United States. However, these traditions have mixed with African, Hispanic, and Native American traditions to create uniquely North American folk traditions.

The portable, inexpensive diatonic harmonica found a place in North American folk song and dance soon after its arrival from Germany sometime in the 19th century. In this chapter, I take you through some traditional songs and dance tunes that you can enjoy playing.

Choosing Harps for Playing Folk and Celtic Music

How do you choose harmonicas for playing traditional music? Different types of harmonicas are used in different traditions, and each type has strengths and weaknesses in adapting to existing styles. Here are some considerations for using the three main types of melody harmonicas in traditional music.

The simple ten-hole diatonic (the one this book is about) is the most widely used type of harmonica in North American music, and it's often found in English and Celtic music as well. However, the diatonic sometimes runs into a problem: Some tunes have notes that aren't built into the harmonica. In earlier times, people adapted tunes to fit the limitations of instruments such as diatonic harmonicas, accordions, and bagpipes. Nowadays, people are more inclined to adapt the instrument to the music. You can make these adaptations in the following three ways:

- ✔ **Play the harmonica in a position to change the available scale.** When you play a harmonica in its labeled key, you're playing in first position. If you play the harp in any other key, you're playing in a different position (see Chapter 9 for more on positions). Each position has its own unique scale, called a *mode*. For instance, if you take a C-harmonica and play it in G, you don't get a G major scale. Instead, you get the key of G flavored by the notes of the C scale. Many folk tunes use these modes, so playing harmonica in positions is a natural fit for folk tunes.

- ✔ **Use note bending to create missing notes.** When you bend a note, you raise or lower it to a different note by shaping your vocal cavity (see Chapter 8 for bending notes down and Chapter 12 for bending notes up). Note bending can be useful for supplying missing notes on the harmonica. Some of the tunes in this chapter use bent notes.

- ✔ **Use harmonicas with alternate tunings.** You can permanently retune individual notes on a harmonica to change the available notes (see Chapter 18 for information on how to tune reeds). For instance, as you may know, the note A is missing in Hole 3 on a diatonic harp. To supply this note, you can retune the note G in Blow 3 to play A instead (you still have G in Draw 2). This particular alternate tuning is known as *Paddy Richter,* and some harmonica manufacturers, such as Seydel, are beginning to offer this tuning for sale.

The tremolo harmonica

The *tremolo harmonica* is a type of diatonic harmonica that uses two reeds to play each note. One set of reeds is tuned slightly higher than the other, and when the two are played together, the difference in fine-tuning creates a quavering pulsation in the sound of the note. This quavering sound is called *tremolo.* Tremolo harps are rarely used for traditional music in the United States, but they are part of the characteristic sound of harmonica music in Scotland, Ireland, and Quebec. Check out Chapter 19 to read more on the tremolo harmonica.

On Track 98 (0:36), you can hear some tunes from this chapter played on tremolo harp.

Tremolo harps are available in a few alternate tunings, such as the minor-key tremolos made by Suzuki and Tombo, and the Hohner Highlander, designed by Donald Black for Scottish bagpipe music.

The chromatic harmonica

The chromatic harmonica has the advantage of allowing you to play in any key without any missing notes. Chromatic harps aren't widely used in folk music, but there are a few Irish-style players doing some cool things with them. For instance, check out Brendan Power and Eddie Clarke if you get the chance.

Playing Fast Fiddle Tunes

The instrumental dance tunes in folk music are often called *fiddle tunes,* because the fiddle is the most popular instrument for playing these tunes. Fiddle tunes include the traditional dance music of Scotland, Ireland, England, Cape Breton, Québec, and the United States (including old-timey, bluegrass, and contradance music). If you want to play traditional music in these styles, you need to become acquainted with playing fiddle tunes, and I've included a few fiddle tunes in this chapter.

When you play fiddle tunes in a group with others, everyone plays the melody together (except those people who are playing accompaniment). Melodies in these tunes are played very fast. How do you keep up? Try the following:

✔ **Practice the tunes slowly at home with a metronome and slowly build up your speed.** See Chapter 10 for more on learning to play fast.

✔ **Play only the notes you can manage and avoid everything else.** Look for notes on the strong beats. You can do this when playing along with recordings. However, be careful about doing it at jam sessions. If the session welcomes beginners and enough people are playing to carry the melody strongly, and you don't play too loudly, then perhaps no one will mind.

✔ **Find a slow session.** *Slow sessions* are where people gather to play through fast tunes at a slow speed. This way everyone can manage all the notes at a reasonable speed. Often someone at the session will teach the tunes by ear, one phrase at a time, which gives everyone a chance to become thoroughly familiar with the tune. When you can play a tune with confidence slowly, you have a basis for learning to play it fast.

To find a slow session, look for local folk music or fiddling societies. Or check out bars that feature Irish or Scottish music; they may have slow sessions on Sunday afternoons or other times when business is also slow.

Trying Out Some First-Position Tunes

First position on a harp plays the major scale. Your home note is Blow 4 or Blow 7, and the blow notes together form your home chord. (Refer to Chapter 9 for more on playing in first position.)

The harmonica was designed to play in first position, and hundreds of folk tunes can be played in this position successfully without any special adaptations. In this section, I show you two songs and two fiddle tunes to get you started playing folk and traditional tunes in first position.

"Careless Love"

"Careless Love" is an American song that may have originated in New Orleans. It was a favorite of trumpeters Buddy Bolden and Louis Armstrong. Lying in the middle and low registers, it's easy to play and works nicely in first position, as shown in Tab 15-1. You can hear the tune played on Track 87 on the CD.

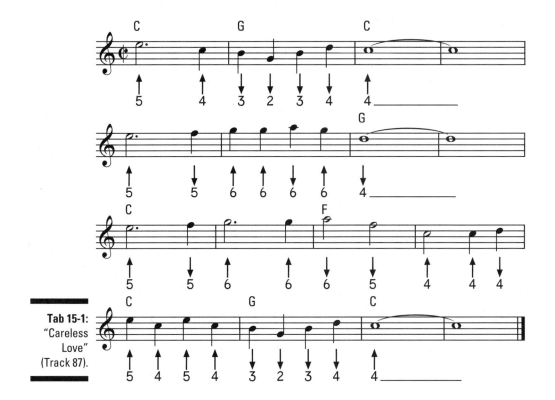

Tab 15-1: "Careless Love" (Track 87).

"Wildwood Flower"

Originally titled "I'll Twine 'Mid the Ringlets," "Wildwood Flower" (see Tab 15-2) dates to 1860. Revived by the Carter Family in the 1930s, it has remained popular ever since, both as a song and as an instrumental tune. Be careful about the leaps from Blow 4 up to Blow 6, as Blow 6 begins a new phrase; you need to play it cleanly and distinctly. If you can bend the high blow notes, try bending Blow 8 a little when you play it, just for effect.

To hear what this tune sounds like, listen to Track 88.

Tab 15-2: "Wildwood Flower" (Track 88).

"April's Jig"

In Scottish and Irish traditions, a jig is danced to a tune whose rhythm divides the beat evenly in three. Jigs can be a lot of fun to play, and I wrote "April's Jig," shown in Tab 15-3, to play easily on the diatonic harmonica with no leaps or tricky moves. (Can you guess which month I wrote it in?) The first half of the tune is based on the blow chord, while the second half of the tune is based on the draw chord but ends up returning to the blow chord.

To hear "April's Jig," check out Track 89 on the CD.

Tab 15-3: "April's Jig" (Track 89).

© Winslow Yerxa

"Mrs. MacLeod of Raasay"

A reel is a type of tune that's common in Scottish, Irish, and North American fiddling traditions. Reels go very fast, with four notes per beat most of the time, making them exciting (and sometimes challenging) to play. "Mrs. MacLeod of Raasay" (sometimes she's referred to as a Miss as well) is a Scottish reel that's well-known in Ireland, the United States, and Canada under a variety of names. This tune, which is shown in Tab 15-4, can help you get the hang of making clean leaps from note to note. For instance, you have to try and make the leap from Hole 4 up to Hole 7 and from Hole 7 down to Holes 5 and 4. This tune is usually played in A on an A-harmonica.

You can see whether you recognize the tune by listening to Track 90 on the CD. To hear part of this tune played on tremolo (0:58) and octave (1:31) harps, check out Track 98.

Tab 15-4: "Mrs. MacLeod of Raasay" (Track 90).

Energizing Some Tunes in Second-Position

When you play in second position, your home note is Draw 2, and the surrounding draw notes form the home chord. However, notes are missing from the scale directly above and below the home note. In earlier times, people played second position fiddle tunes in the upper register where those missing notes were available. However, today, the compelling sound of the low draw chord has caused players to learn how to bend notes in Holes 2 and 3 so they can play tunes in the middle and low register instead.

Second position gives you a scale called the *Mixolydian mode* (see Chapter 9 for more on this mode). The seventh note in this scale is flat (lowered), giving it a distinctive sound.

The tunes in this section take advantage of the unique qualities of second position. The songs are fairly easy to play, while the fiddle tune version of "Old Joe Clark" will help you work up your chops for some hot dance tunes.

"John Hardy"

"John Hardy" (see Tab 15-5) is an American folk song that fits well in second position on harmonica and makes prominent use of the flat seventh in the scale (found in Draw 5). Originally written about a 19th century murder, this tune was later used by Woody Guthrie for his song, "Tom Joad." You can play it as a chordal piece — you don't have to play it in single notes and it doesn't make any fancy leaps. A lot of the moves are just sliding to the neighboring hole without even changing between blow and draw.

You can hear a rendition of this song on Track 91.

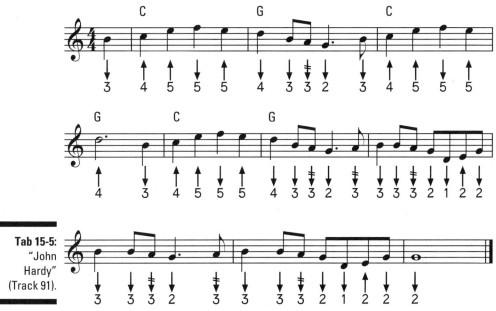

Tab 15-5: "John Hardy" (Track 91).

"Old Joe Clark"

"Old Joe Clark" is famous both as a song and as a fiddle tune. The fiddle tune follows the outline of the song but adds a lot of fast notes in between the notes of the song. I suggest that you learn to play the song version first, and then tackle the fiddle tune. The song does make one demand on your technique, which is to bend Draw 3 down accurately to play one of the melody notes.

The song version is shown in Tab 15-6, and you can listen to it as the first verse on Track 92.

The tab for the fiddle tune version (see Tab 15-7) looks like it has a lot of notes, but at least half the tune repeats other parts. Check out the first and second lines — they both begin the same way. The third and fourth lines also begin the same way. You need to play draw bends in both Hole 2 and Hole 3. In the third line, note how you alternate between Draw 2 and Blow 3 to play the same note. This can help you get through the tune at high speeds while playing the repeated note distinctly.

To hear the fiddle version of this tune, check out Track 92 (0:19) on the CD; it's played as the second verse, after the song version.

Tab 15-6: "Old Joe Clark" as a song (Track 92, first verse).

Tab 15-7: "Old Joe Clark" as a fiddle tune (Track 92, (0:19), second verse).

Soaring with Third-Position Tunes

Third position is based in Draw 4 (also Draw 1 and Draw 8). The draw notes from Hole 4 through Hole 10 form the home chord. The scale in third position is called the *Dorian mode,* which sounds minor, but with a slightly exotic character. (Check out Chapter 9 for more on third position.)

Many folk songs and fiddle tunes are in the Dorian mode and therefore adapt well to third position on the harmonica. In this section, I show you two traditional songs that have beautiful melodies and aren't hard to play in third position.

"Scarborough Fair"

"Scarborough Fair" is an English folk song with several melodies to accompany the words. The version in Tab 15-8 is the best known, thanks to the famous 1960s recording by Simon and Garfunkel. Be sure to make clean upward leaps from Hole 4 to Hole 6 and from Hole 6 to Hole 8. Be careful when you come down from Draw 8 to Blow 7 and then to Draw 6. This sequence of moves isn't hard to play, but it may feel unfamiliar because it involves two hole changes in a row.

You can find a rendition of this tune on Track 93.

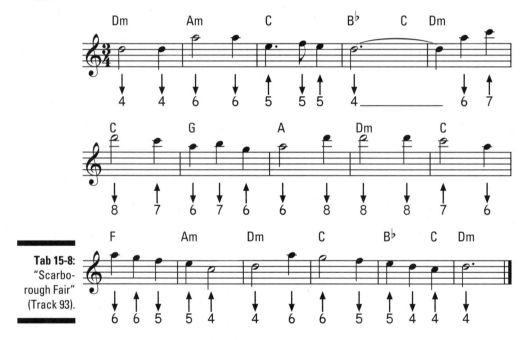

Tab 15-8: "Scarborough Fair" (Track 93).

"Tha mi sgith"

"Tha mi sgith" (pronounced *Ha-me-skee*), which means "I am weary" in Scots Gaelic, is a Scottish air that plays nicely in third position (see Tab 15-9). This tune requires an upward leap from Hole 4 to Hole 8. But after you get the hang of that leap, you'll be swirling in the Highland mists. (If you need a refresher on the best way to leap from note to note, check out Chapter 5.) You can hear this tune on Track 94 on the CD. To hear part of "Tha mi sgith" played on tremolo (0:36) and octave (1:11) harmonicas, listen to Track 98.

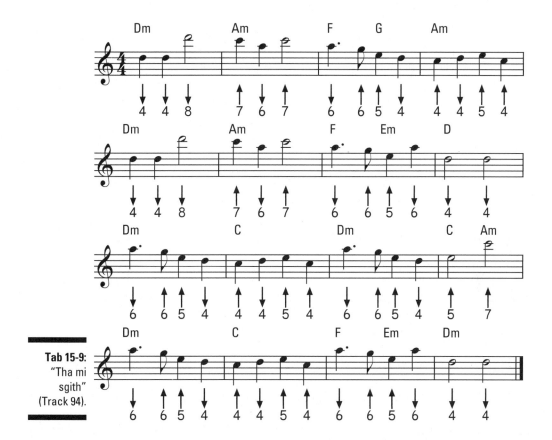

Tab 15-9: "Tha mi sgith" (Track 94).

Exploring Fourth and Fifth Positions with a Single Tune

Fourth and fifth positions play minor scales called the *Aeolian mode* and the *Phrygian mode*. Some tunes don't use all the notes of the scale and can be played in either position without sounding strange.

For example, "Saint James Infirmary" works in both fourth and fifth position. This tune has its origins in an 18th-century English song called "The Unfortunate Rake." Because the home note for fourth position doesn't exist in the low register (though you can get it by bending Draw 3 down two semitones), you play it in the high register. The tab for "Saint James Infirmary" in fourth position is shown in Tab 15-10, and you can listen to it on Track 95.

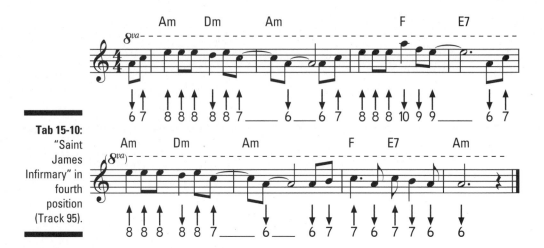

Tab 15-10:
"Saint James Infirmary" in fourth position (Track 95).

You can also play "Saint James Infirmary" in fifth position in the low register, as shown in Tab 15-11. To do this, you have to bend Draw 2 and Draw 3 down for some of the notes. _**Tip**_: In Chapter 6, I describe how you can cup a coffee mug in your hands to create a hollow, brooding tone and an exaggerated wah-wah effect. On Track 96, you can hear me using a coffee mug to add these effects to "Saint James Infirmary."

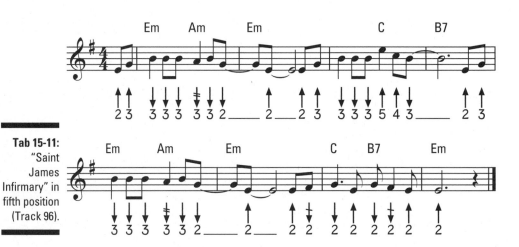

Tab 15-11:
"Saint James Infirmary" in fifth position (Track 96).

Part V
Taking Your Music to the World

The 5th Wave
By Rich Tennant

"Okay—I'll front the band. But I want someone other than Dopey on harmonica."

In this part . . .

This part helps you deal with the world of harmonica beyond learning to play. As you start excelling on the harmonica, you may want to have a little fun and make music with your friends, join a band, or even start playing in front of an audience. You also may want to get more harps, fix and improve the ones you have, and find a handy way to carry them along with your growing collection of harmonica-related stuff. I cover all this and more in this part's chapters.

Chapter 16

Putting It All Together — Your Tunes, Your Band, Your Listeners

*Y*ou can express yourself musically with the harmonica, and you can use this tiny instrument in a big way to share music with others and to make friends. Do you need to be at a professional level to play with other musicians or play for listeners? Not at all. All you really need is the desire to get together over music and find others who want to do the same. With other people involved, social skills and musical skills are equally important and involve many of the same things — listening, understanding, cooperating, sharing, knowing who to follow, and figuring out what's interesting and appropriate in any given situation.

It may be a while before you're ready to start letting the world in on your secret harmonica fascination. Or you may have been itching to bust a move since the moment you picked up a harp. Either way, don't rule out the possibility that you'll soon be ready to start getting together with others to share in the fun and satisfaction of making music with the harmonica. This chapter is designed to get you (successfully) out there in the big, bad harmonica world.

Putting Your Tunes Together

As you get good on the harmonica, one of the first things you'll want to do is find tunes that you'd like to play (as described in the later section, "Selecting tunes for the harmonica"). After you've selected a tune, you want to *arrange* it — present it with its best foot forward by choosing a good key and tempo and figuring out a beginning, middle, and ending. (See the later section,

"Make it your own: Arranging a tune" for more on how to do this.) You may even feel bold enough to step forward and sing a tune or two. If so, check out the later section "Adding vocals to your tunes."

As you add tunes to your playlist and come up with good arrangements and a few featured vocals, you'll start to develop your own unique repertoire. Who knows? Perhaps it won't be long before you're a grand artiste with a new life performing on the cruel stage for an adoring public. Then again, maybe you'll just have some fun making music in your living room with some of your closest friends.

Notice that I said tunes and not songs. After all, a song is something you sing. A tune, on the other hand, can be anything — a song with words, an instrumental piece of music, or even a hummable melody from a symphony. (Beethoven and Mozart had some pretty cool tunes!) This brings me to an important question: With the endless supply of delightful music out there, how do you choose what to play on the humble harmonica? Read on to find out.

Selecting tunes for the harmonica

Choosing tunes for the harmonica can lead you to some that are already known and played on the harmonica, or it can lead you to tunes that are completely innocent of any association with the mouth harp. But before you begin selecting your tunes, consider these guidelines:

- ✔ **Pick tunes you feel good about.** Maybe these tunes inspire you, maybe they mean something special to you, or maybe they just sound good to you. Later in this section, I outline some things to think about when selecting tunes to play on the harmonica.

- ✔ **Choose tunes within your reach.** Maybe you can already play them, or maybe you feel that you can get the hang of them quickly — a challenge is always good. Some tunes will be way tougher than they seem, but others will be surprisingly easy. The important thing is to pick a tune and attempt it — you'll never know what you can do until you try.

- ✔ **Select tunes you can share, such as:**
  - • Tunes that use the instruments that your friends play
  - • Tunes that your friends would like to play
  - • Tunes that fall within everyone's playing ability
  - • Tunes that your listening friends would like to hear

The next few sections outline some of your tune choices.

Tried-and-true harmonica tunes

Some well-known tunes feature harmonica either as the lead instrument or as a prominent accompaniment. This existing harmonica repertoire is worth exploring. The tunes work, audiences know them, and you'll really advance your playing by learning them.

A few of the best known include

- Bob Dylan's "Mr. Tambourine Man"
- The country favorite "Orange Blossom Special," featuring Charlie McCoy
- The rocking "Whammer Jammer" from the J. Geils Band, featuring Magic Dick
- Blues Traveler's "Runaround," featuring John Popper
- "Low Rider" by War, featuring Lee Oskar

If blues is more your style, you can choose from hundreds of harmonica tunes, including these favorites:

- Little Walter's "Juke" and "Blues with a Feeling"
- Sonny Boy Williamson II's "Bye, Bye Bird" and "Help Me"
- Jimmy Reed's "Honest I Do" and "Bright Lights, Big City"

Traditionally, harmonica players have learned repertoire (especially blues) by ear, but do check the Internet for tab sites (just be aware that much of what's out there may vary in accuracy). If you can read music (see Chapter 3 for the basics), the world is your oyster, but also check local stores or online sellers like Amazon.com for songbooks that include harmonica tab.

Many of these tunes will seem impossibly difficult, but they give you goals to aspire to. With practice, you'll be able to attempt the tune you want to play. And that day may come sooner than you think.

Tunes that you can adapt to the harmonica

Never be afraid to try a new style of music or a particular tune just because you've never heard it done with a harmonica. The harmonica is a surprisingly flexible instrument, and you can improve your skills by trying new things. (See Chapter 3 for some music-reading basics, in case you want to learn tunes from sheet music, and see Chapter 11 for hints on how to learn new tunes.)

Harmonica novelty tunes

You can have some fun and draw attention to your harmonica playing by picking up some of the tried-and-true harmonica tricks, which can be fun to play, fun to watch, and even fun to hear. Here are some of the best known and loved:

✔ **The talking baby.** Say, "I want my ma-maaa." Now pick up the harp and try to say the words while playing Draw 3 or Draw 4. Start each syllable with your hands closed around the harp, and then open them quickly as you start the syllable. Try starting each note bent down slightly, letting it rise as you open your hands. Bend the note down again as you close your hands before the next syllable. (You can read more about bending notes down in Chapter 8.)

This technique can be surprisingly effective at conveying all sorts of syllables — "water," "uh!-uhhh," "uh-huh," and so on. The classic "I want my mama" routine was a favorite of old-time harp players.

✔ **Trains and fox chases.** Old-time rural harmonica repertoire includes dozens of tunes that mimic things like trains, hunting, and barnyard animals. You can learn some of these tunes or you can make up your own. (Check out Chapter 21 for some CDs that include imitative tunes.) You may even think of ways to use a harmonica to imitate sounds more typical of modern life — car alarms and ringing cell phones, for instance.

✔ **Noisemakers and fast switches.** Some harmonica players, like Peter Madcat Ruth, make several fast switches between different harmonicas, duck calls, party noisemakers that puff up or unfurl, and other items, while playing in strict rhythm. These fast switches and noisemakers are visually exciting, and the sounds of the different noisemakers playing in rhythm are sure to get a chuckle. The different harps can be identical, or they can be in high or low ranges for dramatic contrast. They can even be in different keys to add excitement.

How do you go about adapting new tunes to the harmonica? Here's the obvious answer: You can simply try playing them. After you try them, here are some things to think about:

✔ **Does the tune sound good on harmonica?** If not, why bother?

✔ **Do all the notes play easily on the harmonica, stay in tune, and sound with good tone?** Bent notes can sound squawky and out of tune if you're not careful. Notes that seem awkward to reach or don't sound good may reveal areas where you can improve your playing technique. (Check out Chapters 4 and 6 for playing with resonance and good tone, and see Chapters 8 and 12 for more on bending notes.)

✔ **Will the tune surprise an audience?** Surprise can quickly turn to delight, and you can have fun playing against type by presenting a tune that the audience would never expect to hear from a harmonica.

> ✓ **Will the rendition interest an audience of folks who don't play harmonica?** Sometimes harmonica players get wrapped up in their own world and need a little perspective. After all, what's amazing to harmonica players for technical reasons may seem ho-hum to an audience that doesn't share an insider's perspective.

If you can answer all these questions in the affirmative, you're in good shape for making a fresh addition to your repertoire.

Make it your own: Arranging a tune

When you arrange a tune, you work out the details of how you'll present the tune to an audience in order to make it interesting and create the effect you want. Even a solo harmonica tune can benefit from arranging. The following points are all important elements to consider when you arrange a tune:

> ✓ **Picking a tempo:** Should the tune be played fast or slow? Find the *tempo,* or speed, that sounds best with the tune. But make sure it's a tempo that's within your ability to play.

> ✓ **Choosing a key:** Choose a key that everyone is comfortable playing in. If someone will be singing the song, make sure that the key doesn't make the melody too high or low for the singer. The singer may already know what key works for him or her, or you may have to try the song in a few different keys to be sure.

> ✓ **Beginning the tune:** When deciding how to begin a tune, you have to ask yourself whether you want to launch right into the melody or play an introduction first. An introduction may consist of the last phrase of the tune and a little pause, or it may involve playing rhythm without any melody and creating a mood or even suspense until you start the tune.

> ✓ **Ending the tune:** You have to end somehow. Simply stopping on the last note may or may not work. Listen to other arrangements in the same style as your tune. Are there standard ending phrases that musicians tack on? Or do they use big, banging, crashing blowouts? Focus on endings when you listen to music, and you'll start to get some ideas.

> ✓ **Repeating the tune:** When planning an arrangement, ask yourself how many times you want to play through the tune. You should play it enough times that it starts to become familiar to listeners (at least twice), but not so many times that you or they get tired of it (even the most gorgeous tune may get a little stale after seven or eight repetitions).

> ✓ **Changing to a different key:** Changing key during a tune can add excitement, and if you can handle the change on one harmonica, this can be a fun challenge. Similarly, if you switch harmonicas in the middle of a tune without stopping, you can impress the audience.

✔ **Playing in contrasting ranges:** Switching to the high or low register of the harmonica for part of the tune can create interesting contrasts. Chapters 9 and 10 help you become familiar with playing in different ranges.

✔ **Contrasting solo melody with accompanied melody:** If you're playing with accompaniment, try switching to unaccompanied melody. In fact, with some tunes, the entire performance may be most effective as solo melody. You can start with just melody, and then add accompaniment. You can also drop out the accompaniment, and then bring it back in later.

✔ **Passing the lead to another instrument for a change:** If you're playing with other musicians, you may want to freshen things up by bringing another instrument — or a singing voice — to the forefront.

Working out these details can help make a tune fun to play and fun to hear. If you're on stage in front of an audience, a good arrangement can make the difference between just reciting the tune and *performing* it.

Adding vocals to your tunes

Songs sung by harmonica players are an integral part of the harmonica repertoire, and you should think about cultivating a few. However, if you think you can't sing (you're probably wrong), don't rule out including some vocals in your repertoire.

One type of tune worth investigating is the *talking blues,* where you mostly talk in rhythm, and maybe sing a tiny amount. Talking blues (which are sometimes rock-and-roll tunes) include Sonny Boy Williamson II's "Don't Start Me to Talking" and Chuck Berry's "Little Queenie" and "No Money Down." You can find plenty of talking tunes that allow you to be the lead vocalist and wail on harmonica between verses.

If you're looking to play in a band, you'll be more attractive as a prospective member if you have a repertoire of songs you can sing (as well as play harmonica). Even if you're just looking to get together and play tunes with your friends, you can add to your fun by singing harmony or joining in on the chorus.

Making Music with Others

Why make music all by yourself when you can multiply your fun by sharing with a partner or a group? In this section, I take you through a few of these combinations and point out some things that can help you make your chosen combination work musically, socially, and in relation to an audience.

When you play music with others, you need to find out what keys everyone wants to play in, and you need harps that match those keys. Owning all 12 keys of harmonica will cover most situations, but if you aren't ready to spring for a full set of 12, check out Chapter 19 for a harp acquisition strategy that can help you zero in on the keys you really need without breaking the bank.

Setting some ground rules when you play with others

When you play music with other people, whether for your own enjoyment or in front of an audience, you develop a way of working together. Sometimes things just naturally fall into place without discussion. Other times you have to discuss and resolve these issues:

- **Who's going to lead?** Most groups have a leader who directs what happens when. Everybody looks to the leader to:

    - Set the tempo, and then count off the beginnings of tunes

    - Direct people when to solo and when to stop

    - Signal when to keep repeating something in a given situation and when to move on to the next part of the tune

    - Tell the group when to speed up or slow down and when to end the tune

    - Determine what tune to play next

    If the role of leader falls to you, be sure to give clear signals with looks, gestures, and body language when something is about to happen. And always encourage whoever is the center of attention.

- **Who's the center of attention?** At any given moment, the main role may be that of the lead singer or someone playing an instrumental solo. If you aren't the center of attention, your job is to support the person who is and make him or her sound good. Sometimes the best way to do that is to stop playing, or as musicians say, to *lay out.* You can read more about laying out later in this chapter.

- **What type of music will we play?** Face it, if you want to play down-and-dirty blues and your friend wants to play ethereal space music, you may not have much common ground. If you have an area of shared interest but no repertoire in common, explore some new tunes in that style. If the style doesn't appeal to you, find other people to play with.

- **How will we make sure that we're fitting together musically?** If two or more instruments simply play a melody together, the tune may not be interesting for long. The same goes for a bunch of people just ignoring each other while they play whatever they feel like. It's much more fun to look for ways to contrast and complement each other.

You can listen and adapt while you're playing, or you can work out arrangements in advance. For instance, you may work out something like this: "You sing this verse, and then I'll play lead while you back me. Then you drop out, and I go solo, and then we both come back in harmony." (For some tips on arranging a piece, refer to the earlier section, "Make it your own: Arranging a tune.")

Knowing when to lay out

Laying out is the art of sounding good by not playing. (I know it sounds contradictory, but sometimes listeners and even musicians will complement you on playing well when you didn't play at all — because the music sounded good.) However, especially for harmonica players eager to jam, discretion can be a difficult lesson to learn. After all, you're there to play, not to sit on your hands. But you can win a lot of friends by knowing when less is more.

Here are some key times to lay out:

- During a part of the song that you don't know well.
- When someone else is playing a solo.
- When someone is singing. If you've been invited to accompany the singer, remember that it's your job to make the singer sound good, not to draw attention to yourself. Play only when the singer isn't singing, and don't try to fill every tiny space between vocal phrases.
- During a *breakdown,* which is a time when just a small group of instruments play, such as just bass and drums or just guitar and vocals.
- Just after your own solo. Finish, and then lay out for a while before coming back. How can the crowd miss you if you don't go away?

Playing in a duo

A harmonica can pair with nearly any instrument, and playing as a duo offers intimacy and flexibility when you have a sympathetic partner. But you have to consider how the two instruments will fit together musically. To do so, ask yourself these questions, and then find a musical way to use the answers:

- **Are the tone qualities of each instrument similar or different?** If they're different, try trading off playing the melody to create contrast.
- **Are the instruments in the same range where they can play the same melody or harmony notes?** Being able to harmonize is always a plus, and sometimes simply playing the melody together can be effective.
- **Is one instrument in a lower range that could play (or simulate) bass?** Try doing this to create an accompaniment.

> ✓ **Can one player produce notes or chords that the other can't?** Think about using those notes to provide accompaniment to a melody or solo.

Jamming with a band

Everyone in a band has one or more roles in playing a tune. If you understand the functions and roles of other instruments in a band, you can find ways to complement the roles played by other instruments. You may find that you can fill some of those roles on harmonica. Here are the main roles:

> ✓ **Melody instruments and vocals** render the melody, or play a solo that temporarily replaces the melody. They may also play a harmony line that follows the shape of the melody but uses different notes that support the melody line and make it sound fuller.

> ✓ **Horn sections** play long chords that swell. They also play short punctuating bursts and simple melodic lines called *riffs,* which help emphasize the rhythm.

> ✓ **Rhythm guitar and keyboards** play the *chords,* which are several notes played at once that coalesce into a single sound. Chords set the mood and fill in the middle of the sound spectrum to provide the background to melody. The chords are usually played with a recognizable rhythm.

> ✓ **The bass player** has two important functions:
>
> • Interact with drums to enhance the underlying rhythm
>
> • Anchor each chord played by guitar or keyboards with low notes that give depth and fullness to the chord
>
> In addition, bass players often play a recognizable, hummable line called the *bass line.* Usually this isn't the melody but a special, catchy part of the tune.

> ✓ **The drummer** keeps time and sets the overall rhythmic feel of the tune. The drummer also often helps everyone else know where they are in a tune. He or she does so by using rhythm to signal changes in a tune, such as getting to the next verse or major section.

On harmonica you can play all the chordal, melody, harmony, and horn section roles. However, you need to be sure that you're playing notes, chords, and rhythms that don't clash with what someone else is doing. You also need to avoid interfering with the singer or the soloist. It's best to follow one simple rule here: When in doubt, leave it out.

When you're working out your harmonica part for a tune, listen, imagine, experiment, and try to come up with a lick, riff, rhythm, or harmony line that fits with the rest of the band and makes the music sound better. Don't be afraid to ask for input and advice from your band mates — bounce ideas off each other.

Strutting Your Stuff on Stage

When you're having fun casually making music with your friends, listeners may happen to be present. In this situation, you're probably focused on the music. You can ignore the listeners, or you can include them in the circle of friends that you're sharing with. But when you're out in front of an audience, the focus is on making them happy by making music.

When you play for an audience, you and any other musicians playing with you typically will face the audience instead of each other, and instead of being surrounded by friends, you may feel confronted by strangers. In this section, I take you through both the opportunities an audience presents and some techniques for dealing with the insecurities you may experience.

Looking good, feeling good

With or without an audience, good posture gives you energy and confidence, and it lets you breathe properly so you can play harmonica well. But in front of an audience, you're also presenting an appearance. Strike a confident pose that invites attention. Stand up straight and look around you at eye level.

Also, be sure to show interaction with your band mates. If you're the center of attention, move around the stage when appropriate. At dramatic points in the music, make gestures to heighten the moment. Don't feel like you have to leap around in a way that makes you feel foolish, however. Some of the most effective onstage body language uses subtle gestures to communicate with audiences. Watch good performers for cues. James Harman is a harmonica player who can use small, brief bits of body language — like a turn of the head, a torso movement that looks like a dance step, or an extension of a forearm — to captivate an audience.

A harmonica player has a special advantage — hand gestures. The opening and closing of your hands around the harp can command attention; these movements may appear sinuous, affectionate, comic, dynamic, or any combination of the above. And large hand gestures that swing the entire arm or forearm can be exciting to watch. See Chapter 6 for more on hand and arm techniques.

Preparing for an on-stage performance

When you're distracted by nerves, you can blank out and forget what you want to play. The key to getting through a performance despite anxiety is to have your part memorized so well that you could play it in your sleep. After you've memorized your part, remind yourself of the first few notes just before you perform it. Then hopefully you can go on autopilot and play despite blanking out and despite the distraction of being in front of an audience. Are jackhammers making a din right beside you? Is a small dog chewing on your ankle? No matter, because you're prepared.

When you start a tune, make sure that you have a harmonica in the right key for the tune, and that you're holding it right side up. Playing in the wrong key — or blasting out high notes when you meant to play low notes — can throw you off your stride. (Check out the Cheat Sheet for a quick reference on relating the key of a tune to your choice of harp.)

Overcoming stage fright

Say you've just stepped on stage to play in front of an audience. You thought you were totally ready for this, but now you're a jittering bunch of nerves. You can hardly say your own name or put one foot in front of the other (let alone play a coherent tune). Now what?

Stage fright is your body deciding, "Those people want to kill and eat me — I'd better *run*!" (You can thank your caveman ancestors for that adaptation.) You get a heavy hit of adrenaline, but instead of running away you're supposed to face those hungry predators and charm them out of ripping you to pieces. Now that your life seems to depend on it, you're like a deer in the headlights of an oncoming car. What do you do? Simply follow this advice:

- ✔ **Take a deep breath.** Your breathing influences your mood, so breathe gently and deeply.

- ✔ **Remember that you're still sharing with friends.** You've just opened the circle out to some folks who aren't playing along. This is your world; welcome them in and help them feel at home.

- ✔ **Remember that the audience wants to hear you and enjoy your playing.** They like you; they want you to do well.

- ✔ **Break the ice.** Acknowledge the audience by slightly bowing or saying something pleasant, like "Thanks for having me." You can even do something dumb and klutzy to burn off some adrenaline and get a laugh.

- ✔ **Channel your energy into the music.** Nervous energy is good if you can convert it into enthusiasm and use it to fuel the passion in your music-making.

- ✔ **Look above the heads of the audience.** When you're in front of an audience, all those staring eyes can be intimidating. You can avoid that disconcerting impression and still give the audience an impression of eye contact if you just look slightly above their heads.

Forget all about that trap door in the stage leading to the pit full of hungry alligators. You aren't there to be judged by Dr. Evil and his stone-faced henchmen. You're simply sharing some music with those friends of yours out there. Enjoy it together.

Recovering from mistakes

Nobody is immune to making a mistake while performing. What do the pros do? They smile and keep on going — the mistake happened and now it's gone. If you make a mistake, don't make a big face and don't stop — you don't have to wait for the mistake police to come and take you into custody. Just let the moment pass and keep on playing. Everyone wants you to succeed, and they will encourage you if you keep trying.

Taking center stage: Soloing

Now that you're on stage in front of the audience, you may be called on to take a solo. First things first: Make sure you have the first few notes of your part ready to go and that you have the right harp (and it's right side up). Now, make sure you also do the following:

- **Watch the leader to begin.** When it's time for your big moment, the onstage leader will gesture or say something to tell you to start. To make the best of your solo time, keep the following in mind:

  - Avoid closing your eyes and going somewhere else mentally. This helps you to stay connected to your surroundings and the music you're playing.

  - Play to the audience (but remain aware of the band; after all, you're making music together). Feel the energy from the audience. Acknowledge it, play to it, and let it stimulate you — it's a powerful, positive force.

- **Start by playing something easy for your first one or two phrases.** This gives you a moment to get comfortable with being out front. You can give some attention to what you're playing, some attention to the band, and some attention to the audience. You can't divide your attention if you're playing the most difficult, intense passage possible right from the start. Beginning at an easy pace also gives you somewhere to go. As you play, you can build the intensity of your solo and bring the audience with you.

- **Watch the leader to end.** Your solo will usually last for one or more verses of the tune. At the end of the first verse, watch the onstage leader. He or she may motion you to stop or to keep going. Be ready to do whatever the leader indicates.

Chapter 17

Amplifying Your Sound

A harmonica isn't a loud instrument (just try joining a marching band with drums and trombones, and you'll see what I mean). So to make your playing loud enough for others to hear in large spaces and noisy environments, you need what's called *amplification*.

When you amplify the harmonica, you can use three basic approaches:

✔ You can play *acoustic,* for a natural sound, and then amplify that sound.

✔ You can play *clean* amplified harmonica, which has a more concentrated tone than natural sound but still sounds relatively unaltered.

✔ You can play *amplified* (but not clean) by using special effects and distortion to make the harmonica sound more like a saxophone or electric guitar. Harp players usually refer to this approach as *playing amplified* (the distorted part is implied).

In this chapter, I guide you through the basics of amplification so you can make sense of all the equipment and connections, and deliver a sound that pleases both you and the audience. (By the way, all the equipment mentioned here is available in music stores as well as online.)

Getting Acquainted with Amplification Basics

Before you dive into the different amplification approaches, it's important that you understand amplification in general terms. Luckily, the basic idea of amplification is pretty simple. Here's the general outline of the process:

1. **You play into a microphone (or *mic*, as it's often called), which converts the sound into an electrical signal.**

2. **The microphone is connected to an amplifier (or *amp*), which makes the signal stronger.**

3. **The amplifier feeds this stronger signal to the speakers, which then convert the signal back into sound.**

With any luck, the resulting sound will be louder and will sound just as good.

When you play with other musicians, each individual instrument may plug into its own amplifier or into a larger *sound system.* The mic you use for harmonica may also plug into an amp or into a sound system.

A sound system is used to amplify voices, acoustic instruments (like harmonica), prerecorded backing tracks, and anything else that doesn't have its own amplifier. This system feeds microphones and other inputs into a central *mixing board* where all the sounds are mixed together and then amplified and sent to the *house speakers.* (The *house* is the part of the room where the audience gathers to listen and dance.) A performance venue may have its own sound system (and even a *sound technician* or *sound tech* to run it), or a band may bring and operate its own sound system. For now, I'm going to assume that you'll be using a house system.

Playing through a Microphone for the First Time

The first time you play harmonica with amplification, you'll probably be playing into a microphone that's connected to a sound system. Usually the mic will be a *vocal mic* — a mic you would use for singing. And that's fine; mics that work well for vocals usually work well for harmonica.

Later in this chapter, I discuss two types of microphones you can use when amplifying harmonica. For now, though, I focus on how to use the mics you might find on stages in coffeehouses, nightclubs, or other small performing venues.

Playing into a microphone on a stand

When you're playing harmonica through a sound system, the microphone will usually be on a stand, ready to amplify the voice of someone speaking or singing (or playing harmonica). Here are some pointers for getting the most out of using a mic on a stand.

- ✔ **Adjust the mic stand:** Make sure to adjust the stand so that the end of the mic is at the same height as your mouth. You don't want to scrunch down or stand on tiptoe to reach the mic — you'll be uncomfortable and you'll probably look strange to the audience.

- ✔ **Position the mic:** To maximize sound pickup of your microphone, point the length of the mic directly at the sound source. Your sound source is the back of your hands if you're holding the harp, and it's the back of the harp if you're playing Bob Dylan style with a neck rack. (Check out Chapter 19 for more on neck racks and other accessories.) Figure 17-1 shows a good placement of the mic relative to the player.

- ✔ **Position yourself in front of the mic:** Get close to the mic so that it can get a strong signal. If you start to hear a loud howling noise, that's feedback (which I discuss later in the chapter). Back away from the mic until the howling stops. Otherwise, you should get nice and close.

Figure 17-1:
A mic on a stand that's properly pointed at the sound source.

- ✔ **Make room for your hands:** An important part of the acoustic harmonica sound is the use of your hands around the harmonica. (Cupping and uncupping your hands makes the harp sound bright and dark by turns and makes vowels sound like "Wah.") Leave enough room for your hands to move without hitting the mic. Your first microphone experience may not involve a stand, however. Someone on the stage may hand you a microphone to cup in your hands along with the harmonica. In that case you need to know how to handle the situation (quite literally).

Playing with a microphone cupped in your hands

Harmonica players often cup the harmonica and the mic together in their hands (perhaps a vocal mic or a bullet mic; see the section "Getting better acquainted with microphones" later in this chapter for more information). Cupping a mic when you're playing through a sound system gives you a sound that's similar to that of a natural harmonica, but stronger and more concentrated. (Later in this chapter I discuss getting a distorted sound, which also uses a hand-cupped mic.)

Cupping the mic has some of the following positive effects:

✔ The sound is louder than if you don't cup the mic.

✔ Other loud sounds, such as drums and electric guitars, won't get into your mic.

✔ You can move around the stage and still be heard because the mic goes where you go.

Cupping the mic also causes other effects that you may or may not want. Consider the following:

✔ You have less ability to shape tone with your hands because the mic now occupies the space needed to create an acoustic chamber.

✔ The difference between loud and soft sounds will be less pronounced.

✔ The tone of your harp will be different. High frequencies become less pronounced, giving your tone a darker, mellower sound.

Don't grab a mic to cup in your hands without letting the sound tech know first. He needs to know so he can turn down the volume on that mic. Otherwise you may hurt everyone's ears and even damage the speakers, either with some very loud harmonica notes or with feedback.

Always hold the mic one finger width away from the harp. Doing this keeps the harp from bumping the mic and making noise. You also create a small tone chamber that you can work for tonal effects by changing the shape of your hand cup around the harp and mic. Figure 17-2a illustrates this tone chamber while cupping a vocal mic, and Figure 17-2b illustrates the same with a bullet mic.

Figure 17-2:
Leaving a
tone cham-
ber when
you cup a
vocal mic
and a bullet
mic.

a   b

Hearing yourself through the chaos

The first time you play on stage, you may have a difficult time hearing yourself and other players on stage because of loud amplifiers, audience noise,
and the distance from the other musicians. And when you can't hear yourself,
you may lose your place on the harp and play wrong notes.

However, a good sound system provides *monitors,* which are little speakers
on the stage floor that are aimed up at you so you can hear yourself. Before
your performance, ask the sound tech to do a *sound check.* During the sound
check, you play and the sound tech sets all the sound levels for the house
sound and the *monitor mix.* The monitor mix lets you hear yourself and the
band so you can all stay in synch and on key.

If you can't hear yourself while you're playing, you can do two things:

✔ **Request more volume in the monitors.** Motion to the sound tech by
first pointing to your ear and then pointing upward. This tells him to
raise your volume level in the monitor.

If you can't get the sound tech's attention with hand signals, say something over the mic between songs. For instance, you may say something
like, "Can I have more harmonica in the monitors, please?"

✔ **Put a finger in your ear.** No seriously, I mean it! If all else fails, a finger in
your ear will help you hear your playing or singing. Hold the harmonica in
one hand, and then use your other hand to create your body monitor.

With high sound levels on stage, you may feel overwhelmed, and then you may start pushing too much air into the harp — even if you can hear yourself. Resist the urge to honk, screech, or beat up on the harp. If you play at a normal level, you'll have better control of the harp, and you'll sound better too.

Avoiding the dreaded howl of feedback

Feedback is the painfully loud howling sound that happens when a microphone "hears itself" — the mic picks up a sound, feeds that sound through a speaker, and then picks up the same sound again and starts feeding it back through the system again.

Feedback happens in the following situations:

- ✔ **When speakers and microphones are pointed at each other.** This is why the house speakers are pointed away from the stage and why the monitors point up from the floor at an angle. The sound crew should have mics and speakers set up to avoid feedback.

- ✔ **When amplifiers are so loud that mics pick up sounds no matter which way they're aimed.** The solution is for a musician (usually a guitar player) to turn down the volume on his or her amplifier.

- ✔ **When a hollow space amplifies certain frequencies and makes them ring.** This ringing can get so loud that mics pick it up and start a feedback loop. If the room itself is ringing, the sound crew has to deal with the problem. However, the hollow ringing space could be something small right in front of the mic, such as the body of an acoustic guitar, your cupped hands, or even your open mouth. You can easily deal with these feedback sources by closing your mouth, changing the shape of your hands, or backing away from the mic a little.

Taking Amplification to the Next Level: Clean and Distorted Amplified Sound

Playing with an amplified sound starts with cupping the harp and mic together in your hands. The mic may connect to the sound system, or it may connect to an onstage amplifier. As the signal from the mic travels toward the speakers, the mic, special effects, amplifiers, and even the speakers themselves may all play a part in shaping the sound of the harmonica.

If your goal is a clean amplified sound, you want to stay as close to the natural sound of the harmonica as possible. But you may want to include a few enhancements (or *effects*) that make the harmonica sound fuller and richer. Your mic, effects, amplifier, and speakers should deliver clear sound at all volume levels without any *distortion,* which is any unwanted change to an electrical signal. If you want clean sound, you avoid distortion.

Distortion was discovered long ago by guitarists and harmonica players who were *cranking* low-powered amplifiers to maximum volume in noisy bars just to be heard over the din. The resulting sound came out distorted, and musicians quickly discovered that they could use that distortion in a musical way, and they began finding ways to create and shape it. They found that they could create distortion by overloading an amplifier, speakers, or even a microphone with a signal that's more powerful than that device could process without alteration. The overload that creates distortion is sometimes called *overdrive* or *saturation.*

In the upcoming sections, I follow the sound of your harmonica from your cupped mic through various effects to your amplifier (or to the sound system). I also discuss the things that can give you either clean or distorted sound at each stage.

Getting better acquainted with microphones

As a harmonica player, you have many choices among vocal mics and mics designed for harmonica. Here are the two most popular types.

✔ **General purpose vocal mics:** *Vocal mics* work well for harmonica. They deliver a clean, natural-sounding signal that can be processed to give a wide variety of sounds, from clean and airy to distorted and boxy.

When you look for a vocal mic, make sure that it has these characteristics:

- **Unidirectional response.** This response pattern picks up sound only from the direction it's pointed in. This helps avoid feedback and picking up unwanted sounds.

- **Ease of holding and cupping.** Make sure you can get your hands around the mic and that it isn't too heavy to hold. And test it to make sure you can cup it without getting feedback.

Vocal mics often used by harmonica players include the Shure SM57, SM58, and 545 series, and ElectroVoice RE10. The Audix Fireball is a mic that was specially designed for harmonica by altering a vocal mic design.

✔ **Bullet mics:** *Bullet mics,* named for their characteristic stubby, bullet-like shape, were designed to deliver spoken communications with maximum efficiency in noisy environments, such as bus stations. Blues harmonica players prize the harsh yet muted tonal colors of these primitive mics, together with the distortion you can get from a cupped bullet mic.

The two classic bullet mics are the Shure Green Bullet and the Astatic JT-30. Once cheap and commonly available, these models are rapidly becoming pricey collectors' items. However, Hohner sells a bullet mic based on the JT-30 called the Blues Blaster. See Figure 17-3 for a look at a bullet mic (on the left) and a vocal mic.

Figure 17-3:
A bullet mic (left) and a vocal mic.

Altering a harp's sound with effects

When you play through amplification, whether you cup the mic or not, you can use several effects that enhance your amplified harmonica. Some effects enhance the natural sound of the harmonica, while others are designed to actually alter the sound of an instrument.

Track 97 on the CD takes a short harmonica line through the following effects so you can hear how some of them impact the sound of a harmonica.

✔ **Equalization (EQ):** With EQ you can boost some parts of the sound spectrum and de-emphasize others, to make your overall tone darker, brighter, or warmer. EQ can also counter some of the thin sound associated with the harmonica. For instance, emphasizing frequencies around

250 Hz can make the harmonica tone sound thicker. (*Hz* is the abbre-
viation for Hertz, which measures vibrations per second.) *Rolling off,*
or strongly reducing, the highest and lowest frequencies (below about
150 Hz and above approximately 6000 Hz) can help you avoid feedback.
(Track 97, 0:13)

✔ **Compression:** *Compression,* which is also called *limiting,* reduces the
extremes of loud and soft in your playing so that loud sounds aren't too
loud and soft sounds aren't inaudible. Compression delivers a louder-
sounding signal without turning up the volume. It also helps avoid feedback and gives you a richer sound. (Track 97, 0:25)

✔ **Delay:** This effect sends some of the signal from your mic directly on to
the next point, while at the same time it delays another part for as little
as a few thousandths of a second. At this point, the signal is delivered as
one or more distinct repetitions. Delay helps the harmonica sound fuller
and richer. (Track 97, 0:38)

✔ **Reverberation (reverb):** This creates the impression of ambient sound
reflecting off the walls of rooms of various sizes. Reverb can create the
impression of sound occurring in a large space. However, remember
that reverb is easy to overdo. (Track 97, 0:52)

✔ **Distortion units:** A distortion unit contains two *preamps,* or small amplifiers that boost the mic signal at an early stage in the amplification process. One preamp overdrives the other to create distortion. An effect
unit is only one of many ways to create distortion; I look at additional
ways in the upcoming section. (Track 97, 1:04)

✔ **Feedback suppressors:** As the name implies, these units are designed
to prevent feedback. Feedback suppression is especially useful when
playing through an amplifier at high volume levels.

Most sound systems have EQ, compression, delay, and reverb built into the
mixing board. So when you're playing through the house sound system, you can
ask the sound tech to adjust these effects to give you a fuller harmonica sound.

Musicians often use *stomp boxes,* small metal boxes that contain a single
effect. You adjust the box to the desired setting, place it on the floor, then
turn it on or off with a foot switch. Stomp boxes are usually made for electric guitar, but they can be adapted for harmonica as well. If you walk up
to a stage and look at a harmonica player's onstage *rig,* or amplification
equipment, you may see a whole series of stomp boxes all plugged into one
another in a chain, ready to be activated in various combinations at the tap
of a toe. If you have your mic connected to one or more effects units onstage,
you can send the signal to the sound system or to an instrument amplifier.

Cranking it up with amplifiers, preamps, and speakers

Whether playing clean or distorted, harmonica players usually favor small speakers — either 8 or 10 inches in diameter — that are configured in pairs or in fours. Why? The harmonica is a high-pitched instrument, and smaller speakers deliver high-pitched sound most efficiently. They also respond rapidly — they *bark,* as harmonica players like to say.

For clean amplified playing, look for an amplifier made for acoustic guitar or keyboards. Often these amplifiers have a much higher power output than an electric guitar amplifier (200 to 400 watts versus 20 to 100 watts), giving them the ability to deliver clean sound without distortion — even at high volume. Because acoustic instruments use microphones just as harmonicas do, acoustic instrument amps have inputs that are specially designed for mics, and they may have better feedback rejection than electric guitar amps.

To play distorted, harmonica players often use electric guitar amplifiers that have been adjusted and modified to work with harmonica. Guitar amps tend to emphasize high frequencies and bright sound, which sound great with guitar but harsh with harmonica. The high power gain in the preamp stage can cause a microphone to produce feedback at low volumes. Harmonica players deal with these problems in several ways, including the following:

- ✔ **Adjust the tone controls.** To do so, turn off the bright button, turn the treble way down, turn the bass way up, and adjust the middle to taste.

- ✔ **Turn down the preamp stage.** This can only be done if this stage has a control.

- ✔ **Swap the tubes, which are internal plug-in parts that look like tiny science-fiction light bulbs.** Substituting one type of tube for another can reduce treble frequencies, lower the preamp gain, and make the amp distort more easily.

Don't attempt to swap tubes unless you know what you're doing and you understand how to avoid death and injury from electric shock.

If you value your hearing more than loudness for its own sake, you can experiment with the following ways to achieve distortion without blasting the world out of existence:

- ✔ **Play through a small amp.** A small, low-powered amp can give you distortion without ear-splitting volume. If the small amp isn't loud enough for the band or the room, put a mic in front of the amp and feed the sound through the house sound system.

- ✔ **Use a distortion effect or preamp.** Distortion effects units that work with any amp are available, and you can usually adjust the distortion to suit your desired sound.

✔ **Explore amp modelers.** An *amp modeler* is a book-sized unit that models the characteristic sound of several different effects units, preamps, amps, and even speakers. You can create and save your favorite settings and switch between them at will. Why lug around a huge amp and tons of effects units when you can just toss an amp modeler in your bag along with your harps and a mic?

Connecting Mics, Amplifiers, and Effects Units

Vocal mics and sound systems are made to work together, but harmonica players often use equipment that isn't designed to work with modern sound systems. For instance, they often use archaic bullet mics as well as amplifiers and special effects units that are designed to work with electric guitars.

To make all this stuff work together, a harmonica player has to match up the different types of physical connecters and also match an electrical value called *impedance.* Impedance is measured in *ohms* (sometimes represented by the symbol Ω). If the impedances of two connected devices don't match, the sound may be weak, thin, or muffled.

Connectors are wired onto the ends of cables and can be either ¹/₄-inch phone plugs that plug into phone jacks or 3-pin XLR connectors (either male or female; male plugs into female). Check out Figure 17-4 to see these phone plugs and XLR connectors.

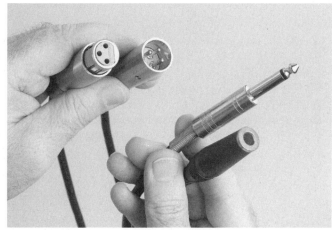

Figure 17-4: 3-pin XLR male and female connectors (left), and a ¹/₄-inch phone plug and jack (right).

Finding your sound

No matter what anyone says, the best sound for you is the one you like best. You get your sound with the right mic, the right effects, and the right amp and speakers. But how do you find what sounds best when so many choices are out there? After all, you can't afford to buy and try every possible equipment combination. Don't worry; the following tips can help you narrow down your choices:

✔ **Try out equipment at music stores.** If you already have one piece of equipment you like (such as a mic or an amp), take it with you to the music store and try it with other equipment that interests you.

✔ **Cruise harmonica discussion groups (see Chapter 20) for evaluation of different models of mics, amps, speakers, and effects, and techniques for using them.**

✔ **Talk to other harmonica players.** If you hear a pro whose sound you like, ask her about her equipment and how she gets her sound. Most harmonica players, even top professionals, love to talk about harmonicas and related subjects.

Keep the following information in mind when connecting and matching impedances for the equipment that you use to amplify harmonica:

✔ Vocal mics, sound systems, and devices that connect with them use XLR connectors. Most are low impedance (or *lo-z*) that is measured in hundreds of ohms.

✔ Guitar amplifiers and guitar effects units use phone plugs and jacks and are high impedance (or *hi-z*), with impedances of anywhere from 1,000 ohms (a *kilohm*) to about 1 million ohms (or one *megohm*).

When you connect a vocal mic to an effects unit or a guitar amplifier, you need a *matching transformer* to convert the low impedance of the mic to the high impedance of the guitar input. Matching transformers are small and come handily wired to an XLR connector on one end and a phone plug on the other.

If you run your mic through a guitar effects unit and then to the house sound system, you need a *direct box* (sometimes called a *DI box*) to match the two impedances and connector types.

✔ Bullet mics are extra-high impedance (around 5 megohms), even though they typically use guitar-compatible phone plugs. A bullet mic may need a matching transformer to connect with guitar equipment. (To find out for sure, you'll have to experiment.) A bullet mic definitely needs a direct box to go through a sound system.

Chapter 18

Improving Your Harmonica with Repairs and Upgrades

In This Chapter

▶ Picking up some helpful tools

▶ Practicing good repair habits

▶ Improving a harp's performance

▶ Repairing an ailing harmonica

*B*ack when harmonicas cost five cents and were good for a simple tune, who cared if a harp broke or played badly? You just tossed it over your shoulder and got another one. But over time harps have become better — and more expensive. And it's not just harmonicas that change over time. As your playing abilities begin to improve, you may become more demanding of your instruments. You may even form personal, intimate relationships with them. So now, if your harp breaks, it hurts — emotionally and financially. If your harp doesn't work well, it's worse than a bad hair day. It's like having a fight with your best friend.

The good news is that broken harps can be fixed, bad harps can be made good, and good harps can be made amazing. Even new, out-of-the box harps can benefit from post-factory setup. With just a little work, you can get that one stuck reed singing again, you can stop air leaks that leave you gasping, you can put your harps in sweet tune, and you can turn your instruments into high-performance barnburners.

Most of these repairs and upgrades are within your grasp if you're careful and have a little pluck. You just need a few simple tools, some know-how, and, to be honest, a fair investment of patience. With the information in this chapter, you should be able to fix most problems — as long as you're willing to try. You may even be able to soup up your harps and make them play better than the way they played out of the box.

Warranty service and repair techs

Major manufacturers guarantee harmonicas against manufacturing defects, such as reeds that don't sound or warped combs, but not against wear and tear. Harmonica manufacturers Hohner, Lee Oskar, Seydel, and Suzuki maintain repair facilities in the United States to repair manufacturing defects, and they may also perform other types of repairs for a small fee. Policies change over time, so you have to contact each company to find out what they're willing to do and how much they charge.

Independent repair techs and customizers perform a valuable service, filling the gap left by manufacturers. These folks can not only fix a harp, but they can make it play amazingly well. However, be sure to always check out the reputation of an independent tech before entrusting your harps and your cash to them.

Never toss out a broken harmonica unless it's radioactive or emitting poison gas. Instead, keep the parts to fix other harps. Every harmonica player keeps a boneyard of dead harps to raid when another harmonica's comb or reeds break or the covers get crushed. If a harp is physically broken into two or more pieces, or a reed has broken off, put it in the boneyard. Otherwise, fix it yourself or send it for repair.

Gathering the Tools You Need

Fixing your own harps is a matter of self-preservation. A harp may play beautifully out of the box and work fine for years, but more likely the playing action could be better, or a reed will stop working or go out of tune. To help you keep your harps working well, several manufacturers produce harmonica toolkits; the most economical is the Lee Oskar Toolkit, which comes with excellent instructions.

If you're really the do-it-yourself type, you can assemble a decent toolkit (and maybe save some money) by buying the following tools from your local music shop and hardware store:

- **Two small screwdrivers, one straight slot and the other cross-slot (Philips #0).** You use these tools to take apart and reassemble your harmonicas.

- **A steel shim, .002 inch (0.51 mm) thick, cut from shim stock or taken from an automotive feeler gauge set.** You use a shim to support reeds when tuning or stroking and to clear obstructions along the sides of reeds.

- **A sturdy toothpick or other small wooden or plastic stick.** This tool comes in handy when trying to poke reeds up and down.

✔ **A reed plinker made from stiff brass.** The plinker should be about $^1/_8$-inch wide, with a thin, sharp end that slides easily under a reed. If you want to, you can also use a shim in place of this tool.

✔ **A sanding detailer.** A sanding detailer is a pen-like wand with a taut band of sandpaper around it. You use it to tune reeds. It's gentler and safer than using a file or a chisel.

✔ **An embossing tool.** This can be a smooth-edged coin, wrench socket, or other smooth, rounded object that you can use for slot embossing.

✔ **A reed stylus made from a stiff strip of brass about $^1/_4$-inch wide and 4 inches long, smoothed along one end.** You can get the brass stick from a hobby shop, cut it to length, and file one end smooth. Use this tool to stroke reeds for curvature.

✔ **A shallow container, such as a jar lid.** You can use this container to hold screws and other small parts from disassembled harmonicas.

✔ **A chromatic tuner.** A portable, battery-operated tuner allows you to set the reference pitch anywhere from about A435 to A446, and it can show you differences of as little as two cents (a cent is 1/100th of a semitone). (I discuss tuning in more detail later in this chapter.)

Following Good Repair Practices

Keeping track of tiny parts in a grassy, wind-blown field in the middle of the night while trying to pry apart a small, delicate object with twigs, pebbles, and bits of scrap metal probably isn't your idea of fun. It's not mine, either, so I offer the following simple practices that will save you time and aggravation when you work on your harps:

✔ **Use reed-safe tools.** Tools that are both sharp and hard are good for tuning reeds or removing burrs and obstructions. The rest of the time, however, they risk making unwanted cuts and scratches to reeds. Most of your tools should either be dull or made of something no harder than the brass reeds. I suggest using tools made of brass, plastic, or wood.

✔ **Keep track of tiny parts.** Those tiny screws, nuts, and nails that come out of a harmonica can easily bounce away into deep carpet. To avoid losing the parts, always disassemble harps over a table, work over a smooth, bright surface, and place fasteners and other small parts in a shallow dish (or jar lid) for safekeeping.

✔ **Make small changes and test frequently.** When you're removing metal from a reed or changing a reed's shape, you can easily go too far. So be sure to make changes gradually, and test the results frequently. Working slowly may seem like a time-consuming chore, but it can prevent mishaps and save you time (and perhaps cash) in the long run.

- ✔ **Plink the reed.** When you make any change to a reed, you should *plink* it. To do this, lift the tip of the reed a few millimeters above the reedplate, and then release the reed and let it vibrate. Plinking allows the reed to settle in place, and the resulting sound tells you whether the reed still vibrates freely.

- ✔ **Test the results of tuning or adjustments.** All the parts of a harmonica affect how individual reeds play. To test the results of tuning or adjusting a reed, play the note with the harp assembled. You don't need to screw or nail it together completely. Just assemble the reedplates with the comb and the covers. Hold them together, making sure that the parts are all in alignment and reasonably airtight, and then test the reed by playing.

Making Three Simple Improvements

Even if your new harp is working okay, manufacturing processes often miss some of the finer points, and parts can rattle loose during long sea voyages. In the following sections, I show you three simple improvements you can make to a harmonica that will make it more responsive and more pleasant to hold and play.

Disassembling and reassembling a harp

For a harmonica that is screwed together, the easiest thing you can do to make it play better is to take it apart and put it back together! (See the later section, "Taking a harp apart and putting it back together," for more on how to do this.) By doing this, you can make the harmonica more airtight and improve the alignment of its parts. Harps that are nailed together are harder to assemble and reassemble and won't benefit from this procedure except in the hands of an expert.

How does taking a harp apart and putting it back together help its performance? Well, when harmonicas are assembled in the factory, the screws sometimes don't get screwed in all the way. Later, during the long ocean voyage from the factory, vibration can loosen the screws.

When you have the harp apart, take a look at the reeds, the reedplates, and the comb to get familiar with the insides of the harp.

Flexing the reeds

Harmonicas often come from the factory with reeds set high above the reedplate. High reed action can help you when you first start playing harp, because a reed set high functions even when you breathe too hard or use too much suction or mouth pressure. But as you gain finesse, you'll find that the reeds are more responsive and require less air if you can lower them a bit. So when you're ready, one simple improvement you can make is to gently flex each reed downward through its slot, as shown in Figure 18-1. (I go into reed adjustment in more detail later.)

Figure 18-1:
Flexing a reed through its slot to lower its action.

To make this performance adjustment, poke the reed through the slot with a toothpick, and then slowly and gently flex it. Don't yank or pull hard on the reed — you don't want to break or crease it. When you're done, the reed should sit a little closer to the reedplate. The reed shouldn't end up pointing down into the slot, and it should have a small gap at the tip about the same as the thickness of the reed tip. If you lower the reed too far, flex it upward until it doesn't dip into the slot and has a gap at the tip.

Smoothing sharp edges and corners

Some harps have sharp corners and edges. You can smooth and round these spots with sandpaper or a file so they don't cut into your hands and lips. To sand the edges, you need a hard, flat surface. A piece of plate glass is ideal, but a countertop will do fine. To break edges and corners, use 180-grit or 240-grit sandpaper. For finishing, a finer grit somewhere between 320 and 600 will do.

If you have a harp where the edges of the reedplates are exposed, you can drag the edges and corners against the sandpaper. If the front edges of the reedplates are exposed to your lips, remove the covers from the harmonica, and then either break the edges of the reedplates by running a file along the edge, or sand the edge, being careful not to sand the "teeth" of the comb itself.

On some harps, the rear edges of the covers may have sharp points or edges that can poke or cut your hands. Use a file to dull them.

Diagnosing and Fixing Problems

With the information in this section, you can become a harp surgeon (though you may not get to play one on TV). In the following list I describe the symptoms, give you the most likely diagnoses, and then refer you to the procedures that will bring a harp back to good health.

- ✔ **The note won't play at all.** When a note just won't play, one of four causes may be to blame. Here they are from the most trivial (and easy to fix) to the most serious and difficult:

    - Something is obstructing the free movement of the reed. To fix this issue, check out the later sections "Clearing obstructions from your harp" and "Fixing reeds that are misaligned."

    - The harp may be assembled incorrectly. Refer to the section "Taking a harp apart and putting it back together" to find out how to improve the assembly.

    - The reed action may be set incorrectly. Check out the section "Setting reed action" for more details.

    - The reed may be dead and ready to break off. In this case, you should send the harp to your boneyard of spare parts.

- ✔ **The note plays, sort of, but you hear a funny buzz.** Buzzing may be caused by debris (see the later section "Clearing obstructions from your harp"), but it also may mean that the reed is out of alignment and is hitting the sides of its slot. To see how to realign the reed, check out the upcoming section, "Fixing reeds that are misaligned."

- ✔ **You get a high-pitched squeal when you bend — or sometimes when you just play the note.** This squeal is caused by *torsional vibration* — when a reed rocks from side to side. Careful attention to your breathing and the formation of your mouth, tongue, and throat can help with this problem (see Chapters 4, 5, 6, and 7), but you can also address it by dabbing a little nail polish or beeswax in the corners at the base of the reed. Some players attach a tiny strip of adhesive tape or a drop of glue to the middle of the reed near the base to dampen the torsional vibrations.

- ✔ **A note takes too much air to play.** The harp may not be properly assembled. Specifically, the screw closest to that reed may be loose. Check out the later section, "Taking a harp apart and putting it back together," for specific directions. If this fix doesn't help, the reed action also may be set too high. See the section "Setting reed action" for details.

- ✔ **It takes too much air to play the harp, and the notes sound weak.** The reedplates may not be securely fastened to the comb (see "Taking a harp apart and putting it back together"). Or the comb and reedplates may not be fitting together.

✔ **The note sounds out of tune.** If the note is the draw (inhale) note in Hole 1, 2, or 3, and you're a novice player, you may be pulling the pitch down inadvertently. Try playing a chord with those three notes. If the chord sounds good, the notes are in tune. You can tune a harmonica to the correct pitch with tuning tools and an electronic tuner. See the later section "Tuning your harmonica" for details.

✔ **The note sticks — it doesn't play right away.** This problem indicates that the reed gap is too low and needs to be raised. Check out the section "Setting reed action" to see how to do this.

✔ **The note stopped playing and a little strip of metal fell out.** The reed has fatigued and broken. You can purchase a new harp or a new set of reedplates (if the manufacturer offers them). Or check your harmonica boneyard to see whether you have a matching reedplate that's in good shape. In any case, don't throw the harp away. Keep it for spare parts.

Taking a harp apart and putting it back together

To get at the reeds in a harmonica for tuning, adjustment, or to clear obstructions, you have to take the covers off. You may also need to remove the reedplates from the comb. If you're careful, you can disassemble and reassemble a harmonica without mishap. Just make sure there are no parts left over when you're done.

Some harps are screwed together and some are nailed together. The processes for disassembling and reassembling are different for each type of harp. I explain both in the following sections.

Dealing with harps that are screwed together

To remove the covers of a harp that's screwed together, hold the harp in the palm of one hand and use your index finger to steady the cover nut while you unscrew the bolt. Place the bolt and nut in your holding container and remove the other screw.

When replacing the covers, follow these directions:

1. **Make sure the top cover (the one with the name of the harp and any numbers) is over the blow reedplate (with the reeds inside the harp).**

   If there are grooves in the fronts of the reedplates, align the front edges of the covers in those grooves.

2. **Place one of the nuts in or over the hole (depending on what type it is) and hold it in place with the index finger of your holding hand.**

3. **Turn the harp over, place the bolt in the hole, and tighten part of the way.**

   Install the nut and bolt in the other end of the cover the same way.

4. **When you're sure both covers are properly aligned, do your final tightening.**

To remove the reedplates, use an appropriate screwdriver to loosen the screws. Be sure to place the screws in your holding container so they don't get lost.

Before removing the reedplates, mark the outside of each one with a permanent marker so that later you can easily identify which reedplate is the top and which is the bottom. The top reedplate has the blow reeds and the bottom reedplate has the draw reeds.

Here's how you reassemble a harp after removing the reedplates:

1. **Place the blow reedplate on top with the reeds inside and the draw reedplate on the bottom with the reeds outside.**

   Make sure the long reeds match the long chambers in the comb. Line up the screw holes in the reedplates with the matching holes in the comb.

2. **Insert the screws in any order, and turn each one to make sure it grabs the thread in the bottom reedplate (but don't tighten it all the way yet).**

3. **Place the harp on a table with the holes facing down to ensure that the front edges of the reedplates are aligned with the front edges of the comb, and then tighten the screws.**

   When tightening, start at the center of the harp and move outward to the right and left ends of the harp. This procedure helps keep the reedplates flat against the comb.

Never over-tighten a screw or bolt. Tighten it only until the screwdriver resists your finger pressure (except when you're cutting threads in a brand-new reedplate, which requires some additional pressure).

Contending with harps that are nailed together

Harps that are nailed together have to be pried apart with a stiff blade that's slim enough to work between the cover and the reedplates and between the reedplate and the comb. The blade needs to be at least as long as the surface that you're prying, and it needs to be stiff enough to lift it. A jackknife blade is fine for covers, but you may need an inexpensive kitchen knife to lift reedplates. When prying up reedplates, try not to cut the comb or press an indentation into the wood.

Nails often go in at funny angles, and their heads aren't at right angles to their shafts. Try to preserve the nails in formation so you can return each nail to its original hole. You can stick the nails into a piece of soft putty or clay, or you can place them in sequence on the surface of some sticky tape.

When reassembling nailed-together harps, press each nail into its original hole, and then press it down with pliers or a hard object or tool that can press the nail without touching the reeds.

Don't press so hard that you break the comb or warp the harp.

Clearing obstructions from your harp

When a reed won't play or makes some kind of sound other than a clear note, it's usually obstructed for one of the following reasons:

- ✔ Gunk (such as lint, hair, breakfast remnants, or something else that doesn't belong) has lodged between the reed and its slot.

- ✔ Burrs have been created by something hard or sharp nicking the edge of the reed or the slot.

- ✔ The reed is out of alignment and is hitting the edge of the slot (in this case, the solution is in the later section "Fixing reeds that are misaligned").

If you suspect that gunk or burrs are to blame, figure out which hole number the obstruction is in and whether it's the blow or draw note. Then remove the covers. If the stuck note is a draw note, look at the reedplate with the reeds on the outside. If it's a blow note, look at the reedplate with the reeds on the inside. Starting either from Hole 1 (with the longest reed) or from Hole 10 (with the shortest reed), count over to the hole with the problem. When you're at the correct hole, follow the directions for the particular obstruction that your harp is afflicted with:

- ✔ **Gunk:** Look for lint, hair, or anything else that's stuck under the reed, and then remove it. Always remove debris by sliding it toward the free tip of the reed. That way you avoid wedging it farther between the reed and the reedplate. By doing this, you'll also avoid snagging or deforming the reed or yanking it out of alignment.

  If the stuck note is a blow note, you may need to shine a light on the reedplate or in through the holes to find the obstruction. Carefully remove any debris you find. You may need to disassemble the reedplates from the comb to get the obstruction out.

- ✔ **Burrs:** Examine the spaces around the reeds by laying a piece of white paper on a table and shining a bright light on it. Remove the reedplate from the comb and hold it so that you're looking through the reeds to see the light reflected from the paper shining through the reedplate and around the reeds. With this technique, you can see any obstructions, such as burrs.

  To clear a burr, slide a piece of steel shim (about 0.02 inches thick) between the reed and the edge of the slot. You're trying to sweep out obstructions and slice off anything that sticks out. Be careful not to shift the reed to one side, however; otherwise, you'll have to shift it back into alignment.

Fixing reeds that are misaligned

If you suspect that you have a reed that's misaligned, remove the reedplate and hold it up to a bright light. As you look at the light around the reed, slowly rotate the reedplate from left to right to ensure that you aren't fooled into thinking the reed is out of alignment as a result of looking at it from an extreme angle.

If a reed appears to be touching one side of the slot, move the reed a little in the other direction. You can do this by nudging it with a fairly stiff shim in the direction that you want it to go. If you have a reed wrench and the misalignment is severe, you can use the wrench to turn the pad at the base of the reed. Whichever way you do it, be sure to hold the reedplate up to the light so you can see what you're doing — this is finicky work, and a small move yields a big result.

Narrowing reed slots

When your breath makes a reed vibrate, some of the air escapes along the space between the edge of the reed and the edge of the slot in the reedplate. You can narrow this space so that less air escapes. This narrowing allows the reed to respond more efficiently and with increased volume. You narrow a slot by pressing the edges of the slot inward with a hard object. Harmonica players call this *embossing*.

You can emboss a slot with a rounded object that's harder than the reedplate metal; has a smooth, regular surface without sharp edges; and has a diameter that's larger than the width of the slot. For example, you may use a coin, a socket from a socket wrench, or even the knob on the end of a tuning fork.

When embossing a slot, you start at the tip end of the reed. There, press firmly but lightly, and pull the embossing tool back along the slot, as shown in Figure 18-2a. When you press on the slot, you're also pressing the reed down into the slot, and that pressure may lower the height setting of the reed. To avoid lowering the reed setting, stop about two-thirds of the way along the reed for longer reeds. With very short reeds, you may be able to emboss only a short portion of the slot length without displacing the reed.

Too much pressure when embossing will make the slot touch the edge of the reed and will prevent the reed from vibrating. So always emboss one stroke, and then plink the reed to make sure it can still vibrate freely (refer to the earlier section, "Following Good Repair Practices," for more on plinking). If you emboss too much and cause reed obstruction, try plinking the reed several times to clear the obstruction. If that doesn't work, use a shim like you would to clear obstructions, or lightly drag the edge of a screwdriver or knife blade against the edge of the slot until the reed can move freely again.

Figure 18-2:
Embossing action along (a) the main part of the reed and (b) at the base of the reed.

To emboss close to the base of the reed without mashing the reed down into the slot, try using a sharp blade, such as a router blade. The corner edge should be pressed downward and inward against the edge of the slot. Run the corner of the blade along the edge of the slot, as shown in Figure 18-2b. Be careful not to score the edge of the reed or shift the reed out of alignment. If you have a reed wrench from a manufacturer's toolkit, you also can pivot the reed away from the slot, emboss, and then swing the reed back into place.

Setting reed action

Reeds can be adjusted so that they respond to a player's breath in a particular way — for instance, to strong or gentle attacks or to heavy or light breathing. The result of these adjustments is called reed action. You set reed action by changing the height and curvature of the reed relative to the reedplate.

For maximum efficiency in responding to your breath, the ideal reed curvature starts with the base of the reed as close to the reedplate as possible. The reed remains parallel to the reedplate for about half its length, and then it curves gently up toward the tip, as shown in Figure 18-3. By changing the curvature of the front half of the reed, you can influence the reed's response to hard and soft attacks and to bending (which I explain in the upcoming sections).

Reed is flush to reedplate
near the base

Reed curves upward
to create gap at the tip

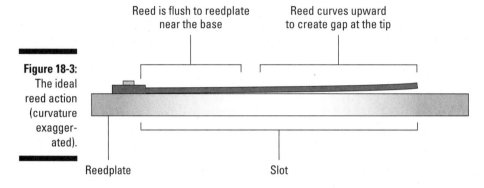

Figure 18-3:
The ideal
reed action
(curvature
exagger-
ated).

Reedplate

Slot

The reed should never dip into the slot and should never curve downward from base to tip. A reed that does this will respond poorly or not at all when you play it.

You start setting reed action at the base of the reed, close to the rivet, and proceed toward the tip. You can raise the base of the reed by inserting a shim and lifting the reed. However, you're more likely to want to lower the base to increase reed efficiency. You do this by gently pressing the base of the reed with your thumbnail, as shown in Figure 18-4.

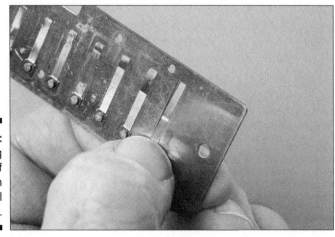

Figure 18-4:
Lowering
the base of
a reed with
thumbnail
pressure.

After you lower the base of the reed, the rest of the reed may be pointing into the slot, which will prevent it from sounding. So you have to raise the rest of the reed out of the slot, and then give it the curvature that will result in your desired response.

If you flex the entire reed upward as I show you earlier in the section, you'll raise the lowered reed base. However, you may want to leave the base of the reed where it is and raise the rest of the reed. You can limit the effect of flexing to one portion of the reed by holding down part of the reed with a finger or tool and flexing the tip. (Refer to the earlier section, "Flexing the reeds," for more information on flexing.)

However, the *stroking method* allows you to introduce a curve to a precise area of a reed. When you use the edge of a tool to stroke a reed while applying pressure, the reed will curl toward the edge — like curling a ribbon with a scissor blade. If you stroke the top of a reed, it will curve upward; if you stroke the bottom through the slot, it will curve downward. Always support the reed, and stroke at the point at which you want the curvature to begin. See Figure 18-5 for examples of the flexing and stroking methods of curving a reed.

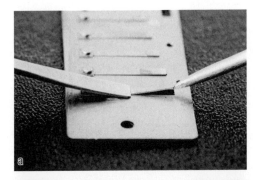

Figure 18-5:
Raising the curvature of a reed by flexing (a) and stroking (b).

A reed's response to breath

If a reed is set so that it sits high above the reedplate, it will respond to hard attacks (when you start to play a note, you *attack* it) and high breath volume, but it will take a lot of breath to play at all. A reed set very low to the reedplate will respond to soft attacks and low breath volume, but it may blank out if you hit it too hard.

A reed needs to have a gap under its tip or it won't start vibrating. The gap width should be approximately equal to the thickness of the reed tip; keep in mind that long reeds require higher gaps than short reeds. A higher gap will favor hard playing (the combination of hard attacks and high breath volume) and a lower gap will favor soft playing. You should gap your harps to respond efficiently to your style of playing while delivering maximum volume and efficiency. Finding the gaps that work for you is a matter of experimenting.

A reed's response to bending

When you bend a note down (see Chapter 8), both the blow and the draw reed respond. The reed that's higher in pitch bends down and moves closer to the reedplate. Notes that bend a long way, like Blow 10, Draw 2, and especially Draw 3, can use a little extra curvature away from the reedplate. This curvature allows these notes more travel toward the reedplate as they bend down.

The reed that's lower in pitch bends up and moves away from the reedplate. This reed can benefit from being gapped slightly closer to the reedplate so that it has more travel range as it pulls away from the reedplate.

On the other hand, when you bend a note up (see Chapter 12), the higher-pitched reed in the hole opens and moves away from the reedplate, while the lower-pitched reed stays motionless. Both reeds can benefit from being set close to the reedplate. The reed that travels away from the reedplate can travel farther from a starting point that's close to the plate, while the reed that stays put can choke out more easily from breath pressure if it's close to the plate.

Overall reed response strategy

An ideal reed response allows you to bend notes down and up with equal ease and play as hard or soft as you like. However, balancing these priorities sometimes leads to conflicts. Bending down and up have slightly conflicting needs, and soft playing and bending up (favored by low reed settings) may conflict with the ability to play hard (favored by higher reed settings).

Sometimes you can help manage these conflicts by altering your playing technique. For instance, you can strengthen your bending-up technique so you can overbend reeds with higher settings. You can also learn to temper hard playing with a softer attack and lower breathing volume so that reeds don't need to be set as high as before.

No matter how much you improve your technique in different areas, reed adjustment always plays a role. Your best strategy is to find a reed setting that gives you maximum reed efficiency — the most vigorous vibration with the least effort. Then you can tweak that setting just slightly to satisfy a specific need — a deep bend in this hole, an overbend in that hole, and an overall soft or hard attack.

Tuning your harmonica

Harmonicas can go out of tune with playing, and even new harps straight from the factory aren't always in good tune. But you don't have to accept what you get — you can correct out-of-tune notes.

Tuning follows straightforward procedures, but it has some ins and outs that you need to know. So in the following sections, I introduce you to the basics of the tuning process, I show you how to test your tuning, and I discuss why you might deliberately deviate from the tuning meter.

Always tune reeds after you have done any other reed work, such as embossing the slots, aligning the reeds in their slots, and setting the curvature and offset of the reeds. Any of these other actions can change the pitch of a reed.

Understanding how to tune your harp

The first two things you need to know about tuning are:

- ✔ To lower pitch, you remove a small amount of metal from the surface of the reed at its base.

- ✔ To raise pitch, you remove a small amount of metal from the surface of the reed at its tip.

You'll find that the easiest way to tune a reed is to have direct access to the reeds you want to tune. A reed will be mounted on one side of the reedplate, and that's the side you want facing you. When you remove the covers from a harmonica, the draw reeds are facing you. However, the blow reeds are inside the comb; to expose them you need to unscrew the reedplates from the comb. You can tune the blow reeds on the comb, but it's much easier with the reedplates removed. Plus, this way you're less likely to damage the reeds or push them out of alignment.

To tune a reed, follow these steps:

1. **Support the reed by placing a shim under it.**

    Metal, thin plastic, or even a piece of stiff paper will work. Just remember to support the reed and not to pry the base of the reed up from the reedplate by using a shim that's too thick.

2. **Remove metal from the reed by stroking it with a sanding detailer that has a medium-to-fine grit sanding belt.**

   The grit number may not be marked on the belt, but you can feel the relative fineness or coarseness of the grit with your finger.

3. **Sand in a small area along the length of the reed.**

   Don't sand across the reed, because doing so may create burrs that strike against the slot edge — and any marks across the reed can weaken it. Also, don't press hard when sanding because pressure can change both the curvature and the offset of the reed. Figure 18-6a shows how to tune a reed using a sanding detailer near the base to lower pitch. Figure 18-6b shows how to tune a reed near the tip to raise pitch.

   When sanding the tip of the reed, the safest procedure is to sand outward toward the tip. (If you sand inward, you might snag the reed and fold it in half.) However, be careful to check for burrs. When you sand near the base of the reed, you can safely sand inward.

4. **Every few strokes, test the tuning by removing the shim, plinking the reed, and then assembling the harp and playing the note.**

   You can read more about testing your tuning results in the next section.

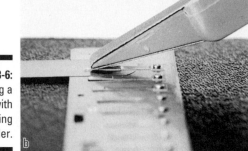

Figure 18-6:
Tuning a reed with a sanding detailer.

Warm reeds vibrate at a lower pitch than cold reeds. Your breath warms reeds up, so it's a good idea to tune warm reeds. Keep reedplates in an electric heating pad for a short time before tuning, and keep them warm while you work.

Testing the results of your tuning

Test your tuning either with an electronic tuner or by playing the note together with another note on the harp. If you can, play the note you're tuning together with the same note an octave higher or lower (you do this by playing tongue blocked intervals; see Chapter 7 for more on this). You may hear a quavering when the two notes play together. That quavering is called *beating*. The faster the beating, the farther out of tune the notes are. As the beating slows down, the notes get closer to being in tune.

How do you know whether the note you're tuning is too low or too high? And how can you be sure that the other note is in tune? That's where a tuner comes in handy. A chromatic tuner tells you whether any note is sharp or flat (and by how much) relative to a reference pitch. At this point, things start to get complicated for three reasons:

- ✔ The standard reference pitch A440 (Middle A vibrating at 440 Hertz) is often ignored by both manufacturers and musicians.

- ✔ Harmonicas are often tuned higher than reference pitch to compensate for the fact that a player's breath will push the pitch of a note down slightly.

- ✔ Temperament — fine-tuning individual notes up or down relative to the reference pitch — varies according to the preference of manufacturers (and players). Just intonation is a temperament that makes one key play beautifully in tune and all others out of tune, while equal temperament puts all keys equally (though mildly) out of tune. Manufacturers and players use a variety of temperaments, too many to describe in this book. If the manufacturer publishes the temperament for your harp (they may call it something like a tuning chart), use that as a reference. Otherwise, I suggest that you either tune to equal temperament or use the chart in Figure 18-7. (For detailed information on harmonica temperaments, visit www.patmissin.com.)

If just one note in the harmonica sounds out of tune, play the same note an octave higher or lower into the tuner and note how much above or below pitch it is. Then play the out-of-tune note. If it shows up lower or higher than the other notes, you'll know whether you need to raise or lower the pitch and by approximately how much. The rest of the job is to tune a little and then test a little until it sounds right. For the final result, your ears are more important than the tuner.

After you tune a reed, its pitch continues to change, especially when you tune it up — the pitch will continue to rise. So whenever possible, leave the reeds alone to settle for a few days after you first tune them. Then you can do some touch-ups.

Figure 18-7 shows the compromise temperament that Hohner uses for Marine Band harmonicas. You can use this temperament if you don't have any other information about the temperament of the harp.

Figure 18-7:
Marine Band compromise temperament.

Blow	0	−12	+1	0	−12	+1	0	−12	+1	0
Hole	**1**	**2**	**3**	**4**	**5**	**6**	**7**	**8**	**9**	**10**
Draw	+2	+1	−11	+2	−12	+3	−11	+2	−12	+3

Chapter 19

Acquiring More Harps and Other Useful Accessories

Somewhere on a dark moor, lightning bolts are flashing over a windswept crag where a mad harmonica scientist is exulting over a towering collection of harmonicas *that he never plays.* You're probably a long way from that level of obsession (but watch out — harmonica fever has a way of sneaking up on you). Still, if you fall for the harmonica even a little bit, I bet you'll want to own a few more harmonicas to play in various keys and styles. And if you do want to play your harmonicas and not just cackle with insane glee over your vast collection, some useful tools can help you practice your harmonica melodies, licks, and riffs.

Collecting Additional Diatonic Harps

The diatonic harmonica is designed to play in just one key. (Check out Chapter 2 for the lowdown on this type of harmonica and why it's great for beginners.) Even though you can play it in several keys or positions (see Chapter 9), you likely want several keys of harps so you can just pick up a harp in the right key for whatever song comes up. The following sections help you formulate a strategy for what keys you should acquire and the order in which you should get them.

The most popular keys are available just about everywhere harmonicas are sold. As you start to seek out harps in the more obscure sharp and flat keys, you may have to special order them, or get them from online retailers that specialize in harmonicas.

Purchasing popular keys

As a general rule, the most popular keys of harmonica are C, A, D, and G, in roughly that order. Add to that the keys of F and B♭, and you have a basic set of six that's versatile and travels light. This set also gives you the most popular keys for playing with guitar players.

If you want to work your way up to a full set with all 12 keys, here are three possible strategies:

- ✔ Acquire the remaining six keys in diminishing order of popularity: E♭, E, A♭, D♭, B, and F♯.

- ✔ Acquire harps for the keys of specific tunes you play or to play in the favorite keys of the musicians and singers you regularly play or jam with.

- ✔ If you play a lot with horns (saxophones, trumpets, trombones), then you'll want harps that play in flat keys, keys that have a flat in the name or in the scale. The best order to get these keys (with some overlap from guitar keys) is: F, B♭, E♭, A♭, and D♭. To those keys, add a harmonica in G♭ (F♯ is the same thing), and you'll have the flat keys covered pretty well.

Expanding your range with harps in high and low keys

A C-harp has Middle C as its lowest note, and its range is more or less in the middle of harmonica ranges. Harmonicas in the keys of G, A♭, A, B♭, and B are all lower in pitch than a C-harp and have a deeper, mellower sound, while harps in the keys of D♭, D, E♭, E, F, and F♯ are higher than a C-harp and have a crisper, brighter sound.

Harp players like to extend the range of harmonica sounds with high G- and high A-harps for an even brighter, crisper response than an F♯-harp. But players also like the deep, mellow, muscular sounds as the harmonica range extends down toward the bass, from low F all the way down to double-low F, two full octaves below a regular F-harp. High and low harps can be a lot of fun to play and can add variety to your sound.

Adding Variety to Your Harmonica Kit

The diatonic harmonica is the most popular in North America, but many other types of harps are worth checking out. (Refer to Chapter 2 if you need a refresher on the basics of the diatonic harp.) In the following sections, I introduce you to three other popular harmonicas that you may want to explore.

You may find chromatic, tremolo, and octave harps in stores that have a broad selection of harmonicas, but many stores stick to the most popular models and keys of diatonics, rounded out by one or two chromatics. You may have to go online to find other types (though, depending on where you live, you may find inexpensive Chinese tremolos in variety stores).

Chromatic harps

A *chromatic harmonica* has a button on the right side, as shown in Figure 19-1. When you press the button, you get a different set of notes tuned one semitone higher than the main key. For instance, if you have a chromatic harp in C, you get the key of C♯ when you press the button. The two sets of notes provide you with a complete chromatic scale, giving you the potential to play any scale in any key. Chromatic harmonicas are used for jazz, classical music, movie soundtracks, and occasionally for blues and popular music, but for some reason the chromatic is most popular in Asian countries, where it's used mainly for classical music.

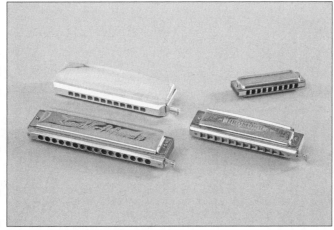

Figure 19-1: Some 12- and 16-hole chromatic harmonicas, with a 10-hole diatonic for scale.

Chromatic harmonicas evolved from the diatonic harmonica, and there are a lot of similarities between the two instruments. The note layout of the chromatic takes the middle register of the diatonic (Holes 4–7) and repeats it through three octaves. This repetition allows the note layout to stay consistent. In other words, there's no top-octave shift and no missing notes in the bottom octave. (See Chapter 5 for more on the registers of the diatonic harmonica.) This note layout is called *solo tuning*. Figure 19-2 shows a comparison between the standard diatonic note layout and the solo tuning layout.

Figure 19-2: Note layouts for diatonic and chromatic harmonicas.

Diatonic:

	1	2	3	4	5	6	7	8	9	10
Draw	D	G	B	D	F	A	B	D	F	A
Blow	C	E	G	C	E	G	C	E	G	C

Chromatic:

	1	2	3	4	5	6	7	8	9	10	11	12
Draw	D	F	A	B	D	F	A	B	D	F	A	B
Blow	C	E	G	C	C	E	G	C	C	E	G	C

Despite what you may have heard, the chromatic is no harder to play than the diatonic, takes the same amount of wind, and yes, you can bend notes on it. The chromatic does require a slightly different approach from the diatonic, but in some ways it's actually easier to play than the diatonic.

Some of the great harmonica music you hear, like most of what Stevie Wonder plays, is played on a chromatic harp. Most good blues harmonica players use a chromatic for some tunes, usually in third position. (Chapter 9 discusses harmonica positions in more detail.)

Most chromatic harmonicas come in the key of C, though you can get them in several other keys. The most popular types are the 12-hole chromatic, with the same three-octave ranges as a diatonic, and the 16-hole chromatic, which has a deep low octave added. Several major manufacturers make solid chromatic harmonicas, including Hering, Hohner, Seydel, and Suzuki.

Listen to Track 98 for some third-position blues played on a chromatic harmonica. This track uses the same backing music as Track 78, where a diatonic harp also plays third-position blues.

Tremolo and octave harmonicas

The most popular type of harmonica worldwide is the tremolo. Tremolo harps are inexpensive and easy to find in the United States, even though few people play them here (Mickey Raphael of the Willie Nelson band is a fine exception). However, in many countries, including Ireland, Canada, Mexico, Scotland, China, and Japan, tremolo is a favorite melody instrument for playing folk music.

Tremolo harps have two reeds for every note, mounted in two stacked rows of holes. One reed is tuned slightly higher than the other, and the slight difference in pitch causes a quavering sound, or beating, that produces the tremolo sound. Octave harmonicas are double-reeded harps that have two reeds tuned an octave apart. The low reed gives fullness to the tone while the high reed gives it brightness. Figure 19-3 shows you what tremolo and octave harmonicas look like.

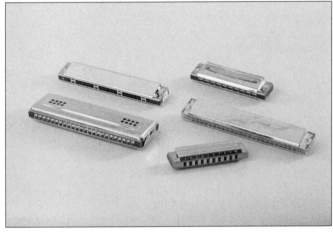

Figure 19-3:
Tremolo and octave harmonicas with a ten-hole diatonic for scale.

Like regular diatonics, tremolo and octave harmonicas come in several different keys. Major manufacturers include Hohner, Huang, Seydel, Suzuki, and Tombo.

Note layouts on double-reed harps are similar to the note layout of a standard diatonic harp but with one important difference: Blow notes and draw notes are side by side in neighboring holes instead of being in the same hole. So one hole on a diatonic is matched by four holes on a double-reed harp (upper and lower blow and draw notes). German and Asian note layouts differ in the low notes (on the left). The German layout omits draw notes from the scale to give a strong chord, just like the diatonic note layout does, while the Asian layout includes all notes of the scale. Most Asian double-reed harps use the German layout. Hohner, however, uses both layouts, depending on the model. Figure 19-4 shows typical note layouts for German- and Asian- style double-reed harmonicas in the key of C. The blow notes are shown with a white background, and the draw notes are shown with a shaded background (holes on double-reed harmonicas are seldom numbered).

On Track 98 of the CD, you can hear tremolo harmonica (0:36) and then octave harmonica (1:11) playing snippets from "Tha mi sgith" (Tab 15-9) and "Mrs. MacLeod of Raasay" (Tab 15-4). To hear these same tunes played on a standard diatonic harp, listen to Tracks 94 and 90.

Figure 19-4:
German and
Asian note
layouts for
double-reed
harmonicas.

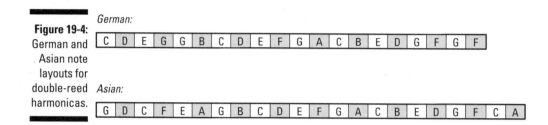

German:

| C | D | E | G | G | B | C | D | E | F | G | A | C | B | E | D | G | F | G | F |

Asian:

| G | D | C | F | E | A | G | B | C | D | E | F | G | A | C | B | E | D | G | F | C | A |

Making Your Harps Portable with Carrying Cases

How do you lug your growing collection of harps around and keep them safe, organized, and ready to play? Harp players tend to come up with highly personal solutions, and you may need to experiment to find what suits you best. Here are a few suggestions:

✔ **Utility cases:** You can adapt available items such as tackle boxes, tool boxes, camera cases, and other portable hard cases. These cases are rugged and offer good protection (though they may be bulky). They often have enough room for a dozen or so harps and spares, electronic cables, microphones, and repair tools. Some cases have built-in partitions that just happen to fit individual harmonicas. Hetrick Harmonica (www.harpcase.com) took this idea a step further and designed a series of utility cases specially designed for harmonicas.

✔ **Harmonica briefcases:** Hohner and Fender both make hard-shell harmonica cases with handles. These cases look cool, offer some protection against crushing, and are good starter cases, but they aren't configurable or expandable. Make sure that they offer enough space for the harps and accessories you want to carry. Even the coolest looking case is a drag if it doesn't carry all your stuff.

✔ **Pouches:** Both Hohner and Lee Oskar offer simple fabric wraparound pouches that hold six diatonic harps. These are great for traveling light, but they don't protect your harps from impact and they aren't useful if you need to carry accessories or larger types of harmonicas, such as chromatics or tremolos. However, you can go up-market with leather pouches that are custom-designed to hold any combination of harps. Cumberland Custom Cases (www.cumberlandcustomcases.com/catalog.php) is one company that offers a wide variety of pouches (along with belts and bandoliers if you really want to get flashy while you're on stage).

Figure 19-5 shows a hard-shell case and a soft pouch.

If you're interested in buying a harmonica case or pouch, you can go online and search for "harmonica case" or "harmonica pouch." Or you can check out the selection at your local music store (or hardware store if you want to check out utility cases).

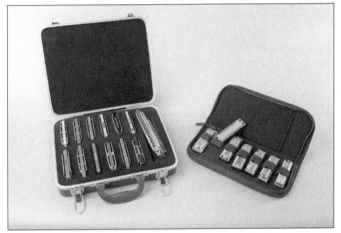

Figure 19-5:
Harmonica
hard case
and soft
pouch.

Exploring Helpful Practice and Performance Tools

All you really need to practice harmonica is some playing time, a harmonica, and the commitment to do the work. But a few tools can help make your practice even more productive and enjoyable. Consider the following tools:

- **Metronomes:** A *metronome* is a small device that ticks out a steady beat at a speed you choose. When you're trying to learn music you haven't played before, you may find yourself slowing down throughout the song, or you may even speed up just to get through it. A metronome keeps you in time and on the beat. Staying in synch with a metronome can be hard work, but it really pays off.

- **Recorders:** What do you really sound like when you play? The only way to be sure is to record yourself and listen back. When you hear yourself while you're not playing, you can really focus on what needs work, and your playing will improve rapidly. Find an inexpensive, portable audio recorder that has decent sound quality, and record parts of your practice sessions and rehearsals. Some players keep a diary of recorded practices over time to evaluate their progress. If you're taking lessons, record the lessons with your teacher's permission. (Getting permission is common courtesy, and some teachers actually forbid recording, so be sure to ask.)

✔ **Backing tracks:** If you don't have a band or guitar-playing buddy who's patient enough to spend half an hour running through a tune that you're trying to learn, you can get *backing tracks* with musicians playing the accompaniment, leaving the tune or solo to you. Or you can pick up a program like Band-in-a-Box, which plays any tune at any tempo (speed) and in any key or style.

✔ **Neck racks:** If you already play guitar and want to start strumming along as you try out your new harp-playing skills, you may want to grow a third arm to hold the harp. However, you can avoid the expense of surgery (and custom-made shirts) by getting a neck rack to hold the harp up to your mouth while you play guitar. Neck racks are made of a loop of stiff wire that hangs around your neck and sweeps up to your mouth, as shown in Figure 19-6. Rack playing is a time-honored tradition of folk, country, and rock music, and you may want to try it if you play guitar.

Make sure you get a rack that brings the harp all the way up to your face so you don't have to crane your neck down. Also, be sure to choose one that allows you to lock the holder in position so the rack doesn't loosen and cause the harp to droop farther and farther away from your face. After all, your neck will only stretch so far.

Figure 19-6:
A
harmonica
neck rack.

Part VI
The Part of Tens

The 5th Wave   By Rich Tennant

"Very nice audition, Vince. Let's talk a minute about that little thing you do at the end with the microphone."

In this part . . .

Harmonica has a rich tradition, and the *For Dummies* series adds something unique: the Part of Tens, which is made up of top-ten lists of fun and helpful information. In this part, I give you ten ways to connect with other harmonica players and enthusiasts, and I provide ten styles of music that include harmonica, along with the greatest players and CDs in each style.

Chapter 20

Ten Ways to Connect in the Harmonica World

In This Chapter

▶ Discovering ways to join the harmonica community

▶ Using online resources to your advantage

*H*armonica players, even top professionals, are amazingly generous and enthusiastic about this odd little instrument. However, finding other harmonica players to jam with, learn from, and just hang out with used to be difficult. Your next-door neighbor could have been a harmonica player or enthusiast and you may never have known. Now it's ridiculously easy to connect with like-minded parties. You have tons of options, including the ten that I list in this chapter.

Take Lessons from a Pro

Dozens of excellent harmonica books and videos are available (you've — ahem — already discovered one of them), but a teacher can quickly show you something that may take pages to describe. A teacher can also offer immediate corrective feedback on dozens of physical nuances of technique. Check out www.craigslist.org and www.learningmusician.com online or local classified ads and music-store bulletin boards for teachers offering their services.

Even though face-to-face interaction is best, harmonica teachers are increasingly using Webcams and online connections to teach by video at a distance. So if you can't find a local teacher that you like, the world is your oyster.

Enjoy Harmonica Performances

If you go to a concert that features or prominently includes harmonica, you're bound to meet other harmonica players and enthusiasts. To find harmonica performances to attend, check listings in your area for concerts and club dates by blues, jazz, and even classical acts that feature or include harmonica players. Also check out BassHarp's International Giglist, where many touring harmonica players list their upcoming performances. You can find the gig list at www.bassharp.com/bh_itin.htm. (BassHarp is Danny Wilson, a harmonica historian and former bass harmonica player for the Harmonicats.)

Seek Out Musical Events That Don't Focus on Harmonica

Harmonica events and activities aren't the only ones worth checking out. Harmonica can play a significant role in events where the instrument isn't the main focus. In fact, even when no harps are on stage, harmonica players still turn out, especially for concerts in styles of music with a strong harmonica association, such as blues. If blues isn't your style, seek out places and events where people get together to play the kind of music you like. You may just meet other harmonica players. However, you also may get involved as the only harmonica player in the territory — sometimes it's fun to be special.

Let Loose at Jam Sessions and Open Mic Nights

Jam sessions exist for many styles of music — rock, blues, jazz, Irish, flamenco, and many more. At a jam session, musicians play for their own enjoyment; the audience is secondary. In this situation, musicians feel less pressure to put on a show. It's more of a collegial atmosphere, though sometimes players compete with each other.

Jam sessions are a great way to become familiar with styles of music. At jam sessions, you can hang out and join in when you feel ready. (Refer to Chapter 16 for more on playing with others.) Some jam sessions are held in bars and nightclubs at off times (such as a Sunday afternoon), and others take place at meetings of clubs that are dedicated to a style of music. Either way, you have to do some digging to find them.

Some bars and nightclubs offer open mic nights once a week. These venues offer anyone the chance to get in front of the crowd and play one or two songs. Karaoke bars do this on a regular basis for people who want to get up and sing. In these bars, you may be able to play harmonica for the crowd, either as a feature or to accompany a friend who sings. Check the entertainment and club listings in your local newspapers.

Contribute to Harmonica Discussion Groups Online

Online discussion groups are a great way to converse with other harmonica players worldwide. You aren't obligated to speak up, however. You can just lurk and read posts by others or research the archives of a group for information on a topic. Never hesitate to ask a question, though — all questions are valid as long as they relate to the general topic of harmonica playing or the specific subtopic of a particular online forum.

Here are the main harmonica forums, starting with the biggest, followed by forums with more specialized subject matter (and smaller populations):

- **Harp-L** (www.harp-l.com): Founded in 1992, Harp-L is the oldest (and probably the largest) harmonica discussion group on the Internet. Free of any commercial or other organizational ties, its only rule is civility and relevance. Anyone from the beginner to the advanced level is welcome. In fact, some of the top pros hang out at Harp-L, along with builders and fixers of amplifiers, microphones, and harmonicas. Discussions can be heated, but civility prevails and a lot of excellent information is freely offered. Posts from the very beginning are archived and searchable.

- **HarpTalk** (launch.groups.yahoo.com/group/harptalk): HarpTalk is sponsored by Coast to Coast Music, a mail-order harmonica specialty retailer. Like Harp-L, HarpTalk is a general discussion forum, but players who aren't on Harp-L show up here, and the passionate disagreements that occasionally crop up on Harp-L almost never occur on HarpTalk.

- **Bluegrassharp** (launch.groups.yahoo.com/group/bluegrassharp): Bluegrassharp, also sponsored by Coast to Coast Music, is one of the few harmonica discussion groups centered on a specific style of music. Some knowledgeable players hang out here, and topics cover an area that often extends beyond the confines of bluegrass to the related areas of country and old-time string band music.

- **Slidemeister** (slidemeister.com): Chromatic harmonica players are a minority in a mostly diatonic world, so chromatic enthusiast A.J. Fedor created this site and discussion group for chromatic harmonica only. No diatonic discussion is allowed except in a special area. This is a great resource for discussion and questions about the chromatic harmonica. (Flip to Chapter 19 for more on chromatic harmonicas.)

If you're interested in a particular style of music, check out discussion groups that focus on a musical style as opposed to a single instrument. This way you may be able to find other harmonica players who share interest in your chosen style, whether it be polka, gypsy swing, Tex-Mex, or whatever. To find groups, cruise Yahoo! Groups (launch.dir.groups.yahoo.com/dir/music), or just Google the name of the style together with "discussion group" (the quotation marks help to narrow the search).

Surf Informational Web Sites

The Internet is bursting with all kinds of harmonica information. Some of it you have to pay for, but most is freely available with a little searching. Here are the best of the best harmonica sites (at least for the moment):

- **Diatonic Harmonica Reference** (www.angelfire.com/tx/myquill): The brainchild of Michael Will, this site offers a huge amount of basic and not-so-basic information about the diatonic harmonica.

- **Harmonica Lessons.com** (www.harmonicalessons.com): If you're willing to pay for online harmonica information, Dave Gage's Harmonica Lessons.com is an excellent site with plenty of modular lessons available (some content is free).

- **Harmonica Sessions** (www.harmonicasessions.com): This bimonthly online magazine from music publisher Mel Bay offers free information on harmonica playing, repair, and gear from knowledgeable authors. (Note that I'm a contributor to this magazine.)

- **Pat Missin's harmonica site** (patmissin.com): Pat Missin could start the University of the Harmonica all by himself. He has done an enormous amount of research in the history of the harmonica. He also knows a lot about the physics of the harmonica and about fine-tuning harmonicas and alternate note layouts.

- **Social networking sites:** Many musicians, including some very fine harmonica players, offer music and information via social networking sites like MySpace (www.myspace.com) and Facebook (www.facebook.com). If you're curious, search for specific players you know about, or search with words like "harmonica" and "harp" and see what you find. After all, one connection leads to another.

- **YouTube** (www.youtube.com): Several noteworthy harmonica players, including David Barrett, Jon Gindick, Adam Gussow, Jason Ricci, and Ronnie Shellist, have offered free instructional videos on YouTube. Just search for their names at the YouTube site, or you can do a general search for "harmonica lesson."

Join a Harmonica Club

Sometimes it's great to get together with other harmonica players to talk shop, jam, and learn from one another. One way to do this is to join a harmonica club. Here are some good opportunities:

✔ **SPAH** (www.spah.org): The Society for the Preservation and Advancement of the Harmonica, or SPAH, is a national-level harmonica club in the U.S. and Canada. It publishes the quarterly magazine *Harmonica Happenings*. You can contact SPAH to find out about local harmonica clubs in your area.

✔ **The National Harmonica League** (harmonica.co.uk): The NHL is the national-level harmonica club in the United Kingdom and can connect you to other players and to harmonica activities in the British Isles. Even if you don't live in the UK, the NHL magazine *Harmonica World* can keep you informed about some of the great harp players over there (Brendan Power, Larry Adler, and Tommy Reilly, for instance).

Share Your Enthusiasm at Harmonica Festivals

You haven't lived as a harmonica player until you've shared a rush of enthusiasm and excitement with several hundred others at a harmonica festival. Here are a few of the harp-fests where you can hear great music, jam, learn new licks and tricks, and share with like-minded fanatics:

✔ **The SPAH Convention:** SPAH, the Society for the Preservation and Advancement of the Harmonica, stages a weeklong convention (really more of a festival) in a different U.S. city every year, with top-level performing acts, seminars by pro performers and teachers, demonstrations by manufacturers' representatives, and plenty of international visitors. You can read more about SPAH at www.spah.org. (Information about each year's convention is usually posted in April.)

✔ **The Buckeye Harmonica Festival:** The Buckeye Harmonica Club doesn't blow the horn very loudly for this little springtime festival in Columbus, Ohio, but it's one of the best small harmonica festivals going. To find out more about dates and times of the Buckeye Harmonica Festival, visit www.buckeyeharmonica.org.

✔ **The Yellow Pine Harmonica Contest:** Billed as a harmonica contest, this Yellow Pine event is really more like a gigantic campout in the mountains of Idaho. The picture of a harmonica-playing chipmunk on the contest's Web site (www.harmonicacontest.com) puts it in perspective. This festival doesn't offer much in the way of hotel accommodation or other amenities, but it does provide plenty of pioneer spirit.

Sign Up for a Harmonica Seminar

Seminars provide an experience somewhere between a harmonica festival and a private lesson. Seminars are social, but they're focused on teaching and learning. You get to rub elbows and learn from several great players in a variety of settings. Here are three traveling seminars that have been offered consistently over the last several years:

- ✔ **Harmonica Masterclass Workshops:** These workshops, which are for intermediate to advanced skill-level blues harmonica players, focus on details of harmonica technique and on concepts such as improvising and accompaniment playing. They also provide a deep study of blues harmonica masters. The workshops are taught by head instructor and founder David Barrett along with other top-level instructors, such as Joe Filisko and Dennis Gruenling, and current touring artists. Visit www.harmonica masterclass.com or call 877-427-7252 for more information.

- ✔ **Harmonica Jam Camp:** This camp is intended for beginner and intermediate players. The camp was founded by Jon Gindick, who's the author of such titles as *Rock n' Blues Harp* and *Harmonica Americana*. Harmonica Jam Camp includes three days of one-on-one lessons, small-group jamming, and large group teach-ins. You even get time to jam with a band. You can get more information by visiting www.gindick.com.

- ✔ **Chromatic Seminar for Diatonic Players:** Taught by classical virtuoso Robert Bonfiglio, this seminar is suitable for anyone who wants to gain more knowledge about the chromatic harmonica at any level. For students with a higher level of expertise, this seminar can provide teaching pedagogy and can reinforce the fundamentals of chromatic play. The skills taught are meant to be applied to any style of music. You can read more about Bonfiglio at robertbonfiglio.com. However, he usually posts notice of upcoming seminars on Harp-L.

Advertise

If you want to find other harmonica players to hang out with or musicians to jam or start a band with, sometimes all you need is a handwritten notice on the bulletin board in the local music store or library. Or you may be able to post a free ad on craigslist.org (www.craigslist.org) or a similar local online service. In your ad, mention the instrument you play, your level (beginner, intermediate, or advanced), the styles of music you're interested in, instruments you're looking to play with, and the goal (start a band, jam, or whatever).

Chapter 21

Way More than Ten Harmonica CDs You Should Hear

. . . .

In This Chapter

▶ Listening to some great harmonica music

▶ Hearing the wide variety of musical styles that feature harmonica

. . . .

Ask any harmonica player — or harmonica lover — to choose ten CDs he'd take with him to a desert island, and watch him squirm while he tries not to give up any of his favorites.

Instead of trying to artificially limit a list to ten good CDs to feed your head (and your harmonica habit), in this chapter I suggest clusters of CDs within ten major style groups. Still, this list is way shorter than I'd like it to be — there's just so much good harmonica music and so many great players to hear.

Blues

The harmonica has always been welcome in blues, and hundreds of great harmonica records have been made in all the varied regional and historical blues styles. Here are my recommendations in the blues category:

▶ **Various artists, *Ruckus Juice & Chitlins, Vol. 1: The Great Jug Bands* (Yazoo Records):** This cross-section of the great jug bands of 1920s and '30s Memphis puts the harmonica in the context of jugs, kazoos, clarinets, and some very witty and racy lyrics.

▶ **Various artists, *The Great Harp Players 1927–1936* (Document Records):** Blues Birdhead with his jazzy, Louis Armstrong-like playing, and the unearthly primitive sounds of George "Bullet" Williams make this collection a worthwhile addition to your collection of early rural blues harmonica.

▶ **Sonny Terry, *Sonny Terry: The Folkways Years, 1944–1963* (Smithsonian Folkways):** Sonny Terry (Saunders Terrell) brought the rural Piedmont style of blues harmonica to the 1950s folk revival and inspired many young players with his fiery playing. This CD presents Sonny either as a solo performer — one of his great strengths — or in small groups that include his longtime partner, singer/guitarist Brownie McGhee, and, on one tune, Pete Seeger.

✓ **Sonny Boy Williamson I,** *Sonny Boy Williamson: The Original Sonny Boy Williamson, Vol. 1* **(JSP Records):** John Lee Williamson was the first Sonny Boy, and his bedrock influence on both blues and rock harmonica can't be underestimated. This set gives a large helping of his recorded output.

✓ **Sonny Boy Williamson II (Rice Miller),** *His Best* **(Chess Records):** Rice Miller may have stolen his stage name from the first Sonny Boy, but his highly original singing, humorous and impassioned songwriting, and laconic, devastatingly witty harmonica playing are unequalled in the history of blues. He's one of the primary influences on modern blues harmonica.

✓ **Little Walter,** *His Best: The Chess 50th Anniversary Collection* **(Chess Records):** This collection is essential listening. Little Walter Jacobs was the defining master of Chicago blues harmonica. His horn-influenced style at times verged on both jazz and rock-and-roll.

✓ **Jimmy Reed,** *Blues Masters: The Very Best of Jimmy Reed* **(Rhino/ WEA):** Jimmy Reed's laid-back groove and amiable lyrics were the complete antithesis of the aggressive machismo of Chicago blues in the 1950s. At the same time, his high-register first-position work was uniquely memorable and remains highly influential to this day, while a handful of his songs have entered the popular repertoire of blues.

Rock

Rock harmonica, like rock itself, has strong roots in blues, as shown by the following recommendations:

✓ **Paul Butterfield, The Paul Butterfield Blues Band,** *East-West Live* **(Winner Records):** Chicago native Paul Butterfield is associated with blues, but his mid-1960s band was one of the earliest psychedelic jam bands, as this fascinating collection of live performances shows.

✓ **Magic Dick, J. Geils Band,** *"Live" Full House* **(Atlantic Records):** J. Geils Band, one of the best-selling rock bands of the '70s and '80s, featured Magic Dick's heavily amplified harmonica that adapted Chicago blues to rock and R&B. This 1972 album comes from the band's early period and includes the exciting harmonica instrumental "Whammer Jammer."

✓ **John Popper, Blues Traveler,** *Four* **(A&M Records):** John Popper has forged an astonishingly virtuosic — and controversial — harmonica style that emulates heavy-metal guitarists such as Eddie Van Halen and Jimi Hendrix. All the music on this CD, including the harmonica solos, was written down and published in the Warner Bros. songbook *Four* (Warner Bros. PG9506).

✔ **Jason Ricci, Jason Ricci & New Blood,** *Rocket Number 9* **(Eclecto Groove Records):** His first studio CD shows off Jason and his tight, rocking band to great advantage, with some virtuosic, exciting rock-harmonica playing delivered with precision and fire.

Pop

Popular music is distinct from both rock and blues in its greater emphasis on melody. Here are my recommendations in the pop category:

✔ **Larry Adler,** *Larry Adler: Maestro of the Mouth Organ* **(ASV Living Era):** Adler's trademark dark, throbbing tone and rhythmic high energy defined the sound of the harmonica for several generations in both the United States and Great Britain.

✔ **The Harmonicats,** *Jerry Murad's Harmonicats: Greatest Hits/Cherry Pink & Apple Blossom White* **(Collectables Records):** The Harmonicats were an all-harmonica trio that had a huge hit record in 1947 with *Peg O' My Heart* and continued to be a popular act for nearly 50 years. Interestingly, as of this writing, Amazon.com indicates that this record is ranked No. 63 in popularity for indie easy listening.

✔ **Lee Oskar, War,** *The Very Best of War* **(Rhino Records):** In the early 1970s, War introduced a new synthesis of pop and R&B that featured Lee Oskar's blues-influenced yet non-blues harmonica both as part of the horn section and as a solo instrument (remember "Low Rider"?).

✔ **Stevie Wonder, Eivets Rednow,** *Eivets Rednow* **(Motown):** Stevie Wonder has made dozens of great harmonica recordings that dot the landscape of his and other artists' albums. This one, made under the pseudonym Eivets Rednow (Stevie Wonder spelled backwards), features some amazing playing that harp players are still enthusing about.

Jazz

Jazz polls have always categorized the harmonica as a miscellaneous instrument along with bassoon and French horn (a harmonica player nearly always wins, though). Here are my recommendations in the jazz category:

✔ **Toots Thielemans,** *Only Trust Your Heart* **(Concord Records):** Jean "Toots" Thielemans has single-handedly defined the jazz approach to the chromatic harmonica while playing with an amazingly broad range of jazz and popular musicians. This CD is a solid introduction to his jazz chops while providing some pleasant listening.

✔ **Howard Levy, Bela Fleck & The Flecktones, *Bela Fleck & The Flecktones* (Warner Bros.):** Howard Levy's revolutionary approach to the diatonic harmonica has taken him on dozens of stylistic and spiritual journeys over the years. His first CD with the Flecktones serves as an easy way to get acquainted with his work.

✔ **Hendrik Meurkens, *Sambatropolis* (Zoho Music):** For several years Hendrik Meurkens has been making solid jazz records that often reflect his years of living in Brazil. *Sambatropolis* is a recent chapter.

✔ **Bill Barrett Quartet, *Backbone* (Bill Barrett):** Bill Barrett takes the chromatic harmonica on a highly original tour through a hip jazz territory that's tonally influenced by blues harp without imitating blues and is decidedly non-Toots in its approach.

Bluegrass/Old-Timey

The old-time traditional music that gave country music its unique flavor continues on its own path to this day. Here are my recommendations in the bluegrass/old-timey category:

✔ **Mark Graham, *Southern Old-Time Harmonica* (Eternal Doom):** A veteran of both Irish and old-timey music, Mark Graham is one of the finest old-time harmonica players active today. This CD finds him serving up the entire range of rural Southern harmonica traditions with minimal accompaniment while generating incredible rhythm and crystal clear melody.

✔ **Mike Stevens, Mike Stevens and Raymond McLain, *Old Time Mojo* (Borealis Recording):** Bluegrass harmonica stalwart Mike Stevens here teams up with Raymond McLain on banjo, mandolin, fiddle, and vocals for a tasty set of old-time songs and instrumental tunes.

✔ **Various artists, *Black & White Hillbilly Music: Early Harmonica Recordings from the 1920s & 1930s* (Trikont):** Many excellent old-time performances came from unknowns who made a single recording in the early days of recorded music. This collection presents a variety of great harmonica performances by Southern rural harmonica players.

Country

From the very first broadcast of the Grand Ole Opry in 1927, harmonica has helped give country music its Southern flavor. Here are my recommendations for some great country harp listening:

- ✔ **De Ford Bailey, various artists,** *Harp Blowers, 1925–1936* **(Document Records):** As the first star of the Grand Ole Opry, De Ford Bailey has earned his place in the Country Music Hall of Fame. His flawlessly virtuosic, precisely arranged solo harmonica pieces, recorded in 1928 and 1929, are still amazing listeners today, just as they did radio audiences all across the South generations ago.

- ✔ **Charlie McCoy,** *The Real McCoy* **(Sony Records):** Charlie McCoy's first solo album still wears well. His clean, single-note approach changed the way harmonica was used in Nashville. His style, exemplified in his adaptation of "Orange Blossom Special," is widely imitated.

- ✔ **Mickey Raphael, Willie Nelson,** *Willie and Family Live* **(Sony Records):** Mickey Raphael has held down the harmonica chair in Willie Nelson's band for something like 30 years. Although Nelson has recorded several albums of popular standards in the company of other stars, this CD shows him playing roadhouse country rock live with his own band and gives a sense of how harmonica integrates into a country band.

Celtic

Celtic is a convenient term for the musical traditions of Scotland and Ireland and their continuations overseas by immigrant communities. Here are my recommendations in the Celtic category:

- ✔ **Tommy Basker,** *The Tin Sandwich* **(Silver Apple Music):** Tommy Basker was one of the stalwarts of the boisterous, close-to-the-floor Cape Breton dance tradition of Nova Scotia. His vigorous, heavily chordal approach to both Scottish and Irish dance tunes is infectious, as this CD amply demonstrates.

- ✔ **Donald Black,** *Westwinds* **(Greentrax Recordings):** Donald Black is perhaps Scotland's finest traditional harmonica player. *Westwinds* packs a large number of Scottish traditional styles into a single CD.

- ✔ **Brendan Power,** *New Irish Harmonica* **(Green Linnet):** Brendan Power's groundbreaking CD ushered in a new approach to Irish music on the harmonica while remaining faithful to the tradition. He uses both chromatic and diatonic harmonicas.

Folk

While many Celtic and old-timey artists could also be classified under folk, I'd like to recommend some choice recordings from the musical traditions of French-speaking North America:

- **Isom Fontenot, various artists, *Folksongs of the Louisiana Acadians* (Arhoolie Records):** Cajun harmonica player Isom Fontenot is prominently featured in some great down-home music with true Cajun flavor and some really fine harmonica.

- **Gabriel Labbé, Gabriel Labbé and Philippe Bruneau, *Masters of French Canadian Music, Vol. 3* (Smithsonian Folkways):** Gabriel Labbé was the last of the old-time tremolo harmonica players of Quebec. The buoyancy of his highly rhythmic style shows the true spirit of French Canadian tradition in this collection of dance tunes.

Classical

The invention of the chromatic harmonica in the 1920s allowed harmonica players to tackle complex music, and pretty soon famous composers were writing concertos for the harmonica. Here are two recommendations in the classical category:

- **Robert Bonfiglio, Robert Bonfiglio with the New York Chamber Symphony, *Villa-Lobos: Harmonica Concerto, Bachianas Brasileiras No. 5: Aria* (RCA Red Seal Records):** Bonfiglio is the world's premier classical harmonicist, regularly playing concertos with symphony orchestras worldwide. This CD presents a concerto written for harmonica by 20th-century Brazilian composer Heitor Villa-Lobos.

- **Tommy Reilly, *Tommy Reilly and Skaila Kanga Play British Folk Songs* (Chandos Records):** Canadian-born Reilly went to Germany to study classical violin just as World War II broke out. During his five years as a prisoner of war, he had ample time to polish his harmonica technique. This CD presents his silvery chromatic harmonica phrasing accompanied by stringed harp.

World

Around the world, musicians have interpreted the repertoire of their national traditions on the harmonica with great flair. Here are a few recommendations in the world category:

- **Hugo Díaz, *Tangos* (Acqua Argentina):** Hugo Díaz adapted the harmonica to both tango and Argentine folk music in an arresting manner that has never been duplicated, as heard in this collection.

- **Sväng, *Sväng* (Aito Records):** Sväng is a high-energy Finnish harmonica quintet whose repertoire encompasses tango, gypsy music, and a bit of Finnish folk music. Their music uses the traditional bass harmonica, chromatic, and chord harp, but they show influence from blues harp and other trends in modern music.

Part VII
Appendixes

The 5th Wave
By Rich Tennant

©RICHTENNANT

"Michael! Michael! You're either having an asthma attack or you've fallen asleep with the harmonica in your mouth again!"

In this part . . .

Every key of harmonica in standard tuning is laid out with the same relationships between the notes and the same note-bending capabilities. However, the actual note names differ. When you're trying to relate a harp to a particular song, specifics can be helpful to know, so the note layouts for all keys of harp are included in Appendix A. Appendix B gives a detailed rundown of the tracks on the CD as well as some instructions on how to use it.

Appendix A

Tuning Layouts for All Keys

• •

*T*he following figures show the note layouts for all keys of diatonic harmonica. For more on how these layouts work, see Chapter 12.

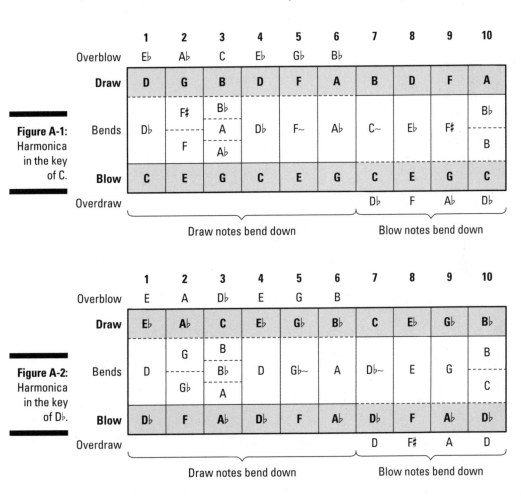

	1	2	3	4	5	6	7	8	9	10
Overblow	E♭	A♭	C	E♭	G♭	B♭				
Draw	D	G	B	D	F	A	B	D	F	A
Bends	D♭	F♯ / F	B♭ / A / A♭	D♭	F~	A♭	C~	E♭	F♯	B♭ / B
Blow	C	E	G	C	E	G	C	E	G	C
Overdraw							D♭	F	A♭	D♭

Figure A-1: Harmonica in the key of C.

Draw notes bend down — Blow notes bend down

	1	2	3	4	5	6	7	8	9	10
Overblow	E	A	D♭	E	G	B				
Draw	E♭	A♭	C	E♭	G♭	B♭	C	E♭	G♭	B♭
Bends	D	G / G♭	B / B♭ / A	D	G♭~	A	D♭~	E	G	B / C
Blow	D♭	F	A♭	D♭	F	A♭	D♭	F	A♭	D♭
Overdraw							D	F♯	A	D

Figure A-2: Harmonica in the key of D♭.

Draw notes bend down — Blow notes bend down

		1	2	3	4	5	6	7	8	9	10
	Overblow	F	B♭	D	F	A♭	C				
	Draw	**E**	**A**	**C#**	**E**	**G**	**B**	**C#**	**E**	**G**	**B**
	Bends	E♭	A♭ / G	C / B / B♭	E♭	F#~	B♭	D~	F	A♭	C / C#
	Blow	**D**	**F#**	**A**	**D**	**F#**	**A**	**D**	**F#**	**A**	**D**
	Overdraw							E♭	G	B♭	E♭

Figure A-3: Harmonica in the key of D.

Draw notes bend down — Blow notes bend down

		1	2	3	4	5	6	7	8	9	10
	Overblow	F#	B	D#	F#	A	C#				
	Draw	**F**	**B♭**	**D**	**F**	**A♭**	**C**	**D**	**F**	**A♭**	**C**
	Bends	E	A / A♭	D♭ / C / B	E	A♭~	B	E♭~	G♭	A	D♭ / D
	Blow	**E♭**	**G**	**B♭**	**E♭**	**G**	**B♭**	**E♭**	**G**	**B♭**	**E♭**
	Overdraw							E	G#	B	E

Figure A-4: Harmonica in the key of E♭.

Draw notes bend down — Blow notes bend down

		1	2	3	4	5	6	7	8	9	10
	Overblow	G	C	E	G	B♭	D				
	Draw	**F#**	**B**	**D#**	**F#**	**A**	**C#**	**D#**	**F#**	**A**	**C#**
	Bends	F	B♭ / A	D / C# / C	F	A~	C	E~	G	B♭	D / D#
	Blow	**E**	**G#**	**B**	**E**	**G#**	**B**	**E**	**G#**	**B**	**E**
	Overdraw							F	A	C	F

Figure A-5: Harmonica in the key of E.

Draw notes bend down — Blow notes bend down

	1	2	3	4	5	6	7	8	9	10
Overblow	A♭	D♭	F	A♭	C♭	E♭				
Draw	**G**	**C**	**E**	**G**	**B♭**	**D**	**E**	**G**	**B♭**	**D**
Bends		B	E♭							E♭
	G♭	—	D	G♭	B♭~	D♭	F~	A♭	B	—
		B♭	D♭							E
Blow	**F**	**A**	**C**	**F**	**A**	**C**	**F**	**A**	**C**	**F**
Overdraw							G♭	B♭	D♭	G♭

Figure A-6: Harmonica in the key of F.

Draw notes bend down — Blow notes bend down

	1	2	3	4	5	6	7	8	9	10
Overblow	A	D	F♯	A	C	E				
Draw	**G♯**	**C♯**	**E♯**	**G♯**	**B**	**D♯**	**E♯**	**G♯**	**B**	**D♯**
Bends		C	E							E
	G	—	D♯	G	B~	D	F♯~	A	C	—
		B	D							E♯
Blow	**F♯**	**A♯**	**C♯**	**F♯**	**A♯**	**C♯**	**F♯**	**A♯**	**C♯**	**F♯**
Overdraw							G	B	D	G

Figure A-7: Harmonica in the key of F♯.

Draw notes bend down — Blow notes bend down

	1	2	3	4	5	6	7	8	9	10
Overblow	B♭	E♭	G	B♭	D♭	F				
Draw	**A**	**D**	**F♯**	**A**	**C**	**E**	**F♯**	**A**	**C**	**E**
Bends		D♭	F							F
	A♭	—	E	A♭	C~	E♭	G~	B♭	D♭	—
		C	E♭							F♯
Blow	**G**	**B**	**D**	**G**	**B**	**D**	**G**	**B**	**D**	**G**
Overdraw							A♭	C	E♭	A♭

Figure A-8: Harmonica in the key of G.

Draw notes bend down — Blow notes bend down

Figure A-9: Harmonica in the key of Ab.

	1	2	3	4	5	6	7	8	9	10
Overblow	B	E	G#	B	D	F#				
Draw	Bb	Eb	G	Bb	Db	F	G	Bb	Db	F
Bends	A	D / Db	Gb / F / E	A	Db~	E	Ab~	B	D	Gb / G
Blow	Ab	C	Eb	Ab	C	Eb	Ab	C	Eb	Ab
Overdraw							A	C#	E	A

Draw notes bend down (1–6)   Blow notes bend down (7–10)

Figure A-10: Harmonica in the key of A.

	1	2	3	4	5	6	7	8	9	10
Overblow	C	F	A	C	Eb	G				
Draw	B	E	G#	B	D	F#	G#	B	D	F#
Bends	Bb	Eb / D	G / F# / F	Bb	D~	F	A~	C	Eb	G / G#
Blow	A	C#	E	A	C#	E	A	C#	E	A
Overdraw							Bb	D	F	Bb

Draw notes bend down (1–6)   Blow notes bend down (7–10)

Figure A-11: Harmonica in the key of Bb.

	1	2	3	4	5	6	7	8	9	10
Overblow	Db	Gb	Bb	Db	E	Ab				
Draw	C	F	A	C	Eb	G	A	C	Eb	G
Bends	B	E / Eb	Ab / G / Gb	B	Eb~	Gb	Bb~	Db	E	Ab / A
Blow	Bb	D	F	Bb	D	F	Bb	D	F	Bb
Overdraw							B	D#	F#	B

Draw notes bend down (1–6)   Blow notes bend down (7–10)

	1	2	3	4	5	6	7	8	9	10
Overblow	D	G	B	D	F	A				
Draw	**C#**	**F#**	**A#**	**C#**	**E**	**G#**	**A#**	**C#**	**E**	**G#**
Bends	C	F / E	A / G# / G	C	E~	G	B~	D	F	A / A#
Blow	**B**	**D#**	**F#**	**B**	**D#**	**F#**	**B**	**D#**	**F#**	**B**
Overdraw							C	E	G	C

Figure A-12: Harmonica in the key of B.

Draw notes bend down ⟵⟶ Blow notes bend down

Appendix B

About the CD

*T*he CD that accompanies this book contains every musical example and tune that I include in the book — a total of 98 tracks! You can listen to any or all of them and play along as often as you need to in order to learn the techniques and tunes that will bring your harmonica playing to the next level.

A great way to use *Harmonica For Dummies* is to scan the chapter for tabbed music examples or tunes and then listen to the corresponding recordings on the CD. (You can find these examples and tunes by locating the On the CD icon. I explain this icon in the Introduction.) When you hear something on the CD that interests you, read the text that goes into detail about that particular example or tune. Or, it's also fun to go to a chapter that interests you (say, Chapter 8 on bending notes down), skip to the appropriate tracks on the CD, and try to reproduce the sounds you hear.

Always keep the CD with your book. The plastic sleeve protects the CD from scuffs and scratches. Plus, this way you'll always have the CD handy when you want to hear an example or tune from the book. Try to get in the habit of following along with the printed music when you listen to the CD. Even if you aren't a fluent music reader, you'll be surprised at what you can absorb just by reading along.

Relating the Text to the CD

Whenever you see written music or tab in the text and want to hear what it sounds like, refer to the caption, which tells you the track number to skip to. If the track contains multiple examples, such as a series of numbered licks, the start time within the track (in minutes and seconds) is listed later in this appendix.

To get to the CD track you want to hear, use the track-skip button on the control panel or remote for your CD player. To access a specific segment within a track, use the cue button of the cue/review function. Use the time, indicated in minutes and seconds, to find the segment you're looking for.

To play along, go to a point a few seconds before where you want to start. Then use the pause button to give yourself time to pick up your harp, find your note, and get ready to play. *Note:* On this CD, every tune or example that's played to a beat starts with a count-off that gives you the *tempo* (how fast the beat goes) and tells you when to start.

When a recorded example is accompanied by another instrument or a band, the harmonica is isolated in the right channel. If you want to hear more of the harmonica and less of the accompaniment, turn the balance control to the right (but not all the way if you want to still hear the band). If you want to hear just the band and not the harmonica (for instance, so you can play along without hearing another harmonica), turn the balance control all the way to the left. You'll still hear the count-off, and you usually can hear a hint of the melody embedded in the accompaniment.

Using the CD

You can listen to the CD on a standard CD player or in a computer's CD-ROM drive. You can also load the audio tracks onto a portable media player. I show you all three ways to listen in the following sections.

Audio CD players

The CD included with this book will work just fine with any standard CD player. Just load it into the tray, and then press play or skip to the tracks you want to listen to and play along with.

Computer CD-ROM drives

If you'd like, you can pop the CD into your computer's CD or DVD drive to access the MP3 files that are included. However, make sure your computer meets the minimum system requirements shown here:

- A computer running Microsoft Windows or Mac OS
- Software that's capable of playing MP3s and CD audio (for example, iTunes, Windows Media Player, or RealPlayer)
- A sound card (almost all computers these days have the built-in ability to play sound)
- A CD-ROM or DVD drive

To browse the contents of the CD, follow these steps:

1. **Insert the CD into your computer's CD-ROM drive.**

   The license agreement should appear. ***Note to Windows users:*** The interface won't launch if you have Autorun disabled. If you do have the Autorun disabled, click Start⇨Run (for Windows Vista, Start⇨All Programs⇨Accessories⇨Run). In the dialog box that appears, type D:\ start.exe. (If your CD drive uses a different letter, replace D with that letter. If you don't know which letter to use, see how your CD drive is listed under My Computer.) Click OK.

2. **Read through the license agreement and click the Accept button.**

   The CD interface appears. The interface allows you to listen to or copy the MP3 files on your hard drive with just a few clicks.

3. **If you would like to copy the MP3 files from the CD on to your computer, click the MP3 button; the MP3 directory will open.**

   You can now copy the MP3 files from the CD to your hard drive.

The Tracks on the CD

The following table lists all 98 tracks on the CD along with the corresponding tablature numbers from the chapters in the book.

All the audio tracks on the CD have been stored on the CD in the MP3 format, which means that if you follow the steps in the preceding section, you can copy the MP3 files from the CD onto your computer. From there, you can listen to the MP3s with your audio software or even copy them to your portable MP3 player.

Track Number	Time	Tab or Figure Number	Track Description
1	0:00	Tab 3-1	Inhaling and exhaling on the quarter note beat
	0:13	Tab 3-2	Playing quarter notes and half notes
	0:26	Tab 3-3	Playing quarter notes and whole notes
2		Tab 3-4	Playing a melody with triplets

(continued)

Track Number	Time	Tab or Figure Number	Track Description
3		Tab 3-5	Playing a tune with swing
4		Tab 3-6	Counting off a tune with a pickup
5		Chapter 4	The smooth swimming exercise
6	0:00	Tab 4-1	Rhythm pattern #1
	0:41	Tab 4-2	Rhythm pattern #2
	1:23	Tab 4-3	Rhythm pattern #3
	2:04	Tabs 4-1, 4-2, and 4-3	A verse of combined rhythms
7	0:00	Tab 4-4	Train rhythms
	0:18	Chapter 4	A train whistle and steam
8	0:00	Chapter 4	Breathing rhythms 1, 2, and 3 with hands
	0:41	Chapter 4	Train rhythms with hands
9		Tab 5-1	"Hot Cross Buns"
10		Tab 5-2	"Good Night, Ladies"
11		Tab 5-3	"Mary Had a Little Lamb"
12		Tab 5-4	"Frère Jacques"
13		Tab 5-5	"When the Saints Go Marching In"
14		Tab 5-6	"Twinkle, Twinkle, Little Star"
15		Tab 5-7	"Taps"
16		Tab 5-8	"On Top of Old Smokey"
17		Tab 5-9	A note shift exercise
18		Tab 5-10	"Joy to the World"
19		Tab 5-11	"Shenandoah"
20		Tab 5-12	High register float
21		Tab 5-13	"She'll be Comin' 'Round the Mountain"
22		Tab 5-14	"Silent Night"
23		Tab 6-1	Pulsing long notes abdominally and playing a scale with abdominal articulation

Track Number	Time	Tab or Figure Number	Track Description
24		Chapter 6	Comparing abdominal articulation with tongue articulation using Tab 4-1
25	0:00	Tab 6-1	Articulating long breaths into a series of notes glottally and playing a scale starting each note with a glottal stop
	0:15	Tab 6-1	Playing glottal attacks and cutoffs on long notes and playing a scale with glottal staccato
	0:31	Tab 6-1	Pulsing long notes glottally and playing a scale starting each note with a glottal pulse
26		Tab 6-2	Combining a throat rhythm with an abdominal rhythm
27	0:00	Tab 6-1	Using single tonguing T and K attacks and playing a scale with T attack and a scale with K attack
	0:27	Tab 6-1	Starting and stopping repeated notes with "Tat" and "Kak" and playing a scale with these articulations
	0:55	Tab 6-1	Using T-K double tonguing and playing a scale with double tonguing
28		Tab 6-1	Playing P and !Ha-pa tongue-blocked articulations and playing a scale with these articulations
29	0:00	Tab 6-3	The Ooh-Eee lick with tongue vowels
	0:14	Tab 6-3	Playing a closed and open hand cup and "ooh-wahs," and then playing with combined hand cupping and vowels
30		Chapter 6	The coffee cup exercise
31	0:00	Chapter 6	An example of hand pulsation with hand, pinky, and forearm; ascending scale only

(continued)

Track Number	Time	Tab or Figure Number	Track Description
31	0:30	Chapter 6	Fanning a note with hand and forearm
32		Chapter 6	An example of four types of vibrato: diaphragm, throat, tongue, and hands
33		Chapter 6	Timing vibrato to divisions of the beat
34		Tab 7-1	"Mary Had a Groovin' Little Lamb"
35		Tab 7-2	"Chasin' the Beat"
36		Tab 7-3	"Slappin' the Blues"
37		Figure 7-4	Using a tongue split (Holes 1 and 4)
38	0:00	Tab 7-4	Tongue texture demonstration line played with a locked split
	0:15	Tab 7-4	Tongue texture demonstration line played with a chord rake
	0:27	Tab 7-4	Tongue texture demonstration line played with a chord hammer
	0:40	Tab 7-4	Tongue texture demonstration line played with a hammered split
	0:53	Tab 7-4	Tongue texture demonstration line played with a shimmer
39		Tab 7-5	A line to practice corner switching
40		Chapter 8	Bending for expression and for missing notes
41		Chapter 8	The sound of bending Draw 4
42		Chapter 8	The sound of going from four notes to just Draw 4
43	0:00	Tab 8-1	The Yellow Bird lick in the middle range
	0:16	Tab 8-2	The Bendus Interruptus lick in the middle range
	0:35	Tab 8-3	The Close Your Eyes lick in the middle range
	0:55	Tab 8-4	The Shark Fin lick in the middle range

Track Number	Time	Tab or Figure Number	Track Description
44	0:00	Tab 8-5	Draw 2 bends with the Yellow Bird lick
	0:15	Tab 8-6	Draw 2 with the Bendus Interruptus lick
	0:28	Tab 8-7	Draw 2 with the Modified Shark lick
	0:44	Tab 8-8	Draw 2 with the Close Your Eyes lick
45		Tab 8-9	Draw 1 with Yellow Bird lick
46	0:00	Tab 8-10	Shallow, intermediate, and deep bends in Hole 3
	0:18	Tab 8-11	The Bendus Interruptus lick on Draw 3
	0:35	Tab 8-12	The Close Your Eyes lick on Draw 3
	0:56	Tab 8-13	The Shark Fin lick in Hole 3
	1:16	Tab 8-14	The Cool Juke lick in Hole 3
47	0:00	Tab 8-15	The Yellow Bird lick in the high range
	0:21	Tab 8-16	The Bendus Interruptus lick in the high range
	0:40	Tab 8-17	The Close Your Eyes lick in the high range
	1:05	Tab 8-18	The Shark Fin lick in the high range
48	0:00	Tab 9-1	First-position licks 1 and 2
	0:21	Tab 9-1	First-position licks 3 and 4
	0:39	Tab 9-1	First-position licks 5 and 6
	0:56	Tab 9-1	First-position licks 7 and 8
	1:12	Tab 9-1	First-position licks 9 and 10
	1:29	Tab 9-1	First-position licks 11 and 12
49	0:00	Tab 9-2	Second-position licks 1 and 2
	0:21	Tab 9-2	Second-position licks 3 and 4
	0:39	Tab 9-2	Second-position licks 5 and 6
	0:56	Tab 9-2	Second-position licks 7 and 8
	1:13	Tab 9-2	Second-position licks 9 and 10
	1:30	Tab 9-2	Second-position licks 11 and 12

(continued)

Track Number	Time	Tab or Figure Number	Track Description
50	0:00	Tab 9-3	Third-position licks 1 and 2
	0:21	Tab 9-3	Third-position licks 3 and 4
	0:38	Tab 9-3	Third-position licks 5 and 6
	0:55	Tab 9-3	Third-position licks 7 and 8
	1:13	Tab 9-3	Third-position licks 9 and 10
	1:30	Tab 9-3	Third-position licks 11 and 12
51	0:00	Tab 9-4	Fourth-position licks 1 and 2
	0:21	Tab 9-4	Fourth-position licks 3 and 4
	0:38	Tab 9-4	Fourth-position licks 5 and 6
	0:56	Tab 9-4	Fourth-position licks 7 and 8
	1:13	Tab 9-4	Fourth-position licks 9 and 10
	1:30	Tab 9-4	Fourth-position licks 11 and 12
52	0:00	Tab 9-5	Fifth-position licks 1 and 2
	0:21	Tab 9-5	Fifth-position licks 3 and 4
	0:38	Tab 9-5	Fifth-position licks 5 and 6
	0:56	Tab 9-5	Fifth-position licks 7 and 8
	1:13	Tab 9-5	Fifth-position licks 9 and 10
	1:30	Tab 9-5	Fifth-position licks 11 and 12
53	0:00	Tab 9-6	Twelfth-position licks 1 and 2
	0:21	Tab 9-6	Twelfth-position licks 3 and 4
	0:39	Tab 9-6	Twelfth-position licks 5 and 6
	0:56	Tab 9-6	Twelfth-position licks 7 and 8
	1:13	Tab 9-6	Twelfth-position licks 9 and 10
	1:30	Tab 9-6	Twelfth-position licks 11 and 12
54	0:00	Tab 10-1	The major scale in the middle register
	0:13	Tab 10-1	The major scale in the high register
	0:26	Tab 10-1	The major scale in the low register
55	0:00	Tab 10-2	A scale with a 1-3 pattern (middle register)
	0:15	Tab 10-2	A scale with a 1-3 pattern (high register)

Track Number	Time	Tab or Figure Number	Track Description
55	0:30	Tab 10-2	A scale with a 1-3 pattern (low register)
56	0:00	Tab 10-3	A scale with 1-2-3 pattern (middle register)
	0:13	Tab 10-3	A scale with 1-2-3 pattern (high register)
	0:27	Tab 10-3	A scale with 1-2-3 pattern (low register)
57	0:00	Tab 10-4	A scale with 1-2-3-5 pattern (middle and high registers)
	0:24	Tab 10-4	A scale with 1-2-3-5 pattern (low and middle registers)
58	0:00	Tab 10-5	A scale with 1-2-3-4 pattern (middle register)
	0:19	Tab 10-5	A scale with 1-2-3-4 pattern (high register)
	0:30	Tab 10-5	A scale with 1-2-3-4 pattern (low register)
59		Tab 10-6	A chord progression with alternating patterns
60	0:00	Tab 10-7	A first-position scale with chord tones
	0:15	Tab 10-8	A melody alternating between resolution and tension
61	0:00	Tab 10-9	The major pentatonic scale in first position
	0:18	Tab 10-10	The minor pentatonic scale in fourth position
62	0:00	Tab 10-11	The major pentatonic scale in second position
	0:18	Tab 10-12	The minor pentatonic scale in fifth position
63	0:00	Tab 10-13	The major pentatonic scale in twelfth position

(continued)

Track Number	Time	Tab or Figure Number	Track Description
63	0:18	Tab 10-14	The minor pentatonic scale in third position
64		Tab 10-15	A melodic line with shakes
65		Tab 10-16	Rips, boings, and fall-offs
66		Tab 10-17	Grace notes
67	0:00	Tab 12-1	A blues line using a bent note and an overblow
	0:12	Tab 12-2	A blues line using bent notes, an overblow, and an overdraw
68	0:00	Tab 12-3	Push-through to Overblow 6 with preparation in Holes 8 and 7
	0:15	Tab 12-4	Push-through to overblow in Holes 6, 5, and 4
	0:33	Tab 12-5	The springboard approach to overblows in Holes 6, 5, and 4
69		Tab 12-6	Hole 1 overblows
70	0:00	Tab 12-7	The springboard approach to overdraws in Holes 7–10
	0:29	Tab 12-8	The pull-through approach to overdraws in Holes 7–10
71		Chapter 12	Playing Overblow 4 and Overdraw 8 in tune against a drone
72		Tab 12-9	"Gussy Fit," a tune with overblows
73	0:00	Tab 13-1	"Outline Blues"
	0:17	Tab 13-2	"Rhythm Chord Blues"
	0:32	Tab 13-3	"Red Sock Blues"
	0:46	Tab 13-4	"Wailing Note Blues"
74	0:00	Tab 13-5	1st anywhere lick
	0:12	Tab 13-5	2nd anywhere lick
	0:23	Tab 13-5	3rd anywhere lick
75	0:00	Tab 13-6	1st second-part lick
	0:12	Tab 13-6	2nd second-part lick
	0:23	Tab 13-6	3rd second-part lick

Track Number	Time	Tab or Figure Number	Track Description
76	0:00	Tab 13-7	1st come-down lick and turn-around lick
	0:12	Tab 13-7	2nd come-down lick and turn-around lick
	0:23	Tab 13-7	3rd come-down lick and turn-around lick
77	0:00	Tab 13-8	1st lick to end a tune
	0:08	Tab 13-8	2nd lick to end a tune
	0:15	Tab 13-8	3rd lick to end a tune
	0:21	Tab 13-8	4th lick to end a tune
78	0:00	Tab 13-9	Third-position blues in the top and middle registers
	0:36	Tab 13-10	Third-position blues in the low and middle registers
79	0:00	Tab 13-11	First-position blues in the top register
	0:36	Tab 13-12	First-position blues in the bottom register
80		Tab 14-1	"Blue Eyed Angel"
81		Tab 14-2	"Wabash Cannonball"
82		Tab 14-3	"Foggy Mountain Top"
83		Tab 14-4	"Since I Laid My Burden Down"
84		Tab 14-5	"One Frosty Morn"
85		Tab 14-6	"Lonesome Whistle Waltz"
86		Tab 14-7	"Muscle Car Boogie, Part 1"
87		Tab 15-1	"Careless Love"
88		Tab 15-2	"Wildwood Flower"
89		Tab 15-3	"April's Jig"
90		Tab 15-4	"Mrs. MacLeod of Raasay"
91		Tab 15-5	"John Hardy"
92	0:00	Tab 15-6	"Old Joe Clark" as a song
	0:19	Tab 15-7	"Old Joe Clark" as a fiddle tune
93		Tab 15-8	"Scarborough Fair"

(continued)

Track Number	Time	Tab or Figure Number	Track Description
94		Tab 15-9	"Tha mi sgith" (Scottish air)
95		Tab 15-10	"Saint James Infirmary" in fourth position
96		Tab 15-11	"Saint James Infirmary" in fifth position
97	0:00	Chapter 17	A short harmonica line played with no effects
	0:13	Chapter 17	A short harmonica line played with equalization
	0:25	Chapter 17	A short harmonica line played with compression
	0:38	Chapter 17	A short harmonica line played with delay
	0:52	Chapter 17	A short harmonica line played with reverb
	1:04	Chapter 17	A short harmonica line played with distortion
98	0:00	Chapter 19	A melody played on a chromatic harmonica
	0:36	Chapter 19	A melody played on a tremolo harp
	1:11	Chapter 19	A melody played on an octave harp

Troubleshooting

If you have trouble with the CD, please call the Wiley Product Technical Support phone number: 800-762-2974. Outside the United States, call 317-572-3994. You can also contact Wiley Product Technical Support at support.wiley.com. John Wiley & Sons will provide technical support only for installation and other general quality control items. For technical support on the programs themselves, consult the program's vendor or author.

Index

removing
  moisture, 27
  reedplates, 274
repair techs, 268
repairing. See also
    upgrading, diagnosing
    and fixing problems,
    272–284
  overview, 267–268
  tips, 269–270
  tools needed for, 268–269
  warranty service, 268
research
  advertising, 300
  clubs, 298–299
  festivals, 299
  informational Web sites,
    298
  jam sessions, 296
  lessons, 295
  online discussion groups,
    297
  open mic night, 296
  performances, 295–296
  seminars, 300
resizing mouth chamber, 113
resolution, 168
resonance, 82
resources. See Web sites
rests, 33–34
reverberation (reverb), 263
rhythm
  counting time, 32–33
  defined, 31, 56
  guitar, 251
  intensifying with hand
    cup, 60–61
  shuffle, 38
"Rhythm Chord Blues," 207,
    208
rhythmic feel, 185
rhythmic patterns, 56–59
Ricci, Jason (*Rocket Number
    9*), 303
riffs
  defined, 251
  relationship with
    jamming, 185

relationship with
    overbending, 188–189
  second-position blues,
    210–212
rig, 263
rips, 173
rock. *See also* blues
  harmonica, 203
  recommended CDs,
    302–303
Rocket Number 9 (Ricci), 303
rolling off, 263
*Ruckus Juice & Chitlins, Vol.
    1: The Great Jug Bands*
    (Various), 301
Ruth, Peter Madcat
    (harmonica player), 246

•S•

"Saint James Infirmary,"
    239–240
Sambairopolis (Meurkens),
    304
sanding detailer, 269
saturation, 261
scale
  defined, 40
  first position, 169
  key signature, 44–45
  major, 161
  modes, 41
  patterns, 162–167
  pentatonic, 169–171
  relationship with
    jamming, 184
  relationship with
    overbending, 188–189
"Scarborough Fair," 238
screwdrivers, 268
seal, forming, 21–22
second position
  avoid notes, 148
  bendable notes, 148
  blues, 206–212
  country music, 220–225
  "Foggy Mountain Top,"
    220–221

folk music, 234–237
  home note/chord,
    146–148
  "John Hardy," 235
  licks, 147, 210–212
  "Lonesome Whistle
    Waltz," 223–224
  modal scale, 148
  "Muscle Car Boogie, Part
    1," 224–225
  "Old Joe Clark," 236–237
  "One Frosty Morn,"
    222–223
  overview, 146, 206
  pentatonic scale, 171
  related positions, 149
  riffs, 210–212
  "Since I Laid My Burden
    Down," 221–222
  12-bar blues, 207–210
selecting
  harmonicas for
    overbending, 190
  keys, 247
  tunes, 244–247
seminars, 300
semitone, 42, 123, 191
setting reed action, 277–281
shakes, 172, 213
shaping mouth, 64–67
sharing music, 15
Shark Fin lick, 127–128,
    131–132, 134–135
(sharp), 41, 44
"She'll Be Comin' 'Round the
    Mountain," 77–78
sheng, 12
shift, 74
shifting up
  "Joy to the World," 75
  from the middle, 74–76
  "Shenandoah," 76
shim, 268
shimmer, 103–104
shopping for harmonicas,
    17–21
shuffle rhythm, 38

Wiley Publishing, Inc.
End-User License Agreement

READ THIS. You should carefully read these terms and conditions before opening the software packet(s) included with this book "Book". This is a license agreement "Agreement" between you and Wiley Publishing, Inc. "WPI". By opening the accompanying software packet(s), you acknowledge that you have read and accept the following terms and conditions. If you do not agree and do not want to be bound by such terms and conditions, promptly return the Book and the unopened software packet(s) to the place you obtained them for a full refund.

1. **License Grant.** WPI grants to you (either an individual or entity) a nonexclusive license to use one copy of the enclosed software program(s) (collectively, the "Software") solely for your own personal or business purposes on a single computer (whether a standard computer or a workstation component of a multi-user network). The Software is in use on a computer when it is loaded into temporary memory (RAM) or installed into permanent memory (hard disk, CD-ROM, or other storage device). WPI reserves all rights not expressly granted herein.

2. **Ownership.** WPI is the owner of all right, title, and interest, including copyright, in and to the compilation of the Software recorded on the physical packet included with this Book "Software Media". Copyright to the individual programs recorded on the Software Media is owned by the author or other authorized copyright owner of each program. Ownership of the Software and all proprietary rights relating thereto remain with WPI and its licensers.

3. **Restrictions on Use and Transfer.**

    (a) You may only (i) make one copy of the Software for backup or archival purposes, or (ii) transfer the Software to a single hard disk, provided that you keep the original for backup or archival purposes. You may not (i) rent or lease the Software, (ii) copy or reproduce the Software through a LAN or other network system or through any computer subscriber system or bulletin-board system, or (iii) modify, adapt, or create derivative works based on the Software.

    (b) You may not reverse engineer, decompile, or disassemble the Software. You may transfer the Software and user documentation on a permanent basis, provided that the transferee agrees to accept the terms and conditions of this Agreement and you retain no copies. If the Software is an update or has been updated, any transfer must include the most recent update and all prior versions.

4. **Restrictions on Use of Individual Programs.** You must follow the individual requirements and restrictions detailed for each individual program in the "About the CD" appendix of this Book or on the Software Media. These limitations are also contained in the individual license agreements recorded on the Software Media. These limitations may include a requirement that after using the program for a specified period of time, the user must pay a registration fee or discontinue use. By opening the Software packet(s), you agree to abide by the licenses and restrictions for these individual programs that are detailed in the "About the CD" appendix and/or on the Software Media. None of the material on this Software Media or listed in this Book may ever be redistributed, in original or modified form, for commercial purposes.

5. **Limited Warranty.**

   (a) WPI warrants that the Software and Software Media are free from defects in materials and workmanship under normal use for a period of sixty (60) days from the date of purchase of this Book. If WPI receives notification within the warranty period of defects in materials or workmanship, WPI will replace the defective Software Media.

   (b) WPI AND THE AUTHOR(S) OF THE BOOK DISCLAIM ALL OTHER WARRANTIES, EXPRESS OR IMPLIED, INCLUDING WITHOUT LIMITATION IMPLIED WARRANTIES OF MERCHANTABILITY AND FITNESS FOR A PARTICULAR PURPOSE, WITH RESPECT TO THE SOFTWARE, THE PROGRAMS, THE SOURCE CODE CONTAINED THEREIN, AND/OR THE TECHNIQUES DESCRIBED IN THIS BOOK. WPI DOES NOT WARRANT THAT THE FUNCTIONS CONTAINED IN THE SOFTWARE WILL MEET YOUR REQUIREMENTS OR THAT THE OPERATION OF THE SOFTWARE WILL BE ERROR FREE.

   (c) This limited warranty gives you specific legal rights, and you may have other rights that vary from jurisdiction to jurisdiction.

6. **Remedies.**

   (a) WPI's entire liability and your exclusive remedy for defects in materials and workmanship shall be limited to replacement of the Software Media, which may be returned to WPI with a copy of your receipt at the following address: Software Media Fulfillment Department, Attn.: *Harmonica For Dummies*, Wiley Publishing, Inc., 10475 Crosspoint Blvd., Indianapolis, IN 46256, or call 1-800-762-2974. Please allow four to six weeks for delivery. This Limited Warranty is void if failure of the Software Media has resulted from accident, abuse, or misapplication. Any replacement Software Media will be warranted for the remainder of the original warranty period or thirty (30) days, whichever is longer.

   (b) In no event shall WPI or the author be liable for any damages whatsoever (including without limitation damages for loss of business profits, business interruption, loss of business information, or any other pecuniary loss) arising from the use of or inability to use the Book or the Software, even if WPI has been advised of the possibility of such damages.

   (c) Because some jurisdictions do not allow the exclusion or limitation of liability for consequential or incidental damages, the above limitation or exclusion may not apply to you.

7. **U.S. Government Restricted Rights.** Use, duplication, or disclosure of the Software for or on behalf of the United States of America, its agencies and/or instrumentalities "U.S. Government" is subject to restrictions as stated in paragraph (c)(1)(ii) of the Rights in Technical Data and Computer Software clause of DFARS 252.227-7013, or subparagraphs (c) (1) and (2) of the Commercial Computer Software - Restricted Rights clause at FAR 52.227-19, and in similar clauses in the NASA FAR supplement, as applicable.

8. **General.** This Agreement constitutes the entire understanding of the parties and revokes and supersedes all prior agreements, oral or written, between them and may not be modified or amended except in a writing signed by both parties hereto that specifically refers to this Agreement. This Agreement shall take precedence over any other documents that may be in conflict herewith. If any one or more provisions contained in this Agreement are held by any court or tribunal to be invalid, illegal, or otherwise unenforceable, each and every other provision shall remain in full force and effect.

BUSINESS, CAREERS & PERSONAL FINANCE

Accounting For Dummies, 4th Edition*
978-0-470-24600-9

Bookkeeping Workbook For Dummies†
978-0-470-16983-4

Commodities For Dummies
978-0-470-04928-0

Doing Business in China For Dummies
978-0-470-04929-7

E-Mail Marketing For Dummies
978-0-470-19087-6

Job Interviews For Dummies, 3rd Edition*†
978-0-470-17748-8

Personal Finance Workbook For Dummies*†
978-0-470-09933-9

Real Estate License Exams For Dummies
978-0-7645-7623-2

Six Sigma For Dummies
978-0-7645-6798-8

Small Business Kit For Dummies, 2nd Edition*†
978-0-7645-5984-6

Telephone Sales For Dummies
978-0-470-16836-3

BUSINESS PRODUCTIVITY & MICROSOFT OFFICE

Access 2007 For Dummies
978-0-470-03649-5

Excel 2007 For Dummies
978-0-470-03737-9

Office 2007 For Dummies
978-0-470-00923-9

Outlook 2007 For Dummies
978-0-470-03830-7

PowerPoint 2007 For Dummies
978-0-470-04059-1

Project 2007 For Dummies
978-0-470-03651-8

QuickBooks 2008 For Dummies
978-0-470-18470-7

Quicken 2008 For Dummies
978-0-470-17473-9

Salesforce.com For Dummies, 2nd Edition
978-0-470-04893-1

Word 2007 For Dummies
978-0-470-03658-7

EDUCATION, HISTORY, REFERENCE & TEST PREPARATION

African American History For Dummies
978-0-7645-5469-8

Algebra For Dummies
978-0-7645-5325-7

Algebra Workbook For Dummies
978-0-7645-8467-1

Art History For Dummies
978-0-470-09910-0

ASVAB For Dummies, 2nd Edition
978-0-470-10671-6

British Military History For Dummies
978-0-470-03213-8

Calculus For Dummies
978-0-7645-2498-1

Canadian History For Dummies, 2nd Edition
978-0-470-83656-9

Geometry Workbook For Dummies
978-0-471-79940-5

The SAT I For Dummies, 6th Edition
978-0-7645-7193-0

Series 7 Exam For Dummies
978-0-470-09932-2

World History For Dummies
978-0-7645-5242-7

FOOD, GARDEN, HOBBIES & HOME

Bridge For Dummies, 2nd Edition
978-0-471-92426-5

Coin Collecting For Dummies, 2nd Edition
978-0-470-22275-1

Cooking Basics For Dummies, 3rd Edition
978-0-7645-7206-7

Drawing For Dummies
978-0-7645-5476-6

Etiquette For Dummies, 2nd Edition
978-0-470-10672-3

Gardening Basics For Dummies*†
978-0-470-03749-2

Knitting Patterns For Dummies
978-0-470-04556-5

Living Gluten-Free For Dummies†
978-0-471-77383-2

Painting Do-It-Yourself For Dummies
978-0-470-17533-0

HEALTH, SELF HELP, PARENTING & PETS

Anger Management For Dummies
978-0-470-03715-7

Anxiety & Depression Workbook For Dummies
978-0-7645-9793-0

Dieting For Dummies, 2nd Edition
978-0-7645-4149-0

Dog Training For Dummies, 2nd Edition
978-0-7645-8418-3

Horseback Riding For Dummies
978-0-470-09719-9

Infertility For Dummies†
978-0-470-11518-3

Meditation For Dummies with CD-ROM, 2nd Edition
978-0-471-77774-8

Post-Traumatic Stress Disorder For Dummies
978-0-470-04922-8

Puppies For Dummies, 2nd Edition
978-0-470-03717-1

Thyroid For Dummies, 2nd Edition†
978-0-471-78755-6

Type 1 Diabetes For Dummies*†
978-0-470-17811-9

* Separate Canadian edition also available
† Separate U.K. edition also available

Available wherever books are sold. For more information or to order direct: U.S. customers visit www.dummies.com or call 1-877-762-2974.
U.K. customers visit www.wileyeurope.com or call (0)1243 843291. Canadian customers visit www.wiley.ca or call 1-800-567-4797.

INTERNET & DIGITAL MEDIA

AdWords For Dummies
978-0-470-15252-2

Blogging For Dummies, 2nd Edition
978-0-470-23017-6

Digital Photography All-in-One Desk Reference For Dummies, 3rd Edition
978-0-470-03743-0

Digital Photography For Dummies, 5th Edition
978-0-7645-9802-9

Digital SLR Cameras & Photography For Dummies, 2nd Edition
978-0-470-14927-0

eBay Business All-in-One Desk Reference For Dummies
978-0-7645-8438-1

eBay For Dummies, 5th Edition*
978-0-470-04529-9

eBay Listings That Sell For Dummies
978-0-471-78912-3

Facebook For Dummies
978-0-470-26273-3

The Internet For Dummies, 11th Edition
978-0-470-12174-0

Investing Online For Dummies, 5th Edition
978-0-7645-8456-5

iPod & iTunes For Dummies, 5th Edition
978-0-470-17474-6

MySpace For Dummies
978-0-470-09529-4

Podcasting For Dummies
978-0-471-74898-4

Search Engine Optimization For Dummies, 2nd Edition
978-0-471-97998-2

Second Life For Dummies
978-0-470-18025-9

Starting an eBay Business For Dummies, 3rd Edition†
978-0-470-14924-9

GRAPHICS, DESIGN & WEB DEVELOPMENT

Adobe Creative Suite 3 Design Premium All-in-One Desk Reference For Dummies
978-0-470-11724-8

Adobe Web Suite CS3 All-in-One Desk Reference For Dummies
978-0-470-12099-6

AutoCAD 2008 For Dummies
978-0-470-11650-0

Building a Web Site For Dummies, 3rd Edition
978-0-470-14928-7

Creating Web Pages All-in-One Desk Reference For Dummies, 3rd Edition
978-0-470-09629-1

Creating Web Pages For Dummies, 8th Edition
978-0-470-08030-6

Dreamweaver CS3 For Dummies
978-0-470-11490-2

Flash CS3 For Dummies
978-0-470-12100-9

Google SketchUp For Dummies
978-0-470-13744-4

InDesign CS3 For Dummies
978-0-470-11865-8

Photoshop CS3 All-in-One Desk Reference For Dummies
978-0-470-11195-6

Photoshop CS3 For Dummies
978-0-470-11193-2

Photoshop Elements 5 For Dummies
978-0-470-09810-3

SolidWorks For Dummies
978-0-7645-9555-4

Visio 2007 For Dummies
978-0-470-08983-5

Web Design For Dummies, 2nd Edition
978-0-471-78117-2

Web Sites Do-It-Yourself For Dummies
978-0-470-16903-2

Web Stores Do-It-Yourself For Dummies
978-0-470-17443-2

LANGUAGES, RELIGION & SPIRITUALITY

Arabic For Dummies
978-0-471-77270-5

Chinese For Dummies, Audio Set
978-0-470-12766-7

French For Dummies
978-0-7645-5193-2

German For Dummies
978-0-7645-5195-6

Hebrew For Dummies
978-0-7645-5489-6

Ingles Para Dummies
978-0-7645-5427-8

Italian For Dummies, Audio Set
978-0-470-09586-7

Italian Verbs For Dummies
978-0-471-77389-4

Japanese For Dummies
978-0-7645-5429-2

Latin For Dummies
978-0-7645-5431-5

Portuguese For Dummies
978-0-471-78738-9

Russian For Dummies
978-0-471-78001-4

Spanish Phrases For Dummies
978-0-7645-7204-3

Spanish For Dummies
978-0-7645-5194-9

Spanish For Dummies, Audio Set
978-0-470-09585-0

The Bible For Dummies
978-0-7645-5296-0

Catholicism For Dummies
978-0-7645-5391-2

The Historical Jesus For Dummies
978-0-470-16785-4

Islam For Dummies
978-0-7645-5503-9

Spirituality For Dummies, 2nd Edition
978-0-470-19142-2

NETWORKING AND PROGRAMMING

ASP.NET 3.5 For Dummies
978-0-470-19592-5

C# 2008 For Dummies
978-0-470-19109-5

Hacking For Dummies, 2nd Edition
978-0-470-05235-8

Home Networking For Dummies, 4th Edition
978-0-470-11806-1

Java For Dummies, 4th Edition
978-0-470-08716-9

Microsoft® SQL Server™ 2008 All-in-One Desk Reference For Dummies
978-0-470-17954-3

Networking All-in-One Desk Reference For Dummies, 2nd Edition
978-0-7645-9939-2

Networking For Dummies, 8th Edition
978-0-470-05620-2

SharePoint 2007 For Dummies
978-0-470-09941-4

Wireless Home Networking For Dummies, 2nd Edition
978-0-471-74940-0